The Way beyond Any Way

— Talks on the — Sarvasar Upanishad

OSHO

JAICO PUBLISHING HOUSE

Ahmedabad Bangalore Chennai
Delhi Hyderabad Kolkata Mumbai

Published by Jaico Publishing House
A-2 Jash Chambers, 7-A Sir Phirozshah Mehta Road
Fort, Mumbai - 400 001
jaicopub@jaicobooks.com
www.jaicobooks.com

THE WAY BEYOND ANY WAY
ISBN 978-93-86867-90-2

First Jaico Impression: 2018
Third Jaico Impression: 2024

The material in this book is a transcript of a series of original OSHO Talks on the Sarvasar Upanishad, given to a live audience. All of Osho's talks have been published in full as books, and are also available as original audio recordings. Audio recordings and the complete text archive can be found via the online OSHO Library at www.osho.com/library

Page design and layout: Yogesh Typesetting, Pune

Printed by
Repro India Limited, Mumbai

The Way beyond Any Way

— Talks on the — *Sarvasar Upanishad*

Contents

Preface

Man is born with a self, but not with an ego. The ego is a social construct, a later growth. The ego cannot exist without relationship. You can exist, the self can exist, but the ego cannot exist in itself. It is a by-product of being related to others. So ego exists between "I" and "thou." It is a relata.

The child is born with a self but not with an ego. The child develops the ego. As he becomes more and more social and related, ego develops. This ego is just on your periphery where you are related with others – just on the boundary of your being. So ego is the periphery of your being, and self is the center. The child is born with a self, but unaware. He is a self, but he is not conscious of the self.

The first awareness of the child comes with his ego. He becomes aware of the "I," not of the self. Really, he becomes aware first of the "thou." The child first becomes aware of his mother. Then, reflectively, he becomes aware of himself. First he becomes aware of objects around him. Then, by and by, he begins to feel that he is separate. This feeling of separation gives the feeling of ego, and because the child first becomes aware of the ego, ego becomes a covering on the self.

Then ego goes on growing, because the society needs you as an ego, not as a self. The self is irrelevant for the society; your periphery is meaningful. And there are many problems. The ego can be taught and the ego can be made docile and the ego can be forced to be obedient. The ego can be made to adjust, but not the self. The self cannot be taught, the self cannot be forced. The self is intrinsically rebellious, individual. It cannot be made a part of society.

So the society is not interested in your self. The society is interested in your ego – because something can be done with the ego, and nothing can be done with the self. So the society helps to strengthen the ego, and you go on living around your ego. The more you grow, the more you become social, educated, cultured, civilized, the more polished an ego you have. Then you begin to function from the ego, not from the self, because you are not aware of it at all.

So your essence goes on into the unconscious, into inner darkness, and a false construct, a social construct – the ego – becomes your center. Now you identify yourself with your ego – with your name, with your education, with your family, with your religion, with your country. These are all just part of your ego, not of your self, because the self doesn't belong to your parents, the self doesn't belong to your country, the self doesn't belong to any religion, the self doesn't even belong to yourself. It doesn't belong.

The self is a freedom. It is total freedom. It exists in its own right. It doesn't belong to anything else, it doesn't depend on anything else. It is.

Osho
The Ultimate Alchemy, Vol. 1

1

One Boat, Two Travelers

Aum.
May the divine protect us both;
may it care for us both.
Together may we strive.
May our knowing be brilliant.
May we hold no envy.
Aum, peace, peace, peace.

To extract the essence from the ordinary, the insignificant, is already difficult enough, but then to extract the quintessential essence of all the essences is much more difficult. To discover the significant from the insignificant is already not easy, but then to extract the ultimate significance from all that is significant is almost impossible. To search for gold in the dust presents its own trials and difficulties, but to find the quintessence of gold from the gold is almost impossible.

The meaning of Sarvasar, of the Sarvasar Upanishad, is: the quintessential essence, the most foundational of all the esoteric knowledge that has ever been discovered. An essence where not even a word can be removed, where nothing remains to be discarded, an essence from where the gross has been eliminated and only the pure self remains, from which the gross that is the gold has been separated out, and only the absolute "goldness" has been saved. Such is this Upanishad.

In understanding this one Upanishad, doors will open to

the most profound understanding known by the genius of man. Hence its name, Sarvasar: the secret of secrets, the mystery within all the mysteries, the essence of essences.

Such a thing is dangerous too, because as a science becomes more subtle, it becomes more difficult to grasp. The purer the truth, the farther away it moves from our understanding. It is not the fault of truth, it is only that our understanding is so contaminated that the gap between us and truth has become vast. The only reason for it is our impurity. Hence, the more subtle the truth, the more impractical it becomes for us in our everyday existence.

That is why, although the ultimate knowledge of life was discovered in this country, all we do is waste our time in merely talking about it. It has never occurred to us that it has to be lived. And even if we want to live it, we don't know which way to approach it – and even if we make this decision, we don't know in which direction to begin to move. It is so profound, so subtle, that we drop all hope of living it. Then, just to deceive ourselves, we talk about it and feel consoled.

So we have talked about it for centuries – and we have talked about that which cannot be understood by talking about it, about that which can only be known by living it. To live it is the only way to know it. We can understand it only if we integrate it into our lives. To live it, is to understand it.

There are some profound dimensions of life where no gap exists between knowing and being; where to know it and to be it are one and the same; where to be it is the only way to know it.

But "to be" seems difficult to us and "to know about" feels easy, because all that we usually mean by knowing is to know a few words, a few doctrines, some philosophies, some scriptures. Our intellect becomes filled with words and doctrines, but the heart remains empty. And there is no situation more dangerous than this – where the intellect is filled up from the outside and the heart is empty – because this sort of intellect will create the illusion that one has attained, while nothing has actually been attained. With an intellect like this one feels that one is full, but inside all is empty and hollow, poor and miserable. The soul remains like the empty bowl of a beggar, while the intellect lives in the illusion that it is an emperor.

More people are misled by intellect than by ignorance, and more people drown sitting in their boats of intellect than sitting in the paper boats of their ignorance, because one appears to know – although one does not know at all. That is why I have said that subtle maxims of ultimate wisdom such as in the Sarvasar Upanishad are also dangerous; the fear is that we may only turn them into objects to think about. We may think about them, grasp them and then be finished with them. Hence, I warn you in advance that to involve oneself in the teachings of an Upanishad is like playing with fire. An Upanishad cannot be understood without also becoming transformed.

Look at it like this: there are some teachings which can be learned even if we remain as we are. One doesn't need to transform oneself in order to learn mathematics or history or something like that. The person can remain the same and his learning will go on accumulating. That person's inner being doesn't need to undergo any transformation: he may remain the same and just go on accumulating knowledge. No inner revolution is required in order to become a historian or a mathematician or a scientist.

But religion is an entirely different matter. In religion a transformation is needed before the knowing can be acquired. Unless you change, you cannot understand; you will have to be transformed in order to understand. Unless the transformation is of your inner being, intellectual accumulations will not do; they become a deception, a self-deception. That is why it is better to remain ignorant instead of deceiving yourself with a false assumption of knowledge, because the ignorant person is at least humble, the learned person becomes egotistical and arrogant. The ignorant person at least feels the pain of emptiness in himself and tears flow from his eyes, but the learned person is just puffed up, his tears have dried up and his thirst has faded away. Even false water is capable of satisfying one's thirst.

We have all had dreams of this kind: you are actually very thirsty, and then you dream that you are drinking water and your thirst is quenched. In this way your sleep is not disrupted. Dreams are only created to support your sleep. If you think that dreams disturb your sleep, then you are unaware of the science of dreams. If you think that if you don't have dreams your sleep will be deeper, then you are mistaken. You will not even be able to sleep if you don't have dreams.

Actually, dreams simply support your sleep. Whenever your sleep is about to be disrupted, a dream will come to deceive you and help your sleep to continue. You are thirsty, but if you don't have a dream that you are drinking water at a riverbank your sleep will have to be interrupted, thirst is such a compulsive thing. But you create a dream that you are at the bank of a river, or taking a bath in a lake and drinking to your satisfaction. You have this dream and your thirst is quenched; it is not correct to say quenched, rather it appears to be quenched, and so the sleep continues. You are hungry, so you dream that you are invited to a feast in the royal palace and therefore your sleep is not broken. You have repressed your sexual urge – now it arises in you in a dream. Dreams provide beautiful women even to beggars…and your sleep continues.

Just as we quench our thirst with imagined water in dreams, the same also happens in our so-called waking state. The Upanishad says that our awake state is also just a dream. In that dream state we are hiding our ignorance by accumulating false knowledge, by learning and memorizing it. Thus our sleep is not disrupted and our worldly affairs can continue in the same way as our sleep continues in the night.

Just as one awakens from sleep and the consciousness enters into another dimension, in the same way, when a person awakens from the sleep called "the world," sannyas happens and the consciousness enters into another realm. Sannyas means that now one no longer chooses to function in the world like a somnambulist, now one simply wants to live consciously.

If by listening to these discourses on the Upanishad you just become more knowledgeable, then I have committed a mistake by speaking, I have become your enemy. If with these discourses you now set out on the journey of self-revolution, then what I have said has been beneficial and good for you.

What I will say can become a poison, an absolute poison, if you turn it into a subject for your discussion, as food for your intellect and a protection for your sleep. What I will say can also become nectar if you do not make it food for the intellect, if instead it develops into a determination, an energy with the potential to transform your heart. It will all depend on you what you do with this Sarvasar Upanishad. If you return from here just having learned a few more things it will not be good, it would have been better had you not come here at all. If you return from here having gained some more information, some more knowledgeability, then your coming and going have been utterly useless.

No, I have no intention or desire to add more information to your store of knowledge. Rather, I would like you to return a little transformed, a little changed; I would like it that your vision changes, not your memory; that your understanding grows, not your knowledge. I would like *you* to grow, not your intellect.

How can that which is your real being grow – not your knowledge, but your very being? That is why I said that this Upanishad is dangerous.

To encounter truth, even a little bit, is not a game; it is dangerous, because truth will not allow you to remain as you are. It will change, demolish, destroy and renew you. It will give you a new birth. Certainly there is pain in the birth, but without pain how can there be a new birth? And when there is so much pain for a mother in giving birth to another being, there will be much more pain in giving birth to one's own self. A mother carries the baby inside her womb for only nine months; we have carried ourselves within our wombs for innumerable lives.

For so many lives we have remained only a womb, only a seed – for eternity we have carried ourselves in our own wombs. We have not been born yet! It is as if a butterfly has been enclosed in its cocoon for many, many lives: neither has the cocoon broken open, nor has the butterfly flown – it has never spread its wings in the open sky. And we are closed within ourselves in the same way.

This Upanishad is about the science which can break that shell. We have taken this shell to be our life, although it is not even the beginning of birth. What life does a seed have? Certainly the seed is there, but is it life? Life is manifested in the tree. What is the life of a seed? – the seed is only a possibility, merely a hope, a future, its present is nothing at all. It is only a potentiality, but it is not life.

What we call life is only a potentiality, a seed in its shell. The tree has life – it spreads in the open sky reaching to touch the sun, it spreads its branches to touch the stars and the moon. Flowers bloom on it and the birds make their nests in it, there are songs, there are storms – the mighty winds, the sunshine and the rains, the struggles and the challenges of death. Moment to moment there is life. What life is there for the seed? The seed is only an embryo.

We are also seeds. And there is much more pain to go through, there is much more pain ahead. We all want bliss, but without any pain. That is why we never attain it. Who does not wish for bliss? Who is not hungry for happiness, and who is not a seeker of bliss? Our each and every fiber asks for bliss, each and every breath longs for bliss. Everybody desires the same, yet bliss does not happen because nobody is ready to pay the price for it. We want to avoid the pain. We are like a mother who wants to avoid having labor pains.

If not today, then perhaps tomorrow, there will no longer be any delivery pain for mothers all over the world; it will be possible to give birth to a child without any pain. It has already become possible. But the day will never come when a person will enter into the rebirth of his own soul, when he will give birth to his own being, without going through birth pangs.

And there is another interesting thing, another truth, which people around the world who are trying to make childbirth painless will only realize later on. It often happens that we only come to realize the implications of something when it is already out of our hands, and the truth is that a mother who gives birth to her child without any pain will also be deprived of certain depths of her motherhood. The mother giving birth to a baby without any pain will lose the depth, the intensity of her motherhood. If the baby is born without pain, the mother too will not be born; she will be deprived of motherhood, she will not become a mother, because when a baby is born with pain, that pain becomes a valley, and beside that valley rises the peak of motherhood.

When we avoid the valleys, we are also avoiding the peaks. If we want to remove the valleys near the Himalayas and preserve the peaks, or preserve Mount Everest, we are mad; we don't know anything about the logic of life. Peaks are there only because of the valleys. In fact, the peaks and the valleys are interconnected.

But man commits the same mistakes again and again. Man thinks that if all the pains and miseries of life are eliminated then there will be much happiness. But it is a strange fact that when all the pain and miseries are gone, we also come to know that there is no happiness left anywhere either, because they are interrelated. That is why the rich man often becomes more unhappy than the poor man; the affluent societies become more distressed than the poor societies.

This is the problem in the West today. Now they have put an end to most of the pain and misery which are still the cause of so much suffering in the East. They have destroyed all those miseries. They have made enormous efforts in the hope that the day would come when there would be no misery and only happiness would remain. And the miseries have ended, but simultaneously they discovered that happiness had also disappeared; the valleys disappeared but the peaks also disappeared. The nights are no more, but with them the days too have disappeared. We separated all the thorns from the rosebush, but while we were busy separating the thorns we looked up and found that the flowers had also been cleared away. They had existed together with the thorns, they were interrelated.

Someday it may become possible for babies to be delivered without pain, but it will never be possible for man to attain to a new life without pain. It cannot happen, and it has a reason. The reason is that whatever we have been up to now has to be discarded to create space for the new.

A mother's trouble in giving birth to a baby is not that *she* will be destroyed, her trouble is in the shock that something completely new is separating from her, is becoming free of her. But when you give birth to your own self you are not giving birth to something separate from you, you are doing double work. You are eliminating yourself and at the same time the elimination is happening, in the same proportion, a new life is beginning to unfold.

That is why I said that the teachings of this Upanishad are dangerous – you have to be ready for the pains of inner revolution. The sage's first sutra is related to the fear of that pain. Try to understand it.

Aum.
May the divine protect us both.

Why this prayer? Why is this sage, in the very beginning of the Upanishad, praying to the divine for protection? Do you think that he had no roof on his hut? Do you think that he had no bread to eat and was dying of hunger, or that he had no clothes to wear? What is it that he wants to protect? What is it that he wishes to have protected? And that, too, in the very beginning! The very first statement is concerning protection.

The journey the sage is about to begin on is that of death, because only after death does a new life begin. "This much is certain: I will die. But it is not certain whether I will be reborn – that is unknown." So he says, "Protect me." He is praying to the divine that, "I am setting out for the unknown, the danger is very obvious, death is apparent." The seed only sees its death – how can it see the tree that is to be born? The seed will vanish, it has to die, this much is apparent. But how could the seed imagine that there will be a tree and that flowers will bloom someday? The songs which will echo through the tree, the music of the flute that will be played under the tree, the gusts of wind which will rustle through the leaves – how could the seed know all this beforehand? What idea could it have of the coming spring? What idea could it have of the raindrops that will fall upon the tree? The only thing the seed knows is that it will die; this much is known, all the rest is unknown; hence this prayer:

Aum. May the divine protect us both. The master and the disciple... This is even more interesting, that the prayer is for both of them – for the disciple and for the master as well. Had it been only for the disciple it would have been easy to understand – but it is for the master also! This feels a little odd. If the prayer was for the disciple who is here to learn, who has just begun the journey, who is just about to launch his boat into the unknown, it would be understandable. He might pray for protection, for safety. But why pray for the master? What is this statement, "both of us"?

There is a reason for it, and it is that the relationship of master and disciple is so deep that if one drowns the other will also drown, then neither one will be saved. This relationship is so intimate that there is no other relationship in the world as intimate as this – neither that of the husband and wife, neither that of the mother and son, neither of brothers nor of friends. This relationship between the two is so intimate that if one drowns the other will also drown. That is why the sage prays:

"Protect us both" – the disciple and the master.

There are also some deeper insights in this statement. The sage is also saying that being a master doesn't mean that he cannot drown, that he cannot go astray. This statement requires our attention. Being a master doesn't mean that he cannot drown. In fact, if there is a state where one cannot falter, cannot go astray, cannot get lost in the darkness, it means that one is almost dead. In life there is always the possibility of going astray – always. That is the only meaning of being alive. Even a buddha could take a wrong step – that he does not take it is another matter; that he will not take a wrong step, that is another matter; that he has never taken a wrong step, that is another matter – but the possibility is there. I say it again: his steps never go wrong, they have never gone wrong. There is no historical evidence that a buddha ever took a wrong step. But even a buddha in his prayer would say, "Protect me." A mistake is possible. And it is strange that one who prays like this never goes wrong, and one who does not pray like this is sure to go wrong, because there is an ego, and that is the original mistake.

That is why the sage begins: "Protect us both" – the master and the disciple. The prayer of a disciple is very ordinary, but with a master joining in it becomes extraordinary. And we call that person a master who has no ego about being a master. One who has no ego about being a master is a real master, and the one who has an ego about being a master is not even qualified to be a disciple.

This prayer is expressing that the sage does not have any such notion that he does not need protection – that "I have known, I have attained, I have reached. I am helping others to reach. Why would I need protection?" He has no such notion; he prays, "Protect both of us."

And this unique humbleness is the secret of his being a master. We can trust that this man can tell us profound things, we can trust that if we even follow this man blindfolded we can reach the goal, that even if we follow this man with closed eyes we can reach the goal. But if we follow the so-called gurus, even with our eyes open and very intelligently, we will fall into a ditch and nowhere else.

A master is one who is not even aware of his individual existence. Such an emptiness can only be full of prayerfulness, there is no other way. There is no way to be otherwise.

...protect us both;
may it care for us both.

It seems that protection is not enough: care is also needed. Does protection not also include care? No, protection is an altogether spiritual phenomenon. It is a spiritual phenomenon. So far, only this much has been prayed for: "We are going into the unknown." The disciple of course does not know, and the master says that he does not know either.

These must have been wonderful people, because to be a master first you have to claim that you know, otherwise who will accept you as a master? It is difficult to get even a single disciple if a master does not claim that he knows. But this master says, "I too do not know anything...protect me. We have set out toward the unknown, we are sailing across an ocean without a map and that there is a shore on the other side has only been seen in dreams, in visions. And this too is only a longing; it is unknown whether or not the other shore exists. We are leaving this shore which we have known up to now, and we are traveling toward that which we do not know at all."

That the disciple should be praying is perfectly acceptable, but the master also says, "Protect me." The master must know the other shore! This is a little complex. In fact the name of the other shore is "the unknown." The very meaning of the other shore is that which is never known; whatsoever we may know, it still remains unknown.

No, the unknown can still be known someday, but the unknowable, no matter how much we know, will still remain unknown; whatsoever we may recognize, even then it remains unrecognizable. It is embraced, still it remains untouched. We discover it, touch it, yet our hands remain empty. One knows it, yet the ego of "knowing" is not created within.

That is why the master says, "Protect me too." And it is right to ask for protection: the journey is unknown, the path is unknown, the other shore is unknown and the destination is unclear.

In the next sutra he says: *...may it care for us both.* Why? Care belongs only to the physical level. But there is a reason for this prayer, and the reason is that whosoever starts seeking truth drops the ego trip of feeling that he himself is responsible for his body. Anyone who thinks, "I earn my bread, I build my house, my clothes are mine, I maintain my body and if I don't maintain all this, everything will fall apart," lives in stupidity. Such a person may do very well in this world but he cannot move toward truth.

That is why the sage says, "You provide for us also, because from now on we will no longer be the doer, from now on we cannot even have the feeling that we are the least responsible for ourselves."

But we are strange people: not only do we think we take care of ourselves, we even assume that we take care of others.

This sage says, "Now our welfare is in your hands; now you care for us. We will live as you keep us. If you protect us it is okay, if you destroy us then that too is okay; now your will is our life. Now we drop even the feeling of being a doer."

To drop the feeling of being a doer is precious, because it helps on the journey. In fact anyone who is attached to feeling like a doer has his boat tied to this shore and he cannot proceed toward the other shore. All anchors are to be removed from this shore; even a single anchor to this shore is dangerous. To think, "I earn and I maintain myself," is enough to create an anchor.

The sage says, "Our care also:"

...may it care for us both.
Together may we strive.

There is the knowledge which a teacher passes on to a student, as is done in the universities and colleges – knowledge which is an accumulation of the known. The teacher knows and the student does not; the teacher passes this knowledge on to the student. The teacher gives it, and the student takes it. This we know very well. Such knowledge is like an object, like money – it is in my hand, I hand it over to you. The father has the money, he gives it to his son; the teacher has the knowledge, he gives it to the student; it is a transfer. But there exists a knowledge which is not transferable. This knowledge the master does not give, he cannot give; there is no way to give it. But if both of them endeavor together it may be transmitted to the disciple. Try to understand the difference.

There is the knowledge we all know, which is given; one gets it, one gives it. I know, you do not know; I give it to you, then you will also know it. Certainly that knowledge is of words, but such knowledge will be superficial. That which can be given through words will not be deeper than the words themselves. It will carry the weight which a word carries, it will have the same value. It is not necessary for me to know that which I give to you; someone gave it to me and I give it to you, you will give it to someone else.

So the ignorant are also engaged in this give and take business of knowledge, they do it a lot. And when knowledge is circulated very fast, it appears that society is becoming very knowledgeable. We are living on such knowledge in this century because knowledge is circulating very fast. Those who know economics understand what this means. If we have one thousand rupees and everyone keeps them in their pockets, they will remain one thousand. But if it starts circulating – I take ten rupees from you, you take from him, he gives it to so and so – hundreds of thousands of rupees worth of transactions can happen through the original one thousand rupees. Circulation! The economists say that money must continue to circulate just like blood in the body, otherwise it diminishes. Money seems to decrease if it is not circulated. The more money circulates in a society, the richer it seems.

Mohammedans remain poor because, in the very beginning, Islam adopted the idea that taking interest on money is a sin. Now, if taking interest on money is a sin the circulation of money is stopped, the flow of money is blocked. So Mohammedans have remained poor in this world because they took the vow not to take interest on money. If you do not take interest the money will be blocked – how can it flow? It flows with the help of interest; it travels from one pocket to another pocket, and one rupee circulating becomes one thousand rupees.

America is the richest country because there money moves fast. If money moves fast, even the poor appear to be rich; if it doesn't move, even the rich are poor. Many rich people in this country are quite poor, their money doesn't move at all. They are sitting on their safes. If their safes were removed from under them, it would not make any difference to their feeling rich as long as they did not know that the safes had been removed. Just the idea that they are sitting on their safes is enough to make them feel that they are rich people. But if money doesn't circulate then even the rich person would be poor, and if it circulates even the poor appear to be rich.

That is how it is with knowledge: it circulates fast. We have universal education; now there is education in the whole world. And knowledge moves fast: the first one passes it to the second one, that one gives it to the third, the third passes it on to still another; everyone goes on passing knowledge to everyone else. There appears to be a great deal of knowledge, but actually there is not.

The sage is not talking about that knowledge which someone can give you. The sage says: *Together may we strive* – "We only need that much blessing. We will live together, we will meditate together, we will pray together, we will worship together, we will move together; we will sit together in silence, in words, in thoughts. We will be together in the longing for ourselves, in our efforts to attain to the being. We will dream together, we will sing together, we will be silent together; together we will look at the sun, together we will look at the stars in the sky at night. We will be together."

This is called *satsang*: we will be together. Perhaps that which cannot be given directly can happen in such a togetherness; that which cannot be given directly can be transmitted silently, that which cannot be said through words may descend in silence, that which cannot be given may be transmitted while living together.

Bodhidharma went to China from India fourteen hundred years ago. One disciple, Hui Neng, was with Bodhidharma for many years and he had asked many times, "When will you give me...when will you impart that wisdom? When will that moment come when my bowl is filled? I have been following you for many years and time is passing by, life is uncertain." Bodhidharma would laugh and say nothing.

Slowly, slowly Hui Neng stopped asking. There was no sense in asking – this man would only laugh. And one day the phenomenon happened. Hui Neng woke up at midnight and shook Bodhidharma: "At least you could have informed me before giving it. And what a time you chose – at midnight, and while I was sleeping!"

Bodhidharma laughed again and he said, "Be silent and go to sleep." Again he laughed as he had laughed before.

Again and again Hui Neng would ask, "Tell me something! How did you give it to me? How did I get it? You should have told me earlier, you should have said something! You have filled me, yet you didn't even inform me."

Bodhidharma said, "I also didn't know when it would happen."

This transmission, when will it happen? Nobody knows. "But we strive together." If we go together, move together and live together, it will happen. If an unlit candle is put near one that is lit, it cannot be known when a gust of wind will bring the flame near the unlit candle, when the flame will jump to the other candle. This is the way, this is how the transmission happens.

So the sage says: *Together may we strive.* Only then, perhaps, it may happen, that that which cannot be given may be given. But for that happening both are needed: one who knows and the other who does not know; one who is called the master and one who is called a disciple – they agree to come close.

One has not to learn from the master, it is enough just to be with him. Learning is easy, but being together is difficult. Learning can be done while standing at a distance; coming closer is not necessary. But a deep intimacy is required in order to be together; an inner opening is required, a trust, a deep reverence, a love, a madness, a capacity to regard someone as closer than one's own self. Then the transmission happens.

If the unlit candle is afraid, keeping a distance, not coming close to the lit candle and if somehow, when the flame comes close to it, it moves farther away and is afraid, then it becomes difficult. So the sage says: *Together may we strive.*

He does not say that only the disciple is to make the effort. That would have seemed appropriate, wouldn't it? – that would have been enough. All so-called gurus ask the disciple to work hard, to make an effort. No so-called guru says that we should strive together – because it is not only that the disciple is to be near the master, it is more important for the master to be available to the disciple. Even if the unlit candle comes very close but the lit candle is conceited and arrogant and not willing to move with the gust of the wind, then too nothing will happen.

If a master feels himself to be a master then nothing will happen, because even though he is ready to give, he is not ready to be together with the disciple, and it cannot be given without being together.

That is why, when the old seekers went in search, the place where they lived with the master was called the *gurukul*, the family of the master. This was the master's family; the seeker just became a member of the family. He became one, joined with the family. But this closeness is two-sided; every closeness is two-sided. That is why the master says: "We strive together, make effort, work hard, meditate together."

This is a great *sadhana*, a great spiritual discipline for the master also. Every person who knows cannot be a master. Try to understand it. Many people in this world know, but they cannot help others to know. To know is not so difficult.

One day, someone came to Buddha and asked him, "You have had ten thousand monks with you for years and you have been teaching them, leading them on the path of *sadhana*, meditation. How many have attained to your state? How many have become buddhas?" Naturally, it is a relevant question. It is the test of a buddha to see how many buddhas he has created.

Buddha answered that many of them have attained to buddhahood.

The man said, "No one seems to be a buddha."

Buddha replied, "Because they are not masters."

To become awakened is one thing and to help others to awaken is quite another. It is not necessary that the awakened one always helps others to awaken, because if the awakened one is to awaken the other, he has to descend from his heights and stand with the other in his dark valley. He has to be near the people who are groping, taking their hand in his own hand. Many times he has to walk a little distance with them on their path where there is nothing but hell. So if he walks a little distance with you now, holding your hand, only then will there be a possibility of a trust arising in you that tomorrow, if he invites you on his path, then you will be willing to accompany him.

The master has to walk with the disciple, so that the disciple may walk with the master. And many times the master has to walk on a path where he should not have gone, he has to come close to the one whom he wants to change. That is why the sage says:

Together may we strive.
May our knowing be brilliant.

There is a spiritual discipline to know the truth, and there is quite another for transmitting that truth; they are different, totally different.

The Jainas have differentiated between the two. A *kevali* is one who has attained to the supreme wisdom; a *tirthankara* is one who has attained to the supreme wisdom and who is also a teacher, also a master – he is called a *tirthankara*. There is no other difference between a *tirthankara* and a *kevali*. A *kevali* has attained to wisdom, he has the ultimate understanding, but he is not a master. He cannot transfer, he cannot give it to others. He does not know how to give it to others.

Understand it this way. There are only a few people on the earth in whose life no poetry ever takes birth. Sometime or other a lyric echoes inside, takes birth in everyone. But there are very few poets. Many people have felt the murmuring of a song, but this does not make them musicians. Even if music is born inside you, it may be that you will not be able to sing it out loud. That is why, when listening to poetry, you feel that this is the poetry which should have come through *me*; this is the song I should have sung; this is the same tune which echoed within me, but I could not produce it. Looking at some painting you feel that you also wanted to paint it, but someone else painted it. In fact when you like a painting, it only means that if you could have, you would have painted it – it represents you, but you couldn't do it.

Many times truth is attained, the ultimate wisdom unfolds, takes birth. But then how to communicate it to others? How to communicate it? How to convey it to others?

To be a master is a different matter. Only one who is ready to strive again along with the disciple can be a master. Only one who agrees to walk again along with the disciple from the very first steps, who agrees to start with the *ABC*'s again, who can take the hand of the disciple and start from where he himself has no need to start can be a master. He who is standing at the destination and has the courage to again take the first step with the disciple, only he can become a master.

That is why the sage prays: *Together may we strive. May our knowing be brilliant.* He continues to pray for both: *May our knowing be brilliant.*

It is strange, but often it happens that the master himself understands many things for the first time while teaching it to the disciple – for the first time! Many times, helping others understand is the easiest way to understand oneself. Many times truth is experienced inside, but the experiencer himself does not fully understand what has happened. What happened? Did it happen? For seven days, Buddha kept brooding: What has happened?

When one faces truth for the first time, one is dumbfounded. One can see all, but nothing is comprehended; everything is understood, but even then nothing is understood in detail. Nothing is grasped. What has happened? That which existed until yesterday exists no more; that which never existed is present; that which was believed to be real has become a dream; that which was unknown even in dream is so real before one's eyes. The one who started the search has disappeared and the one who has attained to this truth is unknown, is unrecognizable.

When Meister Eckhart experienced *samadhi* for the first time, he asked two questions. The first was: "What is happening?" And the second was: "To whom is it happening?"

One of his disciples was near him. The disciple said, "At least this much I can tell you: that it has happened to you. So why do *you* ask to whom it has happened?"

Eckhart replied, "You do not know. The man who started on this search has disappeared in this happening, and the one to whom it has happened is as much a stranger as is this happening."

Many times, what has happened only becomes clear when the master is teaching someone.

So the sage prays: *May our knowing be brilliant.* "May our knowing be bright. May our knowing become sharp, may the flame of our wisdom shine; may it go on shining."

The moment never comes when one can pray to the divine: "Now it is enough." The moment never comes when one prays to existence: "Enough! Now if you want you can dull my intelligence, that will be fine." No, such moments never come. Wisdom is a sword with a blade which can always be made more sharp. Continuous sharpening and still…still, something remains to be sharpened. This is the endless, this is the boundless.

That is why the sage still prays: *May our knowing be brilliant.* In fact the master says that there is no reason to believe that he has become a wise man, there is still more wisdom ahead; still there is ignorance. Perhaps the one who knows can see more ignorance than the one who does not know, and so he can say that there is still ignorance. But now don't misunderstand that he really is ignorant. Don't think that this man actually needs to ask for knowledge and brilliance. But this prayer is right and it is symbolic. It conveys that a wise man is always humble, and that he does not hesitate to pray.

Only the weak are afraid to pray. A weak person is not even courageous enough to ask. Even in front of the divine, from which everything can be received, he stands as if he has everything. Even at the door of the divine he keeps his vanity intact and goes away hiding his begging bowl behind him for fear that it might be seen.

But the one who knows also knows that the knowing is not a static phenomenon. It is not a limited happening like a pond. Knowing is like a river continuously flowing – nonstop. Knowing goes on endlessly growing – it goes on and on. This is the grace of wisdom, that it has no end. If wisdom had an end, it would become dead. The flower of wisdom goes on blooming forever. Just understand it like this: more and more petals go on opening, and the moment never arrives when its flowering is complete. The bud of wisdom doesn't bloom and fade, it remains always a bud, flowering. No matter how much it flowers, it still remains a bud.

May we hold no envy.

On this journey toward wisdom, why is it necessary to say that we should not envy anyone? Between the point where this sutra started and the point where it reaches, this appears to be irrelevant, sudden and abrupt. This is a search for truth. The journey is unknown. Brilliance of intelligence is needed and wisdom is also needed, an awakened consciousness is needed – that is all okay; the master and the disciple should endeavor together; that is okay – but then suddenly the master says: *May we hold no envy.* What is its relevance? Why is it mentioned? Why is he saying not to envy anyone? Try to understand it.

The statements of a sage are never irrelevant, even if they appear to be so. It may look as if the sage has taken a jump from one place to another, and with no link in between. There are many occasions in the Upanishads where it appears as if the sutra started from one idea and concluded somewhere else; there is no link in between, no relationship. Even then don't jump to conclusions, because the sages, the seers, know some inner link which is invisible to you, they are aware of bridges which are invisible to you. They know some inner relevance which has not penetrated your intelligence even today.

May we hold no envy. In fact when a man begins to search for something he is motivated by his envy of the other, by his jealousy of the other. Even in the search for truth one can be jealous of the other. The desire for knowledge can also be based in jealousy and competition with the other.

A friend of mine came to me eight days ago and he said, "I am in great anguish and anxiety: How can I achieve godliness?"

I asked him, "What is the reason for this anxiety? Do you have a strong urge for the divine and that is why you are in anguish? Do you feel pained missing the only meaning in life, the only goal of life? Do you feel life is useless unless it is achieved? Have you tasted its flavor and that taste is haunting you, pulling you, calling you again and again? Have you seen godliness through some window, either close by or maybe from a distance, and now you find it difficult to forget, and again and again, repeatedly, you remember that opening and think of how to reach there?"

He replied, "No, nothing like that. When *you* can achieve it, why can't I? When Ramakrishna can achieve it, why can't I? And when Ramana Maharshi can achieve it, then what is wrong with me? I am disturbed when I listen to you people. I have neither a taste, nor any urge, and I am not even sure whether it exists or not!"

So it may not be visible to you, but the sage's prayer is correct: *May we hold no envy*. We should not begin our search because of the jealousy we hold for others or because we are afraid of lagging behind.

We are all in competition with each other, not only for a house or furniture, but even to realize godliness. If a hundred names were removed from the history of mankind we might even forget the idea of God. Those hundred persons provoke jealousy in us. One Buddha is born and our life is in difficulty: If this man has achieved, how can I lag behind?

So at first we try in every way to deny his achievement; that is our strategy, our self-defense. First, we make every effort to deny his achievement. We think, "One day I saw this man looking so angry, once I saw him eating delicious food, one day I saw this man full of ego." First, we console ourselves in every possible way that he has not achieved, so that we may avoid this problem of envy or jealousy, so that this feeling of competition can be avoided. But a person like Buddha does not consider or care about us. He goes on living in his own way.

Then slowly, slowly we get disturbed realizing that he *has* achieved something. We try him in every way, but he does not care. It seems that he has got something. We test him by throwing stones at him, by giving poison to him, by crucifying him; we test him in all kinds of ways, and then a suspicion grows. One day we feel that yes, he has got it. And then immediately our struggle begins to achieve the same.

It is difficult to conceive that people will begin even the search for truth with jealousy, but this is the reality. Even there, jealousy exists. We neither tolerate the other being rich, nor being wise. We cannot tolerate the feeling that the other has achieved something which we have not.

So the sage prays: *May we hold no envy.*

This is not irrelevant, it is very relevant, because someone who is searching for truth because of jealousy may reach somewhere, but never to the divine. Money can be made because of jealousy, there is no problem in that. In fact money can never be made without jealousy. Competition is a prerequisite for every achievement in this world, and the more poisonous your competition is, the more successful you will be. The deeper your jealousy is, the stronger you become. But this does not apply to the search for the divine, because someone who sees the other as "other," that person cannot realize the divine. And one who is not delighted in seeing the wisdom of the other has no longing for wisdom as yet.

There is another type of person too, who, when he meets a Buddha, is not even concerned whether Buddha has achieved or not. He does not care, does not worry whether this man has achieved or not. He isn't bothered about achieving just because Buddha has achieved – no, he is delighted with Buddha's fragrance, he is touched by Buddha's song; seeing Buddha he becomes convinced, but he is not jealous of him. Seeing Buddha he feels assured and he says, "Okay, whatever thirst is within me, this same thirst has reached to the ocean in this man. Now I can follow my thirst with trust." He attains a trust after looking at Buddha, a trust that even the impossible is possible, a trust that even the faraway truth is very close. Buddhahood is very far from him, but Buddha is very near to him also – he can hold Buddha's feet in his hands. And if he can hold Buddha's feet in his hands, then before long buddhahood can also be achieved – he attains that trust.

Then there is no envy, then there is only a thanksgiving, a gratitude. He feels grateful because someone has blossomed; he is reminded of his own bud, he is reminded of his own self, and an awareness arises. Then the journey has not begun because of jealousy. It is a delightful, loving journey unconcerned with the other.

That is why the sage prays: *May we hold no envy.*

If there is no envy, and only one's own thirst, one can easily reach that state where one can say: "Aum, peace, peace, peace," where one can say, "Everything is at peace, everything has reached to its ultimate rest, everything is bliss."

This much for the Upanishad sutra…

Now a few suggestions for tomorrow morning, and our night gathering will be over.

The first suggestion is for all of these days of the meditation camp. During the coming seven days you have to live in such a way that a minimum amount of life-energy is spent. The minimum has to be spent, because our search goes into a dimension where a lot of life-energy is needed and, if you unnecessarily waste it, you will have no energy for that search. If you burn the oil of your lamp elsewhere, you will not be able to light up the flame for the purpose for which you came here; the oil of your lamp must be conserved.

So for seven days, conserve your energy as much as you can. And in order to conserve your energy, close every possible opening of your senses because they are the way your energy, your strength will be wasted. Keep your eyes closed as much as you can.

So, tomorrow morning you will get a blindfold, or maybe you have one right now. For twenty-four hours, whenever you need to walk, remove the blindfold just so that you can see four steps ahead of you, which is just enough – not even the fifth step. Walk here only looking four steps ahead. As soon as you arrive here, close your eyes and cover them totally with the blindfold. For the whole day, starting from the morning, the blindfold should remain on your eyes.

Most of your energy is spent through your eyes; conserve it inside. The energy of the eyes is to be especially conserved, because that which we are seeking requires the use of the inner eye, and the energy is the same. That which is used for the outer eyes has to be used for the inner eye too – the same energy is used.

That is why we call the sage a seer – one who sees. That is why we call that experience *darshan*, seeing. Your inner eye should receive that energy which your outer eyes are receiving, so keep your eyes closed. For seven days, let all your energy go inside. Keep your eyes closed and remember the whole day that the energy of both your eyes is flowing toward the third eye, just between the two outer eyes, between the two eyebrows, in the middle of the forehead. Whenever you remember, close your eyes, sit silently, and remember that the energy of both eyes is flowing toward the third eye between the two eyes, in the middle of the eyebrows, flowing from both sides, entering into the third eye. Thus your meditation will deepen tremendously.

As far as possible, keep your ears closed. Don't hear anything, because he who is interested in listening to the inner music should avoid outer noises. Otherwise, the inner music is very subtle compared to the outside noises and it will be difficult to hear it, so we need to tune into it. Put some cotton, or anything you wish, into your ears; keep the ears closed the whole time – they are not needed. At the most your ears will be needed for only a few minutes; otherwise there is no need. Do not use your ears except while you are listening to me. Keep them closed, and be aware all the time of anything which you can hear happening inside – just a remembering: is there anything which can be heard inside? Then the energy of your ears will start flowing inside and you will be able to hear the inner sounds in meditation, and you will be able to see the inner visions in meditation.

Ears, eyes and your lips. Thirdly, keep your lips closed and speak the minimum. It is best if you do not speak at all. Keep silent. You are free to choose what you do about your ears and eyes – if you wish you can keep your eyes open, and if you wish you can keep your ears open, because only you will be missing out – but with your lips you are harming others, with your lips you are trespassing, so do not speak at all. Hearing and seeing can be your choice.

Wherever you want to go, whatever you want to do, you can do. However, if you have come to meditate, keep your eyes and ears closed. If you have accidentally arrived here just by wandering around, it is your choice. But even if you have come here accidentally you are not allowed to speak, because in speaking you are attacking others; when you are speaking you are harming others, so please do not speak at all.

Many people may have come here because they could not gossip in their hometowns, or could not find any victims – who will be available here. They hope to chat with them. No chatting is allowed here. The campus should be completely quiet. Silence should prevail in your room, wherever you are; no singing, no songs, no talking, no conversation, nothing of that sort. Keep quiet for seven days.

You have talked your whole life and what have you gained? After seven days, you can do it again for the rest of your life. Or, if you intend to have more than one life, you can keep doing it in several more lives. But for seven days listen to me and stop talking. Then it is possible that you may have a glimpse of silence, of that which could not be known through talking. Then with our total energy we can go deeply into meditation. So you have to keep these three senses closed.

And now, the fourth thing. We will be using a lot of energy

here for meditation, so it is better to do a minimum amount of physical work outside. Do not go wandering around to see this place or that. You will come back tired, and then you will complain that nothing is happening in meditation. Come here totally fresh, because you have to make much effort here. So do not go anywhere else; do not go sightseeing during these days.

Whatever time you get after these three sittings, lie down somewhere in the shade of a tree, keep resting silently, relax; maximum relaxation and maximum cessation of your external senses.

Eat very little, because a lot of energy is consumed in digesting your food, and it is spent in digesting food which produces nothing more than diseases. Take the minimum amount of food, keep the stomach light so that the energy can go upward. The heavier the stomach, the lower the energy goes because it has to reach to the stomach. This is why you feel sleepy after meals, because the brain has to send its energy to the stomach and then the brain becomes idle and goes to sleep. That is why, if you are hungry or you are on a fast, you can't sleep at night. The reason is that the energy continues flowing upward and the brain cells keep awake because they are full of energy. If energy flows more toward the stomach, making an effort to be conscious becomes difficult; so eat less.

You will lose nothing during these seven days with a minimum amount of food, and the benefits can be tremendous – it can even be helpful for the body. Eat less and eat lightly. You should eat so little that you feel as if you have not eaten anything, only that much. So I do not say to stop eating completely, because the person who stops eating completely does nothing but think about eating the whole day. You should just eat less.

And it is strange that the people who overeat find it difficult to eat less. If you tell them not to eat at all, they are ready to agree. The reason for this is that it is always easy to go from one extreme to another, it is difficult to stop in the middle. If you are told not to eat sweets at all you will say, "Okay I will not look at them." But if the sweets are there in the dish and you are told to take only two spoonfuls, then it gets really difficult trying to control yourself when temptation is there.

Eat, but eat less.

This is the basic program for the next seven days.

In the morning there will be *kirtan*, devotional singing and dancing, for fifteen minutes. All of you are to stand up and dance blissfully during the *kirtan*. Blindfolds are to remain on the eyes. You can spread out and, with the blindfolds on the eyes, dance, do *kirtan* delightfully, dance blissfully. You are to let yourself go in *kirtan* blissfully for fifteen minutes; that I will tell you in detail in the morning.

Then the *kirtan* will stop and only music will be played for fifteen minutes; you are to continue dancing, dancing freely. After that, for thirty minutes, you are to relax like a dead man. That will be the morning meditation. Tomorrow morning I will explain to you about the noon and night meditations.

A special experiment has to be added in this camp – to be done before you go to sleep. I will explain it to you now, because that has to be started from tonight, and that is compulsory. If you do it you will create a lot of energy, and that energy will be utilized tomorrow. First, I told you to conserve your energy, not to waste it – that is one thing; now I will tell you the way to create more energy – how to create it. I told you not to spend what you have so that it is conserved, and now I will tell you the next thing – how to create it.

Whatever energy a man has is generally spent in daily routines, and whatever energy is left, gets accumulated at your sex center. That left-over energy provokes you, pushes you into sexual desire. That is why celibacy is easy to practice if you eat less – because that extra energy is not produced. Since extra energy is not produced, it does not accumulate at the sex center. But then *brahmacharya*, celibacy, is a deception, it has no meaning. It happens because you are living at a lower level with only a minimum amount of energy. If you do not take food for thirty days you will lose your interest in the opposite sex. Your interest has not ceased because you are a transformed person, but because the energy needed for this interest is not now being produced. After thirty days, if you eat even for only three days, three days of food will destroy what the thirty days of fasting had created; you will find yourself back in the same place.

The first thing is that the extra energy gets accumulated in your sex center, and the second thing is that the sex center is the dynamo which produces energy in every human being, in every living being. The sex center is the machinery within us that creates the energy. If you wish, you can create more and more energy with it. But we use this machine only to throw out the energy and not to create it. Energy created by this center, flowing upward, becomes kundalini, serpent power, the vital force.

So this night experiment is for the kundalini. And if you do it, these seven days will turn into utter bliss for you; then you will never be able to forget it again.

Tonight, when you go to sleep, and daily, when you lie down on your bed after completing everything, when you are ready to go to sleep, undress and cover yourself with a blanket or sheet. Lie on your back or on your stomach on the bed, whichever way you feel more comfortable – you can decide which after experimenting for a couple of days. Let your body be loose, close your eyes, and bring your attention to the sex center. Imagine that the sex center is getting active and energy is moving around it. You must have seen whirlpools in the water, water revolving so fast it makes a whirlpool. Anything thrown into the whirlpool moves in the circle, so feel like that within you – the energy moving fast around the sex center. If you throw a flower into it, it will revolve and drown in the middle. Imagine it like that. Within three minutes vibrations will start within you.

At first these vibrations will be just like the vibrations during lovemaking; the body will vibrate. When it vibrates, let it vibrate totally, cooperate with it, help it. Just imagine that you are really indulging in lovemaking and the whole body is vibrating. Let the whole body vibrate. Your whole body will become hot.

As soon as you feel that the whole body is vibrating and the energy is moving fast at the sex center, let yourself be loose and concentrate on one thought: that the energy has started rising upward from the sex center, just like a flame of fire going upward. Bring that energy to the middle of your forehead, between the two eyes, between the eyebrows; you have to take it to the third-eye center. This energy will start flowing upward. You have only to be aware that the energy has accumulated between the two eyes and it has started circulating there.

Then forget all about the sex center, and go to sleep with your attention on the third eye. When you get up in the morning, first feel this center between the two eyes and you will find there is a sensation of energy moving fast there. You will feel the movement clearly.

This you have to do every night, for seven days. It will channel the extra energy which used to flow into sex to the third eye. The sex center will create energy, as much as it can, and all that energy will be available to your third eye. In the morning we will experiment on that third eye, so to do this experiment at night is a must.

This will be the experiment for the night. Now we will do *kirtan* for a few minutes. Everyone stand up and dance and participate in *kirtan*, and after that we will disperse.

2

The Inquiry

What is bondage? Katham bandhah – what is bondage? Katham mokshah – what is liberation?

What is vidya, true learning, and what is avidya, false learning?

What are these five bodies? – the annamay, formed of food; the pranamay, formed of life-energy; the manomay, formed of psychic-energy; the vigyanamay, formed of awareness; the anandamay, formed of bliss.

What is the doer? What is this embodied soul? What are the five categories? Who is the one who knows? Who is the witness? Who is the one that resides deepest? Who is the knower of all thoughts and feelings?

What is the jeevatma, the individual soul, and what is paramatma, the universal soul? What is maya, illusion?

After the prayer to the divine, the inquiry begins. Inquiry can only begin after prayer. Prayerfulness brings the heart into such a space, it creates such a receptive and sensitive state of mind, that now the inquiry is not just made out of curiosity, it has turned into a longing for liberation. Inquiry without prayerfulness is only an intellectual game, and someone who inquires without having prayed first has not inquired at all. If someone is sitting in the dark with his door closed inquiring about the sun and about light, he can continue inquiring forever but he will never get an answer.

One of the biggest games of the mind is: when it receives no answer, it fabricates some answers in the darkness, never having known the sun. Someone will state, "The sun does not exist" – not because he knows that the sun does not exist, but because it is easier for him to deny what he could not know about than to allow his anguish, his state of not knowing, to persist. The anguish disappears with the denial; we can remain contented in our darkness. He who has not opened his doors may continue to inquire about the sun and about the light, but he will not get an answer. And, not getting an answer, he may not even deny the existence of the sun, but may instead fabricate an imaginary sun, fabricate his own concept, his own notion. And those concepts are just as false as his denial.

A non-believer standing in the darkness is as untrue as a believer standing in darkness. Without knowing the divine, their statements about the existence or the nonexistence of the divine are meaningless. Both statements are meaningless. And it is really interesting that great disputes and discussions go on in the darkness between these two groups who do not know anything at all.

Ignorance is full of disputes. Ignorance does not know, yet it is very voluble. Disputes can go on, doctrines can be established… In fact doctrines can only be created in darkness; in the light there can be no beliefs. The light is enough; beliefs are not needed. All doctrines are born in darkness, as where there is light, none are needed. Where truth is revealed, words have vanished; and where truth is everything, doctrines serve no purpose. Beliefs are a substitute, a compensation; when truth is not known, we create beliefs and install them in place of the truth.

Right inquiry begins with prayerfulness. When I say this, I mean that someone who wants to know the sun should at least fulfill one condition: that he should open the door of his house. If there is a longing to know the sun, he should at least open his doors so that if the sun wants to answer, it can answer. The sun has tremendous energy; even so it will not break down the doors to enter into your house. The sun will not even knock on your door.

In this world truth never trespasses on one's life, it never meddles in one's life. Truth never brings any slavery into one's life, it never brings any bondage. That is why truth is freedom. Truth never imposes itself forcibly without your will. Unless you are ready, truth will stand waiting without knocking at your doors. Your readiness, only your heartfelt invitation, can become truth's arrival.

But what is the point of your invitation if your door is not open? You should stand and wait at the door for the guest whom you have invited. That is why the Upanishad begins with prayer.

Prayerfulness is the way to open the door to the heart. If an inquiry is without prayerfulness, then it is initiated more by your doubts and not created by the search; then the inquiry is not for the sake of the search, it is to raise more doubts. One who has set out only to doubt, his doubting becomes unhealthy, it is sick.

And it is not that someone who opens his door with a prayerful heart loses the right to doubt – in fact only he has the right to doubt, because now doubt is only a part of the longing for the solution; now doubt is creative, not destructive; now doubt is only to find the way to remove all the hurdles; now the questions are there to get close to the answer. Now the inquiry is not the game of a diseased mind, now this doubt is not the disease of a sick mind, it is now the search of a healthy person.

Trustful doubt – these words appear to be very contradictory, but if we try to understand them from a different angle it will be clear. Try to understand "doubtful trust."

Even when we trust, it is full of doubt. Even if we put our trust in someone it is full of doubt; doubt is the undercurrent. In fact we trust only because inside there is doubt and we want to suppress it. And when doubt is inside and trust is on the surface, trust will be weak, because the inner is more powerful and the outer, the superficial, will be feeble; that which is on the periphery will be weak, and that which is at the center of the heart will be powerful.

So doubt is inside and trust is just imposed on the outside like clothes. Just as clothes do not eliminate your nakedness, they only hide it, similarly, trust imposed on the outside like clothes does not destroy doubt, it only hides it.

The opposite is also possible – what I call "trustful doubt." Trust is there in the heart, doubt is only on the circumference. That doubt becomes a part of the journey to strengthen the trust, because how can someone who has not doubted, trust? But actually he is full of trust.

Maulingaputta, a disciple of Buddha, said to him, "I ask you, not because I doubt you but because I doubt myself; I ask you, not because I doubt what you say but because I doubt whether I have understood it rightly. I ask not because I doubt your achievement, I ask you because I doubt my footsteps – and the journey is very long and the dream so vast. I have doubt about my own footsteps. I ask you so that my trust gets strengthened, I ask you so that my trust becomes profound."

Whenever one asks prayerfully, the doors of his heart are open; he does not come with doubt, he comes with a question. Questions can have answers, but doubts can have no answers, because someone who wants to doubt will go on doubting every answer you give him.

Doubt is an infinite regression: you give an answer, he doubts it; you give another, he doubts it; doubt is his basic premise. Whatever you say, he doubts it. Then there is no way.

But if doubt is only a part of the search, just a methodology – a method, not an end, not a solution, not a goal – if doubt is not the premise, but inquiry is, doubt is very helpful.

So, trustful doubt, and prayerful inquiry.

The very first question asked in the Sarvasar Upanishad is:

What is bondage?

Consider this. People usually ask whether God exists. What is God? What is liberation? Does liberation happen or not? What is the soul? Does it exist or not? People begin from where they should end. A diseased man is asking, "What is health?" But an intelligent person, if he is ill, will ask, "What is this illness?" The diagnosis will start with the illness. The first question raised in this Upanishad is: *What is bondage?* That is the disease, that is the sickness with which we are bound.

Someone is in a prison, tied with chains, enslaved, and is asking, "What is freedom?" He has never tasted freedom; he has been in chains since he was born, always in chains. He has found himself in chains for as long as he has been aware of himself. His awareness and his bondage are both joined together, and he is asking, "What is freedom?" Perhaps he would not be able to understand; he has not asked the right question. He should only be asking that which he can understand.

An intelligent seeker is a person who only asks the question whose answer he will be able to understand. And if he understands one answer, he will also be able to understand other answers.

That is why the first question is: *What is bondage?* – "How am I bound?" – because the person who has always been in bondage does not know what bondage is. Even to recognize it as bondage you must have had some experience of freedom. If you are handcuffed, you will realize that you are handcuffed. But if a child is born in chains, will he ever be able to recognize the chains as chains? They will appear to be a part of his body. And if you try to break his chains he will cry and scream, "Are you trying to kill me?" These chains are his life. They are not separate from him, they are his being.

And that is how we are. As long as we have existed, as long as we have known that we are, our awareness of our existence and of our prison have been joined. We have never experienced freedom. We have never flown in the sky, our wings have never opened in the open sky, we have only known them to be forever closed and unused. We have never known that our wings are meant for flying. We were born and brought up in a prison; this prison has been our very life.

So the right inquiry would begin with *What is bondage?* But we don't even know anything about slavery! We are deep in our slavery, we are slaves. How then can one recognize what slavery is? If a man is born and he suffers from a headache for the whole of his life, he will be unable to distinguish between the head and the ache, because he has always known his head with an ache.

Simone Weil, a great woman thinker of the West, has written that for thirty years she did not know what a headache was. Not because she never had a headache, but because she had *always* had a headache.

She never knew that the head could exist without a headache; she could not distinguish between the head and the headache. At the age of thirty, when her headache was cured for the first time, then she came to know that it was a headache and not the head itself.

You cannot separate yourself from that which you grow up with. That is why you are unable to know your body as separate from yourself – because you grow up with it. Hence the identity, the oneness with the body. That is why you do not know your mind as separate from yourself: because one grows up with it, identification happens.

Here the sage and the disciple raise the first question in this Upanishad: *What is bondage?*

Understand it like this: the disciple is asking the sage, "What is this bondage?" This Upanishad is a deep dialogue, a conversation. If he who is always in bondage can recognize his bondage, he can then have an idea, a dream, a concept, or a sense of freedom.

A perpetually diseased person can conceive only of a negative definition of health. He will understand health only as the absence of his disease. The person who has always lived in prison, in his chains, cannot understand a positive definition of freedom. He can understand freedom only as an absence of chains – when the walls of his prison will cease to exist, when there will be no guard with a gun to prevent him from doing whatever he wishes, to prevent him from going wherever he wishes to go. He can understand only by such negative definitions. But before he can understand this, it is also necessary to recognize that there are walls to his prison, to see the prison itself, to see the guards at the gate, the chains around his hands.

A great mystic from the Caucasus, Gurdjieff, used to say: I have heard about a magician who had tamed many sheep. Every day he would have one sheep killed in order to prepare his food. Hundreds of sheep stood and watched this, but even then it never occurred to them that if not today then tomorrow they would also be killed.

A guest who was staying with that magician said, "These sheep are strange. You kill a sheep in front of all the other sheep every day, and even then they are not worried. Can't they conceive of their own death the next day, that any day the dagger will be plunged into their necks?"

The magician replied, "I have hypnotized them and told them individually that they are not sheep, that all the rest are sheep; all the others will be killed, except them. That is why they are carefree; they don't run away when they see others being killed."

The guest asked, "And it is even more surprising that you do not tether them. Don't they go astray? Don't they get lost?"

He said, "I have also told them that they are totally free, they are never in bondage – because one wants to run away from bondage, but when one is already free there is no question of running away. The desire to run away comes when one is in bondage, but when there is no bondage and one is totally free then fleeing is not needed."

Gurdjieff used to say that man is almost in this situation: he considers his prison to be his palace. So there is no question of leaving it; in fact if someone comes to help him to get out of it, he defends himself as though against an enemy who is trying to get him out of his palace. Man treats his chains as his ornaments, they are a decoration for him. If you want to take away his ornaments he will stand with his sword and fight.

We do not crucify Jesus without reason, we do not poison Socrates without reason. They are our enemies because they try to take away our ornaments. What they call our chains are our ornaments, and what they call our prison is our kingly abode; what they call our slavery is our life, and what they call our sorrows are our pleasures.

So Gurdjieff used to say, the first thing a prisoner must know if he wants to be free is that he *is* a prisoner; everything else is secondary. If a slave is to get free, he first needs to understand that he is a slave.

This should penetrate his consciousness so deeply that he feels an acute agony and becomes filled with a longing for freedom: *What is bondage?*

The second question…then the second question arises: *What is liberation?*

Katham bandhah – what is bondage? Katham mokshah – what is liberation?

If you were to go and ask Buddha, "What is liberation?" Buddha would not answer. But if you asked him, "What is bondage? What is liberation?" you would receive an answer – because if you don't ask the right question, you cannot receive the right answer. Wrong questions do not have right answers.

And what you ask shows the state of your mind. Liberation can be understood only after understanding bondage.

And then the next question is:

What is vidya, true learning, and what is avidya, false learning?

What is bondage? What is liberation? What is true learning? – What is true knowledge? It would have been better if as in the first part – *What is bondage? What is liberation?* – we asked in this order: *What is false learning? What is true learning?* But it is not asked like that. And this is not accidental. What should be asked first is, "What is true ignorance?" then, "What is true knowledge?" But it is not asked like that, because here *vidya* has another meaning. Here *vidya* means: What is bondage? What is liberation? And when the Upanishad asks: What is *vidya*, true learning? it means: What is the method by which to be liberated? *Vidya* has exactly this meaning. *Vidya* means: What is the method by which to be liberated? Here *vidya* does not mean what we generally understand it to mean.

What is the method? After understanding what bondage is, and what liberation is, now: What is the method?

Granted that we are in prison, and granted that there is a vast sky outside the prison and it is possible to fly in that sky, granted that there is a sun beyond the walls of darkness and oneness with that sun is possible, and granted that beyond this body is the abode of the immortal – but then, what is the way there? What is the method?

Even if we know what bondage is and what liberation is, if the door is unknown – the way to get out of bondage and to reach liberation is unknown – then what to do? Then nothing can be done.

Buddha has spoken about the four noble truths, the four foundational truths, the four basic truths. He said, "He who knows the four, knows all."

The first foundational truth is that man is in misery. The second is that there is a cause for that misery, that one is not in misery without reason – because if one were in misery without reason then there would be no way to get free. And the third is that even if there is a cause, the misery is there, so there must be a way out, otherwise it would not be possible to transcend misery. So Buddha has said, "The first truth is misery, the second truth is the cause of misery, and the third truth is that there is a way to be free from misery."

But even if there is misery, a reason for this misery, and a way to get free from this misery, if a possibility of becoming free from this misery did not exist, and if that state of freedom where man could be out of misery did not exist, then he would just plunge from one misery into another. So Buddha has spoken about a fourth foundational truth: the existence of the state of freedom from misery. Buddha said, "Enough, these four are enough."

Here, *vidya* means: How to get free? What is the way? What is the method? What is the remedy?

Maybe there is only bondage, a prison, miseries – and man is standing helplessly, without remedy! Then the struggle would be meaningless; then we would have to be satisfied with what and where we are; then we would just have to accept whatsoever happens as our destiny. Whatsoever we are, that would be our fate; there would be no way to get out of it. Then it would be right to accept this prison as a palace in which we are destined to dwell with no possibility of ever getting out – so then what would be the point in creating unnecessary suffering by calling it a prison?

There have been thinkers who believed that misery just exists and there is no remedy to free ourselves from it; it is the very nature of life, transcendence is impossible.

Diogenes was a Greek thinker. When the Greek emperor visited Diogenes he asked him, "Tell me: what is the greatest truth of life?

Tell me about the highest, the supreme-most truth."

Diogenes replied, "There is no way to get to know the greatest truth, so leave it and ask for the second truth."

The emperor was taken aback, and he asked Diogenes, "But then at least say something about the first one."

Diogenes replied, "No, there is no way to know it, because the supreme-most truth is: not to be born at all. And now you have already been born. The highest truth is not to be born at all. This is the first truth. But now there is no way of knowing this, as you have already been born. I will tell you the second truth, and that is: to die right after birth." To die right after birth!

"Why?" the emperor asked.

Diogenes replied, "Life and its miseries are not separate; unless you die this death, miseries will persist. *To be* is the misery. There is no way out."

Naturally, if this is the situation, then there is no way out except suicide.

There have been thinkers who believe that there is no way to get free of the sufferings of life; that there is no way to get out of the prison, because existence itself is the prison, that nothing exists outside of it. That is why the question is meaningful: *What is vidya, true learning?*

Is there a way, is there a remedy, or are we just helpless? If the latter is the case, then it is right to keep on dreaming, to keep on sleeping, treating the prison as a palace, thinking of the chains as ornaments. Then this would be intelligent. Many people live with this kind of intelligence; they live in delusion in order not to have to be aware of the misery and the prison because there doesn't appear to be a way to come out of it.

What is vidya, true learning, and what is avidya, false learning? Avidya does not mean ignorance. If *vidya* means the method, the way to reach, then what could be the meaning of *avidya*? *Avidya* means the method which appears to be a method but leads nowhere: a false method. Certainly there are false methods also, pseudo methods! There are doors which do not exist but they appear to exist; there are keys which look exactly like keys but they cannot open any lock, they are of no use; one can play with them one's whole life but nothing will open.

Wherever there is a search then false keys can be invented because they are free, cheap; they are easily available, they can be purchased in the market. What *you* call *dharma*, religion, generally ninety-nine percent of it is *avidya*, because a superficial search and the desire to get things cheaply creates false methods in the marketplace.

Many ways exist, most of them false ways which only lead to oblivion. If one falls into oblivion then the prison no longer exists.

If one is intoxicated by the prison, does the prison still exist? No, in intoxication neither the prison nor the person himself exist; everything disappears in unconsciousness. And the intoxicated person becomes the emperor of this prison. The intoxicated person imagines in his prison that he is flying high in the sky. Now he can imagine anything, because when one is intoxicated one can dream and an awareness of the truth is lost. Like this, one can visualize God. Someone who has not even seen himself can see God; someone who does not even know himself knows the ultimate. These are the devices for deception.

And this world is not harmed as much by ignorant people as it is by the so-called knowledgeable people who hand you false keys. They derive much pleasure in giving you the keys, and you have the pleasure, the great pleasure, of getting something for free without paying a price, without doing anything. And most people want to get something without doing anything for it.

The greatest of all human diseases is lethargy, inertia: wanting something for nothing, wanting to reach somewhere without moving. Expecting the goal to come walking toward you without even taking a single step – what could be better than that? The crowd is bound to follow these people. The crowd pleases these so-called gurus and their ego is fulfilled. So a mutual exploitation goes on. So-called gurus with false keys are readily available; and disciples too are available, ready to purchase these keys. And so the trade goes on.

Avidya means those methods which do not open any door, but they give the illusion that an opening exists. That is why the inquirer asks: What is *vidya*? What is *avidya*? Waking, dreaming, sleeping and *turiya* – the fourth – what are these four states?

In fact the distinction between *vidya* and *avidya* cannot be understood if these four states of waking, dreaming, sleeping and *turiya* are not understood.

In the history of mankind, the first seekers on the earth to mention the four states of human consciousness were in India. Western psychology has until now been circling around the waking state; up to the year 1900, Western psychology was completely involved only with the waking state. Any discussion about the dreaming state was thought to be a lack of understanding. Whosoever talked about the dreaming state was thought to be mad. What is there in dreams? A dream is only a dream, what else is there to it? But during the last fifty years, as psychology went deeper into understanding the human mind, going deeply into the investigation of mental diseases, they gradually began to realize that under the waking state there lies a layer of dreams which is even more significant than the waking state. Until then the dream had been thought to be just a dream – a meaningless area, only human imagination; there was no need to pay attention to it. Thinkers of the West used to laugh at the East, where stupid people were even talking about dreams. But now, today, due to the efforts of Freud, Jung and Adler, psychologists are constantly talking about dreams.

If you go to a psychologist he will first inquire about your dreams, because according to him whatsoever is happening in your waking state is just superficial, it does not reflect your reality; only dreams reflect your reality. Reality through dreams?

– because you cannot deceive in dreams. Man has become an expert in deceiving. You may talk of celibacy the whole day, but your dreams will tell how deep your celibacy is; you can easily fast the whole day, but your dreams will tell how deep your desire for food is.

As yet man has not found a way to deceive in his dreams. His dreams expose his reality. In dream a thief is a thief and a saint is a saint. The waking state is not reliable; there even thieves are saints, and sometimes even saints appear to be thieves. The waking state is not to be trusted. The waking state is not at all reliable, because man manipulates the waking state in every way, paints it in every way.

So what you pretend to be in your waking state is completely false and dreamlike. And nothing is truer than your dream, because as yet you cannot be deceptive in dreams. If anyone ever discovers how to do that, your dreams will also begin to be false; but as yet no one has discovered how to do it. If you discover such a technique someday you may choose to be a saint in your dreams. But as yet you cannot manipulate your dreams, as yet you cannot direct your dreams, you cannot yet penetrate into them; you remain standing outside of them. That is why when your dreams are investigated, your deeper reality becomes known; this second layer is deeper.

You have an upper layer, that is the waking state. What do you do in the world from morning till night? All your chanting, worshipping and praying – no, these are not that deep. What you do in dreams is more profound; they bring to the surface your inner state of being.

So psychologists now accept that even a dream is not merely a dream; in actual fact it is truer than the waking state.

The question is, what are these four states? – because without understanding these four states it will be impossible to enter into meditation. People say that they want to know their real self. They perhaps think that there is a direct way to know the real self. No, first you have to know what the waking state is, what the dreaming state is, what the sleeping state is, what *turiya* is. Then, only then, you can enter into your inner being. *Turiya* is your inner being.

This is of great psychological interest. Now the West has accepted that dreams are significant. A genius like Freud devoted his whole life to studying people's dreams. But the West has still not accepted the third layer. The West has not yet inquired, "What is dreamless sleep?" because they think that sleep is merely sleep, as they used to think that a dream is merely a dream. Now they think that sleep is merely sleep, a matter of relaxation – one gets tired and sleeps. But doubts have started arising.

After the year 1950, in these twenty years, doubts arose, and now they have begun to think that sleep is not merely sleep. So now, in America, ten major labs are working on the question of deep sleep.

It has become clear to them during these twenty years that unless we understand sleep, it is going to be difficult to understand man – because a man who lives for sixty years sleeps for twenty years.

This is not a small ratio! Twenty years of sleep during a lifespan of sixty years! One-third just spent in sleep! So sleep must have a deep significance, it must have a purpose. It is an essential part of life. A man can live for three months without food, but not without sleep; a man can fast for three months, but can't do without sleep.

One more amazing thing that has come to the notice of the Western psychologist is that a man will also go mad if he does not dream. He cannot live without dreams. If a man is allowed to sleep but not to dream... They have conducted experiments, because machines are now available which can indicate when you are dreaming and when you are sleeping. When you are dreaming, a needle moves very quickly, because the brain is active when you are dreaming. Even by touching your eyes in sleep it can be known whether you are dreaming at that time or not, because when you are dreaming your eyes are moving in the same way as they move in the waking state when you are seeing.

And slowly, slowly it is becoming clear that the eye movements will confirm what type of dream you are having. When you are seeing a sexual dream your eyes move very fast. The impulses in the brain and the frequency of the eye movements have been observed. Now you can no longer remain unconcerned that others will never know about your dreams; the man sitting in your room can know all that you are doing inside! Sooner or later we will be able to categorize the different eye movements and the different measurements of your brain impulses and what they mean. Then we will know what type of dream the saint is having!

The latest discovery is that if a man is not allowed to dream… A man dreams about eight to ten times during the course of a night. There is deep sleep and in between there are dreams – so when the machine indicates that someone is dreaming he is immediately awakened. As soon as he begins to dream he is awakened; the dream has been discontinued, and again he is allowed to sleep – he is allowed to sleep until he starts dreaming again. As soon as he starts dreaming he is awakened again. The results are surprising: however much sleep you may have, if you are not allowed to dream after fifteen days you start going crazy. Dreams are necessary, otherwise you will go mad.

You may be thinking that dreams disturb you too much; but that is the outlet of your madness. If you are prevented from dreaming you will certainly go mad because that which remains inside will disturb you the whole day. If it is not allowed to be released during the night it will surface during the day. So it is better that it is released in the darkness of the night, because if it were to come up during the day it would be troublesome. If the anger which you would normally throw away by killing somebody in your dream during the night is suppressed for fifteen days, you will actually kill someone – there will be such an accumulation of anger that you will have to kill.

Dreams are necessary. Unless consciousness reaches to *turiya*, dreams are necessary. Only someone who attains to *turiya* neither needs dreams, nor sleep, nor even the waking state; he passes through all three, but he has no need of them. He is awake even in dreams, he is awake during sound sleep; he is also awake during the waking state. We are dreaming even during the waking state, we are even dozing during the waking state.

What are these states?

During the second half of the twentieth century psychologists began to think that deep sleep also needed to be investigated. If someone's sleeping state could be accurately understood it would be easy to know his personality and his real nature. Sleep also has qualities. Everyone does not sleep in the same deep state. But even now, psychologists are not yet aware of *turiya*, the fourth state. But Jung has said, "We have to accept the discovery of the East that dreams are valuable and that they should be investigated."

When the Upanishads were translated for the first time in the West, people were asking, "What are these Upanishads? Is there any spirituality in the inquiry into dreams? To ask about the divine, about liberation, can be understood, but to ask about dreams? What is this inquiry? And this inquiry is being made by Hindus, who believe that this world is *maya*, a dream. And they are inquiring about dreams!" So Jung has said, "Now, bowing our heads, we have to accept that the dreaming state is more important than the waking state."

But Jung had already died; he never came to know that psychologists have now had to accept the importance of sleep. The deeper the phenomenon is, the more valuable it becomes. And yet they are still not aware that there is a state beneath the sleeping state, which is not a state but being itself, called *turiya*.

These are the three states: waking, dreaming, sleeping; and the fourth is not a state – that is our self-nature, our being.

So the inquiry is valuable. We shall probe into the answers in the Upanishad one by one.

What are these five bodies? – the annamay, formed of food; the pranamay, formed of life-energy; the manomay, formed of psychic-energy; the vigyanamay, formed of awareness; the anandamay, formed of bliss.

We have heard about the "soul" and its search, but until we know what the physical body is, we cannot search for the soul. This is a very scientific search.

What is the body? If there had been only one body it would have been easy, but we have five bodies inside ourselves. The Upanishads have divided the layers of our bodies into five parts. What is visible on the outside is the *annamay* body. Hidden behind it is the *pranamay* body – what scientists in the West call bio-energy. The East has called it *prana*; it is an energy body. It is the second layer within this physical body. Behind it is the *manomay* body, the body of mind, of psychic energy. Those who have gone on the inner journey know that the mind is also a body. "Body" only means that you are surrounded by a layer of it.

Behind the mind there is one more body called the *vigyanamay* body. This we call consciousness – that capacity of knowing. The ability to know is also a body. Behind that the Upanishads accept one more body which they call the *anandamay* body, the bliss body. Those glimpses of happiness which we occasionally feel in life are the happenings in our bliss body.

These are the five bodies. Behind these exists our inner being. These are the five walls of our prison; these five are our prisons. The divine is within as well as outside these five walls. With the fall of these five walls, the inner and the outer become one. Sometimes we are able to penetrate through these five walls and touch the divine outside. Sometimes the divine outside is able to send its rays across these five walls and touch us inside. But this happens rarely; this phenomenon happens rarely.

Sometimes, in deep love with someone, you can suddenly cross beyond these five walls and you get a glimpse of the divine in the other. But this is only a glimpse. The glimpse comes and then vanishes. This is why when you are in love with someone, the other does not appear to be just a person, he or she appears to be divine. This is in no way a mistake; it is a glimpse, but it is only a glimpse. This phenomenon happened because the five walls were penetrated – a little bit of fragrance entered you. It will not happen every day. This is why lovers find themselves in great difficulty afterward, because later one finds that the man is just ordinary, or the woman is just ordinary. Where has that glimpse gone? It has disappeared, it was only a momentary thing.

That glimpse will only come in some very sensitive moment. Sometimes it comes seeing a flower in bloom; sometimes, cutting across the five bodies, one gets a glimpse seeing a cloud floating in the sky; sometimes the sun rises in the morning and its rays touch not only the body but penetrate beyond the five bodies, touching something within.

It is in such glimpses that the concepts of the religions have been born in the world. A sage is taking a bath in a river...the sun is rising, and he is standing on the banks freshly bathed and the sun's rays enter him... The sun becomes a deity, the sun becomes a god to him. His experience is complete in itself. But now people stand with their hands folded in prayer because the sun has become a deity, although they can't see any point in it. Science books say that it is nothing but a fireball, and this he can understand, but about this god he has no idea at all.

Sociologists say that perhaps seeing the sun people became afraid and so they took the sun to be a god. That all religions were born out of fear. People may have been afraid of fire, so to show respect to it and to persuade the fire not to harm them or the sun not to harm them, people knelt down to worship them with folded hands. This is a total misconception.

With an awareness of these five bodies, the inner journey starts.

What is the doer? What is this embodied soul?

What are the five categories? Who is the one who knows? Who is the witness? Who is the one that resides deepest? Who is the knower of all thoughts and feelings?

What do these mean? Similarly:

What is the jeevatma, the individual soul, and what is paramatma, the universal soul? What is maya, illusion?

What are these?

These questions are the preface, then the Upanishad enters into the answers. Try to understand the questions correctly. In this morning's discourse, understand the questioning mind; understand the proper dimension of the question. Answers are not so difficult, the question is the real matter – because the answer has to be born within the questioner. The answer does not come from outside, the answer is not without, it is within you. If you can ask the right question, the inner answer starts arising in you. "The right question" means that you have begun to hit at the answer within you. The wrong question means you do not hit it at all and the answer never comes. The answer can be given from without, but it never reaches you.

A communion is needed: the answer should be throbbing within you, and then, when it is also given from the outside, only then can you receive the answer, otherwise not. Until you feel a deep response, until your inner strings feel a resonance when the outer strings are played, until your inner veena resounds, the outer veena may continue playing but it will be of no use.

Throughout the Upanishad, I will give you the answers from without. But that will not be enough. A sensitivity needs to be created within you for the answers to hit at the right place within. And to hit at the right place is all that matters. If you have this resonance within, the answer from outside can be helpful; the answer is revealed at the meeting point of the two. And it is possible that the outer answer is not needed and the inner answer is revealed on its own, but it is never possible for the outer answer to be revealed without the resonance of the inner one. The outer is the secondary – it has its utility, but it is secondary; it is necessary, but not essential.

So it is possible that the answer is revealed without any answer coming from the outside. If the question is so penetrating, so heartfelt, so sincere that one's whole life is at stake, then answers are revealed even without the outer answers. But it is not possible the other way – it is never possible. Buddha may be standing outside, Mahavira may be standing there, Krishna may be standing there and Christ may be standing there, and all of them may be shouting the answers, but if there is no sensitivity, no yearning, no thirst, no longing, there is no way – all those questions, all those answers are a wastage.

From this evening we will begin to understand the answers.

Now we will do the meditation to awaken a sensitivity within. If the sensitivity is there, we can then enter into the answer.

So understand a few things about the method of this meditation. The first: stay seated, first listen to me, then you can spread out.

For the first fifteen minutes of the meditation there will be *kirtan*, devotional singing and dancing. Drown yourself in it completely. If you hold back even a little you will miss the first step, and then there can be no question of taking the second step. So someone who shows even a little bit of miserliness is utterly stupid. It is better he should leave here; he is making a useless effort.

Keep it in mind: either put everything totally at stake, or don't do it at all. A halfhearted effort won't do. Either devote yourself totally, or not at all. Do not work unnecessarily, because a halfhearted effort brings wrong results. You will feel that you tried it and nothing happened. It creates a dejection. No, don't do it at all, then at least a hope will continue and you will gather the courage in some other life. No lukewarm effort.

Boil up to one hundred degrees, then evaporation can happen. Participating in a lukewarm way and then cooling down, again and again repeating this, slowly, slowly you will lose all hope that you too can boil at one hundred degrees and evaporate.

So the first thing to be remembered is to enter totally into the *kirtan* for fifteen minutes. By "total" I mean go completely mad; less than that won't do. Blindfolds must be kept on your eyes, with the eyes closed. Spread out – you have enough space here – spread out all over so that you can dance freely.

Keep dancing for fifteen minutes during the *kirtan*, then the singing will stop and the music will continue. In those fifteen minutes you have to dance individually with the music. Whatever energy you have, use it totally. Become a flow of energy, so that the dancer disappears and only the dance remains. Let the music become all and you dance with that music. If you can do it with total intensity you will immediately feel that you have become separate from the body. It is not very difficult to be separate from the body – separation from the body is very easy. If you use your total energy, you immediately become separate from the body. This is the science behind it.

So *kirtan* singing will go on for fifteen minutes in all, then it will stop and there will be only music – no group singing, only dancing and jumping – and put your total energy into it. The second step will continue for fifteen minutes. If you wish to shout you can shout, but the *kirtan* singing will stop. Do whatever you feel like doing. If the feeling of *kirtan* singing persists with someone he may continue on his own, but the collective singing will stop. Individually you can do whatever you want to do – but you must not stop. Put your total energy into it for fifteen minutes.

Then we will relax for thirty minutes. Lie down on the earth for thirty minutes like a corpse. You can lie on your back or on your stomach – whatever is comfortable for you. If someone feels like standing he can stand; if someone wants to sit he can sit. But be a corpse. Standing, stand in such a way that if you fall, then you will fall like a corpse. Don't interfere. I will give a few suggestions during these thirty minutes. When I suggest to you to rub your forehead with your palm, slide your blindfold up or down a little for these one or two minutes. That is all I will suggest for you to do during the thirty minutes. When you have completed the first thirty minutes, I will then go on suggesting to you what you are to do for the next thirty minutes, and you will be gone on the journey within.

If this journey can be made, the answers of the Upanishad will be understandable; otherwise you will miss.

No one is allowed to come up on the raised area.

Spread out all over the ground.

3

The Sage Answers

Soul is both: the universal and the individual.
Through identification with the body,
which of itself is not the soul,
the soul becomes possessed
with a sense of ego around the body.
This sense of ego is the bondage
of the individual, embodied soul.
When this sense of ego ceases, it is called liberation.
That which gives birth to this sense of ego
is called avidya, false learning,
and that which leads to the cessation
of this sense of ego is called vidya, true learning.

What is bondage? What is liberation? Now come the answers to these questions.

There are two methods, two ways to seek to understand life, to understand existence. One is the method of analysis, the second is the method of synthesis. One belongs to science, the other to religion.

Science reduces things into their smallest unit, and through this it accumulates knowledge. Science dissects objects into their minutest parts, and only through this dissection is the knowledge of science born.

The process of religion is just the opposite. Religion synthesizes each and every unit with the ultimate whole, synthesizes the parts with the whole, unites the divisible with the indivisible. Only when everything is one, does religion become the ultimate knowledge.

Understand it like this. There is a flower: you can dissect it. A scientist will dissect it; to study the flower he will analyze it down to its chemical components, down to its elements – how many minerals it contains, how much water it contains, what chemicals it contains. He will dissect and analyze, and be able to describe the components of the flower. But no poet will agree to that; a lover of beauty will call this analysis murder because in the very analysis the flower is destroyed. What we have come to know is not the flower. What we found through analysis may very well be the constituent parts of the flower, but the flower itself is something else. We come to know the parts of the flower by analyzing them, but the flower itself remains unknown; it disappears in the very dissection and analysis.

The beauty of the flower will not be there in the labeled bottles containing the parts of the flower after the scientist has dissected it; that beauty was in the wholeness of the flower, in the total flowering of the flower. The beauty was not in its parts, it was in its totality.

Understand it like this: someone has written a song – can we know this song better by dissecting it? A linguist, if asked to explain the song, could explain how the song was written, what words were used, what grammatical rules were applied – but the song will be lost, because the song was not in its grammar. A song, when understood deeply, is not only the sum total of its words. It is more than that, something more. That "more" is lost.

So science searches for the subtlest unit, the ultimate particle, but is deprived of the whole – it misses godliness. Religion says that that which emerges out of the organic unity of the whole is godliness. These two kinds of knowledge are totally different, in fact quite contrary. But these are the two ways in which one can know.

Analysis can never lead us beyond matter; it never will. No, it is impossible. It is futile to hope that someday science will declare the existence of God. A scientist may start talking of the existence of something divine, but that is not a statement of science.

In his last days Einstein started experiencing the existence of something divine – but that was the statement of a scientist, not of science. It is like this: a scientist falls in love with someone and says that she is the most beautiful woman on earth. This is not a statement of science but a statement of the scientist. A scientist can feel blissful to see a flower and can dance in ecstasy, but this is not the dance of science, it is the dance of the scientist.

But religious people often think… If sometimes a scientist admits to the existence of God – some Eddington, or Oliver Lodge, or an Einstein – religious people immediately start thinking that now science is also going to be talking of God. That is totally wrong. These statements are individual and personal, they have nothing to do with science.

Science will never be able to talk of God, the ultimate reality, because the very method used by science leads to division, it does not lead to a synthesis, to the whole. It would be another thing if science someday used the method of religion and was then able to talk of the divine, but then it will not remain science anymore, it will have become religion.

The answer of the sage starts with this:

Soul is both: the universal and the individual.

That capacity of awareness, the consciousness, this knower within man, the watcher, the witness, this is what the Upanishads call the soul.

But this statement is very strange. It says: "The soul, the self is God. There is no other God than this self." This is the way of synthesis. The individual self is within you, and the universal self is the name for the whole of existence.

You have a drop of water. If you ask a scientist, "What is the ocean?" he will say it is nothing more than the sum total of many, many drops. And he is not wrong. If you divide the ocean, what will you get except drops? But is the ocean really only just drops? – storms and waves cannot arise in a drop. The ocean *is* something more, more than just drops of water. But science will then ask, "Where is the ocean? – if we take out all the drops of water there will be no ocean left." And they are right.

If you amputate my hands, my feet, cut off my head, cut off all my limbs – then what is left of me? Yet I am more than just my hands and feet, and even when my feet are being cut off I can be aware that I am still here, that it is not me that is being cut off. Even when my head is being cut off I can also be fully conscious – not only will others be watching this head being cut off, I will also be watching it being cut off.

When they were killing Mansoor by cutting his limbs off one by one, he was laughing. Someone in the crowd asked him, "Mansoor, have you gone mad? You are being killed and yet you are laughing."

Mansoor replied, "Previously I was mad; then even the prick of a thorn used to make me cry. But now I am not mad, because just as you are watching my head being cut off, I am also seeing the head being cut off. You are watching it from the outside, I am watching it from within; but we are both onlookers, watchers. You are watching this body from the outside, I am watching it from within."

If we ask a religious person, "What is a drop?" he will say, "It is the ocean itself."

The scientist reduces the ocean to a drop, the religious man finds the ocean in a drop. And this is no small difference, this is a revolutionary difference. Science reduces all things to their lowest denominator, religion connects all things to the highest point.

This is not just an ordinary play of words so that you can say, "What difference does it make whether you say a drop is the ocean or the ocean is a drop?" It *does* make a difference, because science analyzes, and after this analysis it accepts the lowest common denominator as the basis for all life. When a man is dissected all that can be found is matter – the bones, the flesh – but no soul. So science says, "There is no soul, man is only a combination of bones, flesh and marrow – this is the sum total; there is nothing more."

Religion says that the higher cannot be understood through the lower, but the opposite is possible… The ocean cannot be understood through the drops, but the drops can be understood through the ocean; the lower can be understood through the higher, but the higher cannot be understood through the lower. There are reasons for this. Try to understand this correctly, then you will be able to understand the language of the Upanishad.

An old man cannot be understood through a child, but a child can be understood through an old man, because an old man has lived both. A child is only a child, he has not yet become old. Through the ocean we can understand the ocean as well as the drop, but through the drop we cannot understand the ocean. Through matter we can explain only the body, through the divine we can explain both body and soul. The vast universe contains the molecule, but the molecule is unable to contain the universe. Through the vast universe everything can be explained, but through the infinitesimal it is impossible to explain the universe.

Understand it in this way: science always focuses its attention on the first and religion always focuses on the last. Science focuses on the first step and religion focuses on the ultimate destination – because religion says that if there is no destination, then even that first step cannot be explained. How can you even call it the first step when there is no destination? That first step exists because of the last step which is waiting in the future.

So we can explain the first step through the destination; but if we have accepted the first step as everything, then the destination cannot be explained – then even the first step cannot be explained. The means can be understood through the end, but the end cannot be understood through the means. So the drop cannot explain the ocean, but the ocean can absorb the drop.

The sage says: *Soul is both: the universal and the individual.* Two words have been used: *universal soul,* meaning pure consciousness, the divine; then the *individual soul,* or self.

What is the difference between the individual soul and the divine? The sage says there is no difference. There is only as much difference as there is between the ocean and the drop. The drop is also the ocean, it contains everything of the ocean. Only one thing is to be remembered – that the ocean is not only the sum total of its drops. The divine dwells within a person; then it is called the individual soul.

It is like the sun rising in the sky, filling your courtyard with its rays. There is no difference between the sunrays in the sky and the sunrays in your courtyard, but the rays in the courtyard have a boundary; the walls of your courtyard surround the sunrays and a boundary has happened.

The universal soul dwelling within limits is called the individual soul. But is it true that the rays of the sun which fill your courtyard have a boundary, or does the boundary belong to your courtyard? Do the walls create a hindrance for the sunrays? Walls enclose your courtyard, but how can the walls enclose the sunrays? But if the sunshine in your courtyard has the illusion that it has limits, that it is in bondage, then it will be called the sunray's ego.

The universal soul which is within the boundaries of the body is called the individual soul. But if this individual soul has the illusion that it is the body itself, then it is called the ego. There is no difference: even when the sunrays are under the illusion that they are imprisoned in the courtyard, in reality they are not. Rays cannot be bound; that is the very nature of sunrays. Close your fist and you cannot catch hold of the rays. Their very nature is unbounded – that is their very freedom, their very life. The walls are not there for the rays, they are there for the courtyard; but the illusion can be created. Illusion binds the individual soul with ego. With the dissolution of that illusion, the individual soul becomes the universal soul, the whole. Religion sees the whole of life in such a vast perspective.

It is very useful for the seeker to remember this line of thinking because his journey also starts from the courtyard – from the walls of the courtyard to the sunrays, and from the sunrays to the sun itself.

Soul is both: the universal and the individual.
Through identification with the body,
which of itself is not the soul,
the soul becomes possessed
with a sense of ego around the body.

Ego is identification: the illusion of being that which I am not. The sunrays in the courtyard thinking that they are defined by the courtyard, that this is their being: this identification is ego.

This sense of ego is the bondage
of the individual, embodied soul.
When this sense of ego ceases, it is called liberation.
That which gives birth to this sense of ego
is called avidya, false learning,
and that which leads to the cessation
of this sense of ego is called vidya, true learning.

That which creates this ego is called *avidya*, false learning. The method, the way, the process which creates the ego is called *avidya*. And the method or the way which leads to the cessation of the ego, which disintegrates the ego, which melts the ego, which withers the ego, is called *vidya*, true learning.

We all live in *avidya* because we do nothing except create the ego. If we are earning money, we earn only to support the ego; if we accumulate knowledge, we do it only to fulfill the ego. And if we go on the long journey toward prestige and position, climbing step by step to reach the capital and attain to the throne, then what will we do there? It is not *you* who becomes famous on the throne, it is only the ego which becomes famous; it is not your head which is crowned, it is the head of your ego which is crowned.

We are earning nothing more than ego. Our entire life's very process is of how to become something: how to push others' egos back and reach to the front. A meaningless race! But it goes on your whole life; from the cradle to the grave the same race continues, the same race of envy, rivalry and competition.

What is envy? What is competition? What is rivalry? What is this struggle? – and why do they all exist? The basic motivation is not to be left behind, not to remain a pigmy, not to remain poor, but also to be crowned, to be garlanded, for this ego to be studded with precious stones, to shine; not to remain a nothing but to become something.

From the smallest to the biggest, all are engaged in this one race. And this race is so strange that even if it sometimes takes just the opposite turn the basic motivation still remains the same. A man goes on accumulating wealth so that he may reach to the top, to the peak of wealth, to the Everest of wealth. And another man renounces his riches, goes to the jungle and becomes an ascetic, and yet he may still be vain and now start collecting the coins, the rewards of his asceticism, instead of ordinary coins. There is still the ego, that now there can be no one as pure as him; that there is no comparison between him and the rest of the world.

The ego can even feed itself with the search for the divine. Ego can even talk about the divine in order to show that now it is not involved in just ordinary matters, that now it has even got a hold on God!

If the process of earning ego is *avidya*, we all are living in *avidya*. And what we call *vidya*, learning, what we call schools, colleges and universities, places of learning, if we understand the sage properly these are all places of false learning. They are anti-universities, because nothing is taught there except the art of filling the ego. All education is a process to create ego; it is an attempt to arouse ambition. The father tells his son to come first in his class and not to lag behind. And if the son lags behind, the father feels miserable. If the son comes first, it is as if the father himself has come first.

Everyone has to be in the race, that is the only game. If this is *avidya*, false learning, then our whole life is *avidya*. Then we know nothing of *vidya*, the right learning, because the sage says that right learning is that process, that method which melts the ego, which withers the ego – and a moment comes when ego is no more and only the soul remains, only the being is left.

You may call that *vidya*, religion, yoga, meditation, prayerfulness, worship, any name you want to give it – thousands of names have been given to it – but the essence of *vidya* is only one: it should create an inner state where only you remain but not the ego, where consciousness remains, but there is no center inside proclaiming "I."

You should be able to lose this I through any method or process. And this losing does not mean falling asleep or forgetting yourself, it means that you should be left totally awake, fully conscious, with self-remembrance, and yet the I should not remain; only that should remain which has no connection with the I.

One morning someone came and bowed down to Buddha's feet. A skeptic was also there, sitting near Buddha. And the skeptic asked Buddha, "Why don't you prevent this person from touching your feet? – because you yourself have taught us not to go to anybody's refuge, rather to seek one's own self. This man has come to you for refuge and you are not preventing him."

Buddha said, "If I had been there, I would have prevented him." And Buddha continued, "And if I had been there, then preventing him from touching my feet or inspiring him to come to my feet would have been one and the same thing. But the man who might have prevented him or inspired him does not exist anymore. You saw him bowing his head, so did I. But there is a slight difference between us. You saw him bowing down his head to me, whereas I wondered who he was bowing down to. I don't see anybody! To whom has he bowed down?"

The sage calls the methodology which brings one to such moment in life *vidya*, right learning.

What I am calling meditation is simply this science of religion. Whenever I say meditation, I am referring to this *vidya*.

We all live in unawareness. We are living as if asleep.

You may have seen a person under hypnosis walking, or a somnambulist sleepwalking, many persons sleepwalk. There may be many among you here, because at least seven out of one hundred walk in their sleep. At least seven! But the person is never aware of it, because he walks around and then goes to sleep again. He walks with open eyes. People have even murdered in their sleep and in the morning they were totally unaware of it, they could only say that they had had a dream in the night in which they killed someone. People have stolen, and they were not responsible at all because it all happened while they were asleep. But this refers only to those few people who sleepwalk.

And if we look at ourselves closely, we all live in a kind of sleep. Whatever you are doing you are not aware of it, your awareness is somewhere else. When you are walking on the street, are you aware of your walking? Your awareness may be anywhere else except walking. When you are eating, are you aware of eating? Your awareness may be anywhere else except on eating. Yes of course your awareness goes to food too, but that only happens when you are not eating.

Your awareness is not there where you are. Then what is left when there is no awareness? There is sleep, and all the disturbances happen in that sleep. When you were angry with someone, do you remember: where was your awareness? If there had been awareness, anger would have been impossible. Awareness and anger cannot co exist. Anger is not possible with awareness.

For anger, sleep is needed, intoxication is needed.

That is why a person becomes sorry after he has been angry, he is surprised that he could have done such a thing – and for what? What was the sense in it? Even though it was he himself who became angry – and it is not that this is the first time that he has become angry, and it is not the first time that he is regretting it. He has regretted it many times, because he has been angry many times, and each time he has wondered why he had done it, what was the point? And why did he do it when there was no point? This person was not aware, was not present; he only returned home after the anger was gone. He was absent when the anger happened, and when he returned he was sorry. But at this stage there is no use feeling sorry; there is no meaning in it, it is pointless to feel sorry.

There are a few things which are impossible to do with awareness. That which wise men have called sin cannot be done with awareness. This is the definition of sin: something which you cannot do with awareness. And that which you can only do in awareness is called virtue. You cannot steal with awareness, you cannot murder with awareness, you cannot be angry with awareness; but you can be compassionate with awareness, you can be loving with awareness.

Whatever is possible to do with awareness, all that is religion, is virtue. That which is impossible to do with awareness, for which sleep is necessary, which can happen only in unawareness, is sin.

So we are not living in awareness. Sometimes even when we sit in meditation we feel sleepy – even then! In fact then our sleep is even deeper. The reason for it is that we have no experience of awareness. The way we walk, sit and stand – everything happens in sleep, we are accustomed to it.

I said that we do everything without awareness, in a sort of sleep.

I was reading the biography of a man who had a habit of stammering. Psychologists analyzed it for years, and even after the best efforts and thousands of dollars being spent on his cure the stammering wouldn't stop. He was the son of a rich man, but no remedy could be found. He was given medicines, everything was tried, but the stammering did not stop. Then an interesting incident occurred. A play was being put on in the town and they needed an actor who could stammer; the actor who was experienced in stammering had fallen ill, he was unable to perform, so someone told them about this boy in the town who would be as expert in stammering as this actor was. The boy was called. The role was small, and the boy was readily available – training someone would be a difficult task. That young boy was sent onto the stage, and the miracle of all miracles happened that day: the boy could not stammer on stage. He tried his best, but he could not stammer. So what had happened?

I was in a town and a student from a university came to me. He had developed a strange habit of walking like a woman. He had tried a lot of things but he did not improve; often on the street he would find himself walking like a woman. There is no harm in walking like a woman – because women also have to walk – but he was in trouble and felt miserable.

In actual fact, the distribution of flesh on men's and women's bodies is different. Women gather flesh on some parts where men do not, so the difference in their gait is natural; it is a difference of flesh.

But he had no accumulation of flesh which would make him walk like a woman – because sometimes he would also walk like a man. It was just sometimes that he would start walking like a woman. He was in great trouble.

I told him, "Now do this: consciously try to walk like a woman."

He said, "What are you saying? I am already in trouble doing it unknowingly, and now you want me to do it knowingly? I try to prevent it all the time, but whenever I forget I walk like a woman."

I said, "You have tried to prevent it consciously but it didn't stop; now I ask you to consciously try to walk like a woman. Get up and walk in front of me."

He tried his best but he could not manage it. He said, "What has happened today? You must have done a miracle."

I asked him, "Don't tell anyone, because I had nothing to do with it. You have performed the miracle, but you are not aware of it."

A few things cannot be done knowingly, consciously. And a few things just drop by themselves in awareness.

Meditation is the method of *vidya*. It is impossible to assert the ego with awareness. Try to assert the ego consciously and you will understand what I am saying.

Gurdjieff used to play a trick on his disciples. He would put them into a situation in which they were unaware that they were being made deliberately angry. He would create a situation, or would do something so that the disciple became so annoyed, upset, that he would start screaming and abusing and become afire – and it was all planned, and everyone was contributing to this game. Only this one person was unaware that a trick was being played on him.

When he was swept up in the storm of his anger, ready to leave with all his baggage, abusive, then Gurdjieff would say, "Be alert, be aware of what you are doing." And the disciple would suddenly be taken aback and everything inside him would come to a standstill. He would laugh and say, "This was too much! So it was all a game."

Gurdjieff would try to arouse the ego, and when it was there he would shout at the right moment, "Now look within for the ego!" The disciple who was afire with ego would then close his eyes, look within, and sit quietly...until he would open his eyes and say, "No, it is not there – I am searching for the ego, but it is nowhere to be found."

Then who created such a storm? Big storms can arise even out of vanity. Storms can arise even in small teacups! Mighty storms can arise out of the insubstantial.

Vidya is the experiment to drop the false and meaningless forms which we have created within ourselves. There are many methods of *vidya*.

We are experimenting with a few here.

Now I will explain to you the method which we are going to use tonight, and I will give you some explanation about the experiments for tomorrow; then we will enter into the night meditation.

During tonight's method, which we will do now, you are to stare at me for thirty minutes without blinking your eyes, with your eyes as wide open as possible. You are to connect yourself with me through the eyes. The eyes are the doors. You are to bring your consciousness to me through your eyes; you are to extend your consciousness toward me.

If it can be extended to me, you can extend it further. Do not worry too much about that. If you can extend it to me, it will not be difficult to extend it to the sky.

So for thirty minutes you are not going to blink your eyes. You may say that this is very difficult. It is not difficult at all. You are not aware that when you look at a movie you do it without blinking your eyes for hours on end. That is why your eyes get tired; you are not aware that you were not blinking, so the eyes get tired. Whenever you look at something attentively, your eyes don't blink.

It is not difficult. The difficulty is just a trick of the mind. As soon as your mind becomes aware of the danger, that the disappearance of *avidya* is happening and, "This whole game will be over; if this jump happens, I will disappear," then the mind immediately says, "Your eyes are getting totally tired. Close them, blink them – have you gone mad?"

These are the mind's devices. Be aware of them. Don't

worry, tears are good; they will cleanse your eyes, you will feel unburdened. Don't think of anything. You are not to blink your eyes for thirty minutes. This is the first thing.

This experiment needs to be done while standing. Your eyes are not to blink at all, you are to stare at me continuously. Keep your hands raised up toward the sky, because the whole effort is to move the consciousness which is directed at me toward the sky at any moment. So continue holding both hands up. Keep staring at me, keep dancing and jumping and simultaneously shouting "Hoo...Hoo...Hoo..." in a loud voice.

This "Hoo" is being used as a mantra. This "Hoo" hits at the kundalini, the serpent power. When you shout "Hoo" loudly, you will find that it is hitting at your sex center, exactly on *muladhar*, the sex center.

So for thirty minutes, with your eyes staring at me, your consciousness rushing toward me, "Hoo" hitting at your kundalini, hands ready for the journey toward the sky. And you are dancing, because in dance the hit is stronger, the energy will rise within to go upward through your spinal cord.

Meanwhile I will keep silent, but occasionally I will make a gesture with both hands directing you to move toward the sky. When I make that gesture with the hands, then you are to put your total energy into dancing, into shouting "Hoo," into staring at me – you have to go totally mad. Put your total energy into it and keep jumping. When I stretch my arms upward and keep them there, then you have to give your total energy. I will make these gestures ten to twenty-five times to pull you from the lower to the higher. Don't be a miser at that moment, give your total energy. And when... Keep sitting, keep sitting, listen to the whole process.

When I feel that energy is running in your spine and your body has become a dancing flow of energy, when I feel that many people have reached to the point where their union with the universal energy can happen, I will turn my hands palms down. When I turn my palms downward, search within if there is any energy left, then give it totally, and I will bring my hands down. This will be the indication that in that moment, if you give your total energy, the universal energy from above can descend on you, the individual energy.

And where both energies meet there is bliss, and where both of them meet, *vidya* flowers. Where a person's consciousness identifies with the physical body *avidya* happens, that is where ego emerges; and where a person's consciousness meets with the universal consciousness *vidya* blooms, and one attains to the egoless state. Where a person's consciousness is identified with the body ego is born; and where a person's consciousness meets the universal energy the individual soul is realized. This describes tonight's experiment.

A little more information. Today, in today's experiment, to get you accustomed to it, I did not push you to put your total energy into it, and kept the experiment a little liberal. The experiment will be more profound from tomorrow onward.

Now I will tell you the new arrangement of the experiments which will be applicable for the whole camp from tomorrow onward.

The morning experiment which we did today, will now be done in the afternoons from four to five. *Kirtan* for fifteen minutes, dance for fifteen minutes, and relaxation for thirty minutes.

For the mornings, we will start another experiment from tomorrow on. It will be fast breathing for ten minutes; during the next ten minutes there will be dancing, screaming, crying, laughing, throwing out all the physical energy; then for ten minutes shouting the mantra "Hoo" – the same as we will do tonight; and then relaxation for thirty minutes. This will be the morning experiment.

The one we did this morning will be done from now on in the afternoons. And the experiment that we are to do tonight will continue at night.

4

The Four States of Existence

The state in which the soul can perceive gross
objects, such as sound and touch,
is called jagrat, the waking state of the soul.
Gross objects are perceived through the
fourteen instruments – mind, intellect,
accumulated mind, ego and the ten senses
(the five senses of perception
and the five sense organs of action) –
which are supported by the sun and the other gods.

When in the absence of gross objects,
such as sound and touch,
and due to the unfulfilled
and lingering desires of the waking state,
through the fourteen instruments
the soul perceives gross objects
which are but creations of these desires
– this state is called swapna,
the dreaming state of the soul.

There are four states of human consciousness; we will begin our discussion with the waking state. The sage says, "The state of perception achieved through the instrumentalities of the mind and the senses, helped by the sun and other gods that pervade all around, is the waking state."

The state in which the soul can perceive gross
objects, such as sound and touch,
is called jagrat, the waking state of the soul.
Gross objects are perceived through the
fourteen instruments – mind, intellect,
accumulated mind, ego and the ten senses...
which are supported by the sun and the other gods.

Consciousness dwells within. Outside is the infinite existence.

There are two ways for contact to happen with this infinite existence. The one which pervades all, the universal, and the other which dwells inside, the individual – there are two ways for them to meet. One is an indirect way; it happens through the doors of the senses. The other is a direct way, immediate, without a medium; that is possible through the transcendence of the senses.

If this outer world is to be known, there are two ways. One way is that I should use the body and know it, and the other way is that I should leave all mediums and know it directly.

Ordinarily, we can't know the light of the outer world without the eyes, we can't know the sounds of the outer world without the ears. The senses have to be used for knowing the colors of the outer world. Through these senses we know what is in the outer world, the senses are our mediums of knowledge.

So the knowledge acquired through the senses is as if an incident has happened somewhere and then someone comes and informs me. In fact I was not present there, some medium has come to inform me. Certainly I will not hear about it exactly as it happened, because the interpretation of the messenger will be included in it.

When my eyes bring the news to me that a flower has blossomed on a tree – very beautiful, very lovely – this information will not be only about the tree and the flower, but it will also include the liking of my eyes. The eyes have added their own interpretation too. The eyes will have added many things to the flower on the tree, many more colors which are not there in the flower on the tree.

You will be surprised to know that some five thousand years ago man could see only three colors: in the books written five thousand years ago only three colors have been mentioned. Later, human eyes started becoming more sensitive; now they can see seven colors.

Colin Wilson has declared in one of his great books that very soon, within four or five hundred years, man will be able to see colors which we cannot even imagine today. The eyes are becoming more and more sensitive day by day.

Colors appear with the developing of the eyes. They cannot appear if there are no eyes; the world is colorless. One who is born blind has no awareness of colors; one who is born deaf has no world of sounds – for him the world is devoid of sound.

Our knowing is through the senses. We are bound to accept what our senses convey to us because we have no other alternative. But the information that comes through the senses includes the interpretations of the sense organs themselves. You see a face, it looks beautiful.

Then look at the same face through a microscope and you will be perplexed: the face will look so uneven, so full of pits. You will see hillocks and lakes in it; the scars of the face will look like large pits. Is the microscope telling a lie? No, the microscope is giving its own interpretation, it sees deeper than your eyes.

Then look at that same face through an X-ray machine. Now the skin will disappear, only the skeleton will be left inside. Is the X-ray giving wrong information? No, the X-ray machine is giving its own interpretation.

Which face is real? – the one you saw with your naked eyes, the one you saw through the microscope, or the one you saw through the X-ray machine? They are all giving information about the same face, all are correct, but every interpretation is partial and is dependent on the medium through which it is seen.

But is it possible to see the world without a mediator? – because truth can be known only when we see the world without a mediator. The most profound discovery of the sages is that the world known through the senses is the projection of the senses on the world as we see it; that has been called *maya*. What you have seen is not only the objective scene, the viewer has also contributed to the view.

In the story of Majnu and Laila, when Majnu is telling someone that Laila is very beautiful, he is not only saying something about Laila, he is saying something about Majnu also. In fact, it is the eye of Majnu that is able to see Laila as beautiful. It is not necessary that Laila look beautiful to everyone. Those who don't see Laila as beautiful and those who do see her as beautiful are describing the same Laila, but the mediators, the mind and the senses through which Laila has been seen, are also included in their descriptions.

So when a person informs you about someone, "He is a very good man," then this information is not only about that man, he is giving an interpretation of himself also. And when a person says of someone, "He is a very bad man," it is not only about that man, it is also about the person himself. And it is possible that his information about the other may be wrong, but it cannot be wrong about himself. Our senses include their own interpretation. They are not inactive, indifferent mediators, they are active by projecting too.

So this is one way – through the senses – to know the vast manifestation of reality. But those who have transcended the sense organs and seen the world say that this knowledge of reality is illusory, *maya*. When a man like Shankara says that this world is illusory, do not misunderstand him and think that he is saying that this world is nonexistent. Shankara cannot say such an insane thing – that this world is nonexistent. The world does exist, but it is not the same as what you are seeing. It is your vision that makes it look like that, it is your way of looking at it that makes this world illusory; the world as you see it is your own projection, it is your own interpretation.

It will be better to say that there is not one single illusion, there are as many illusions as there are people in this world. Everyone is living in his own created world; everyone has a world around himself. You are living surrounded by your own world, your neighbor is living surrounded by his own world: there is no harmony between the two worlds. And whenever we put the two worlds together there is a struggle, there is a collision. The struggle between the husband and wife is the struggle between two worlds; the struggle between the father and the son is the struggle between two worlds. The son is creating his own world, and the father has already created his world; collision between the two is unavoidable. It cannot be otherwise. We live surrounded by our own interpretations.

The sage says that the state in which the world is known through the senses is called the waking state. The state in which this world is known through the senses as mediators is called the waking state. A few more things are to be understood.

The sage has said: *"...the sun and the other gods."* The sun is the center. Whatever we see around us, if we search for the center of it all, the sun is the center. If the sun cools down, immediately our whole world will be reduced to ashes. The sun is life. Whether it is green leaves on the tree dancing in bliss, or clouds moving in the sky, or someone singing a song on earth, or playing on his flute, or a seed sprouting, or a waterfall falling from a mountain and flowing toward the ocean – the sun is at the root of all these. If the sun cools down, all our lives will cool down and vanish.

That is why he has said: *"...the sun and the other gods."* Everything else is secondary, the sun is the chief god. The sun means life.

You are breathing, your blood is warm, and your heart is beating...the sun has made a contribution to it. If the sun is extinguished, we will never know when it was extinguished because with the sun we will also be extinguished. No one will remain alive to write the history – that the sun was extinguished on such and such a date – because with the cooling down of the sun, we will also be finished, immediately.

Therefore, the sun has always been accepted as the center – but why has it been called divine? Science does not call it divine. And the scientists are surprised: "Why this pantheism? Why is it necessary to see divinity in everything? The sun is the sun, what need is there to see something divine in it?" But Indian seers understand it differently.

This is the way of Indian seers – to feel grateful to that which gives us anything, because the individual soul does not evolve in the absence of gratitude. All that is sublime in man grows with this feeling of gratitude. The more you feel grateful, the more your soul grows.

So when we say the sun is just the sun, it is right, but there is no feeling of gratitude in this statement. It does not appear that we get anything from the sun; it does not appear that we are a part of it, are reliant on it; it does not appear to have anything to do with our heartbeats; it does not appear that we are extensions of it. Yet, although we are about one hundred million miles away, we are the very rays of the sun. It is the sun that is pulsating within us, it is the sun that is living within us. It is the warmth of the sun, it is the heat of the sun.

With science no relationship is created with the sun. But this is sheer lack of understanding, because if we do not feel grateful to our life-giver, the higher within us cannot grow.

The feeling of gratitude is a basic quality of a religious mind. It is through this feeling of gratitude that one receives divine grace. So when some people, full of awe, bowed down to the sun with folded hands, there was more to it than just the fact that it is an enormous fireball. These people had begun to recognize and knew the truth well…that bowing down gives nothing to the sun, but he who is bowing down receives much. As the sensitivity of gratitude is born it creates simplicity, and the mind becomes innocent.

And this does not only apply to the sun, it is a far greater phenomenon. Hence, those who bowed down to the sun also bowed down to the rivers and the trees.

Sometimes amazing incidents happen. Buddhists have been worshipping the *bodhi* tree for two thousand five hundred years. Anyone can say that this is nonsense: it was just a coincidence that Buddha sat under that tree. What is there to worship? He could have sat anywhere! But during the past fifty years, science has discovered a very startling fact. The fact is that the third eye, in the middle of the forehead, had always been thought to be just imagination by scientists and thinkers, and they laughed at it and denied its existence. But during these fifty years, science has found a gland between the two eyes which is the most important gland in the human body. Whatever consciousness has grown in man, it is due to the secretion from that gland. And this gland is the same as that which has been called the third eye by the wise men of the East. The secretion that comes from that gland – and without which consciousness cannot evolve in man, intelligence cannot grow in man – surprisingly is found in large quantities in the *pipal* tree, the *bodhi* tree. When compared to all other vegetation in the world it is a very large amount.

Colin Wilson has written in his new book, *The Occult*, "It would not be surprising if the tree might have had an influence on Buddha's sitting under it and attaining to enlightenment. The tree may have influenced it, it was not just accidental; the tree may have helped it."

India has always worshipped the *pipal* tree. In that sense, the *pipal* is a unique tree among all the vegetation on earth; all other trees are quite different. It is dangerous to sit or to sleep under any other tree in the night, except the *pipal*. Trees exhale oxygen during the day – it is beneficial to be near them – and during the night they exhale carbon dioxide. It is only the *pipal* tree which exhales oxygen for all of the twenty-four hours. You can be near it any time; it is beneficial to life.

Those people who chose the *pipal* tree to worship from

among all the others were full of gratitude. It is not just a coincidence that Buddha attained enlightenment sitting under this tree, it was a conscious choice. To sit and meditate under this tree is a part of a scientific process.

Those who have felt gratitude have felt it in each and every minute thing in the world. Whenever they felt something had helped them, in gratitude they called it a god. "A god" means something which gives to us and does not take anything in return. A god means something from which we always receive, we are always receiving – and receiving without even asking for anything, continuously receiving without even thanking. It is given unconditionally, so we called it a god. And we cannot give anything in return. But, of course, we can show our gratitude.

Every fiber of our being is connected with the existence spread all around us. When consciousness knows this connection through the sense organs, it is called the waking state. To call it the waking state is only symbolic. Because we do not know the greater awakening, we therefore call this the waking state. So this is relative, because we know only three states.

This first state is our relation with the world through the senses, the second state we know is the dreaming state, and the third state we know is the sleeping state. We know nothing about the fourth state. The day we will know the fourth, we will also know that what we had understood as the waking state up to now was also a state of dreaming and sleeping.

Sri Aurobindo has said that when he was awakened, he came to know that until then he had been asleep, and when he knew the real life, he found that what he had taken for life was only death. But it is natural that we cannot conceive of what we do not know, and we cannot even make comparisons.

The waking state is so called in comparison to the other two states. We are acquainted with these three states – dreaming, sleeping, waking – and this can be called the waking state among these three. The day we come to know the fourth, all these three states will have to become sleeping states. Then we will have to define them in some other way. Then we will have to say: deep sleep, less deep sleep, lesser deep sleep. What we now call the waking state, when compared to the other two, is the lesser deep sleep; what we call dreaming, is the less deep sleep; and what we call sleep, is total deep sleep. All these three are the states of sleeping, but at present we call it the waking state.

The second state is dreaming.

When in the absence of gross objects,
such as sound and touch,
and due to the unfulfilled
and lingering desires of the waking state,
through the fourteen instruments
the soul perceives gross objects
which are but creations of these desires
– this state is called swapna,
the dreaming state of the soul.

Sometimes it is really amazing. We say that now the world has become a big village – Marshal McLuhan calls it a "global village." But this does not seem to be actually true. We only appear to be close, because the means of traveling have increased. People have not come closer to each other in consciousness.

This Upanishad defined dreaming thousands of years ago, and during the last fifty years the West has still not been able to explain it totally, it is still groping. It is amazing to realize that human civilizations have discovered many things but these discoveries have remained local and confined to their region, not reaching to the whole of human consciousness.

Thousands of years ago this Upanishad stated that we call it dreaming when the senses have ceased to work and the eyes are closed, yet images can still be seen. The ears become inactive during sleep, outer sounds are inaudible, but even then sounds can be heard within. Hands are lying unmoving as if dead, touching nothing; still touch can be felt within.

The sage says: "The unfulfilled desires, the unsatiated desires – whatever is left incomplete in the waking state, these are fulfilled in dreams. So dreaming supplements the waking state."

And many things can remain incomplete from during the day. You are going along a street and you see a beautiful woman but you cannot stare at her, that is not good manners. The desire to look at her remains in the mind; in the night you will again see her in your dream. While eating, sometimes you cannot eat to your satisfaction for many different reasons. You may have to rush back to your work or you have too many things to do, or it may be due to politeness and hesitation; during the night dreaming will fulfill the remaining desire to eat. What remains unfulfilled in the waking state, dreaming will follow it and fulfill it during the night.

That is why the person who lives totally in the daytime has no dreams. He who lives totally in whatever he does, who does it totally and not halfheartedly, who lives every moment totally, loses all his dreams. A person like Buddha will have no dreams. There is a reason behind it – because nothing has remained unfulfilled which has to be fulfilled during the night.

The sage says: "When the senses are inactive but the consciousness is still seeing the images of objects created by the senses, this state is called dreaming."

There is one difference between dreaming and waking: in waking, the object remains outside and the image is inside; in dreaming, the object is absent yet the image is inside. So a dream is a pure form, there is no object. The man you see in your dream is not present outside, yet his form is present inside. These forms are created by the senses. Remember it: these forms are created by the senses, they are the creations of the senses. How do the senses create them?

Every sense accumulates its experiences. Whatever colors you have seen until now, and whenever you have seen them, all those memories of colors are stored in the mind. In dreaming, that accumulation is utilized; the eyes again use those colors.

Whosoever you have ever touched, those touches, those contacts are collected. Inside this little skull of man is the greatest collection of the world; inside this small brain are ten billion cells, and every cell contains a great world in itself.

This collection is not only of this life, it is from many, many lives. That is why you can see forms in dreams that you have never seen in this life; you can see faces you have never met, that you do not remember; you can see scenes that have nothing to do with the memory of this life. That is why sometimes a dream will leave you stunned, leave you in a fix; you cannot understand what this dream is all about. Impressions from many, many lives have been accumulated – whatever you have known, all that is accumulated. The mind uses it again; it is all recorded there. *Conditioning* means accumulated memories. *Conditioning* means that which has been collected in the cells of the brain.

Now scientists have found a technique where they can activate any part of your memory by inserting an electrode into your brain. You may keep saying that you don't want to see colors but you will not have any control over it. The accumulated memory of colors in your brain can be activated by the electrode and all kinds of colors will spread within you. You may say that you don't want to see all this, but it will be out of your control because this memory has been touched by the electrode.

One more interesting thing is that whenever this same point is touched, those same colors will be repeated, because they are only a record. It is as if you are a gramophone record: it will repeat the same song as many times as you play it. Just like that, every cell in the brain is a record: whenever you touch it with the electrode, it is as if you put the needle on a record and it will play the same thing, again and again the same thing. You can do it thousands of times and the record in the cell will repeat itself. So, one thing is certain now in scientific terms, that your brain is an accumulation of impressions. During the dreaming state you see things again and again from this same collection. It is just like ruminating.

A buffalo grazes the grass during the day, but there is no

time to chew because, who knows, someone else may eat away all the grass while she is engaged in chewing. So first she grazes the grass, then she ruminates leisurely, brings the grass back into her mouth and re-chews it.

The whole day, the whole of our life we go on collecting, for lives together we have gone on collecting, then we ruminate in our dreams. Wherever the mind has remained unfulfilled then we reopen it, we reopen the record again; we spread those impressions again on the screen.

Dreaming is an arrangement whereby we can project our impressions without the help of our sense organs, without the help of the outer world. This is our private wealth. Again we can spread our own world within us. You can create a whole world. That is why, in the dreaming state, you never know that what you are seeing is a dream. In dreaming, what you see appears to be true. Only after waking up from a dream do you know that it was a dream. During the dreaming state it is never recognized as dream.

If someone realizes the dream is a dream while dreaming, then the dream is broken, because in the presence of the knower the record of impressions hides, goes back into the deeper layer. Now the person is awake, waking has begun, the dreaming state is shattered.

The "dreaming state" means the senses have accumulated impressions in our memory, and we can reproduce this imaginary world within us, without even the help of the outer world. That we do daily. This is another state of our mind. This is our deeper state. Because in waking we have had to make choices due to society, civilization, culture – there are thousands of restrictions – but in dreaming we are free.

We have been free until now, but who knows whether we will remain free or not in the future, because now scientists are slowly becoming capable of entering into man's dreams.

During the past two hundred years, all over the world, politicians have been demanding freedom of thought. It will not be surprising if after this century, revolutionaries revolt and begin to demand freedom of dreaming, demand noninterference in dreaming, because in the near future governments will have the power to allow you to dream what they want you to dream, and restrict your dreaming of that which they don't want you to dream. This danger is greater than the atom bomb.

Psychologists are now discovering methods and systems to control the mind from without. Atom bombs can only destroy the body, but these methods are more dangerous because they can create deep psychological slavery. It will not be surprising if one day you are called to some police office and interrogated: "Why did you dream that dream last night? The government is totally against it. That dream is totally anti national; you appear to be a traitor." In the future it will be possible to monitor your dreams, so it will not be surprising if fascist governments of the future begin to use it.

Human dreams can be manipulated. If you know a small technique even you can manipulate them a little bit. For example, if you rub ice on the sole of the foot of a sleeping person, he may soon start dreaming that he is walking on ice. Or maybe a similar dream will begin: he will start dreaming that it is raining heavily and his feet are getting wet. He will create a dream to include this sensation of cold received from the outside and it will activate all the impressions of cold inside the brain.

Sometimes, when a nightmare is happening or a frightening dream, it may be simply because you have put your hands on your chest, and for no other reason. If you put your hands on your chest you may begin dreaming that someone is sitting on your chest. So if you put a pillow on somebody's chest you can manipulate their dream a little bit, you can direct their dream.

This is now well known. But now instruments have been invented which can direct your dreams from inside the mind – because this way your brain cells can be contacted directly, and the impressions can be activated.

Without the aid of the senses, without any connection with

the vast world outside and only on the basis of old memories, man creates a world within himself. That state is called the dreaming state.

These are two states – waking and dreaming. To understand and transcend the dreaming state, freedom from dreams is necessary; only then, in the waking state, can our eyes become innocent, impartial, clean and smokeless.

The eyes of animals have an innocence which human eyes don't have. The only reason is that they have fewer dreams, almost none. Yet animals who live with human beings start dreaming. Cats and dogs dream because living with human beings they catch their diseases.

Dreaming is a continuous anguish, a continuous anguish within you, an anxiety, a tension; it affects your eyes. Look into the eyes of a cow – they are totally clear, smokeless. Their eyes are like a calm, blue lake in which you can see even the pebbles lying at the bottom. Look deep into the eyes of a cow – they are totally empty, there are no layers anywhere in them. But look into the eyes of human beings! – there are so many layers in their eyes. Those layers are the creations of dreams.

The more ambitious a man is the more shallow his eyes will become, because the more ambition he has the more dreams he will have. I said that whatever has remained unfulfilled creates dreams; and ambition can never be fulfilled, it is always insatiable.

So a half-fulfilled ambition fills a man with dreams. These dreams can become so profound that it may become difficult to awaken him.

Perhaps a man like Hitler has no ordinary waking state as we know it. It only became known later, near the end of the Second World War, when psychologists began to realize that the man they were fighting with appeared to be asleep, not awake. While bombs were being dropped on Berlin and fighting was going on in the streets, when Hitler was being defeated on every front and there was no way to escape – bullets were being fired right in front of Hitler's bunker – he was still broadcasting that he was winning in Moscow.

Hitler must have been dreaming: he was not hearing the shooting outside his door. Otherwise, there seems to be no way that he could have announced, "We are winning." When the chief of the army came and informed Hitler that they were losing the battle, Hitler ordered, "Shoot him down, he has gone mad! We can't lose the battle. The question does not arise. It is only a matter of a few moments – Moscow must have surrendered by now." He had lost everywhere – but he was dreaming, he was not in the waking state.

Perhaps an ambitious person lives in his dreams: the more the ambition, the deeper the dream. So if you want to see the shallowest eyes, you will find them in politicians. Profound eyes can be seen in a sannyasin, because sannyas means a state where no ambition is left, no dreams are left. And even if one last dream is left, it is only about how to transcend dreaming, how to get rid of the dream and to be free of it. If there is still an ambition, it is how to be free from ambition, that is all.

If you can disperse your dreams, your waking will be more alert. Or, if you make your waking alert, the dreams will begin to disperse. If you live your life more alert, more awake, your dreams will decrease; or if you decrease your dreaming, awakening will increase. All these states are interrelated. And if dreams decrease and your waking state is stronger, you will know for the first time what deep sleep really is, otherwise you will never know it.

What is deep sleep? Certainly we sleep, but we do not know what sleep is – because how can he who is asleep even in the waking state, be awake in the sleeping state? How can he who cannot wake up in the waking state, wake up in the sleeping state? Getting up in the morning we can say this much, that we have slept soundly – but we don't know anything about it.

You have been sleeping your whole life, but you have never confronted your sleep. Have you ever witnessed sleep descending? As the night descends in the evening, the sun is setting and darkness starts spreading layer by layer on the earth...have you ever witnessed the sleep descending on your consciousness like that? No, you have not. Because when sleep descends, *you* are not present. And as long as you are present, sleep does not descend.

You are sleeping every day, but you are not acquainted with your sleep, and how can the one who is not acquainted with his sleep be acquainted with himself? One who has pitch darkness within himself, a large continent of sleep – one who sleeps for eight hours daily and loses all consciousness – how can he reach to that profound state where consciousness is never lost? He cannot.

Dreaming is to be shattered. The purpose of spiritual practices is to shatter and destroy this dreaming so that the waking state can become more awake, and a moment can come when the waking state is so awake that the dreams disappear. The day when the waking state is so alert that dreams have disappeared, that day you will experience sleep for the first time. You will witness your sleep. Then you will be sleeping, and you will also know that you are asleep.

The day a man is aware in his sleep that he is sleeping, then there is no way to make him behave unconsciously; now he cannot act unconsciously, now anger is impossible. Now he cannot kill, he cannot steal, he cannot lie. Now all this is impossible, because the very source of the sleep which could have made him unconscious is destroyed. That poison which used to make him unconscious, which used to make him drowsy, is no more.

When one is aware while sleeping, one attains to *turiya* – the fourth state. He who is awake in sleep reaches turiya.

Now get ready for the morning meditation. First understand a few things: nothing happens with lukewarm effort; use your total energy. Because the dream state is strong – it has been created over many lives – if you want to break it, then hit hard.

Blindfolds are to remain on the eyes, and fast breathing is to be done for ten minutes. Fast, just like the bellows of a blacksmith. The kundalini has to be hit so hard that it can wake up. Breathe like a madman for ten minutes. Dancing and jumping will start on their own; energy will arise because of the fast breathing.

Then, in the second step, dance for ten minutes, jump, scream and laugh – whatever you wish to do, do it totally. Do not stand inactive; do something – whatever comes to mind, do it.

And in the third step, shout "Hoo," hit the kundalini hard with "Hoo."

In the fourth step we will relax.

5

The Individual Search

When there is inactivity
and rest of the fourteen instruments,
there is a lack of perception,
and gross objects, such as sound and touch,
are not experienced.
This state is called sushupti,
the sleeping state of the soul.
The eternally witnessing consciousness
which knows the presence or absence of the three states,
and which is itself beyond presence or absence,
is turiya.
This is the fourth.

Waking is the first state, dreaming is the second and sleeping is the third state. *Sushupti*, the sleeping state, means that there is neither an awareness of the outside world, nor is there any experience of objects or of any dreams created by their impressions in the mind. Consciousness is totally asleep, there is no trace of any awareness: consciousness is there but no awareness, life is there but completely asleep – without comprehension of any kind. The person becomes inanimate – living, yet inanimate, inert.

So far we have discussed two states: when we open our eyes the outer world is seen, when we close our eyes, then what we have seen outside is seen inside in our dreams. Something is always visible. The outside world may be absent, but still the forms created by it continually move on the mind's screen. Something always remains on the screen of the mind.

When this screen is empty, this state is called sushupti, the sleeping state. Then neither any outer objects nor any inner thoughts are perceived, the flow of all images ceases; the screen is empty, it is blank, no awareness is left – that state is called sushupti.

Now, there are a few very important things to understand here. First, it is necessary to understand that you are never aware of yourself. If you did have some awareness of yourself, then even if the outside world disappeared, and the inside world of dreams also disappeared, yet one point of awareness would still remain, that "I am." The sun, the moon and the stars may not be visible, your eyes may remain closed with no dreams flowing, but even then the awareness of "I exist" would still remain. But as it is you have no awareness of yourself, your awareness is object-oriented; you are aware of others, of objects, but not of yourself.

So when all objects disappear your awareness disappears, the consciousness disappears. Whatever awareness you have is about others; you have no awareness of yourself. When you stub your toe on a stone, you become aware of the stone and the experience of pain in your mind, but you are not aware of yourself, you are not aware of the one who is perceiving everything.

Right now, I am speaking and you are listening. You are hearing my words, you are hearing by the vibrations in your ears, but you do not yet know the listener who is hidden behind all this. If the speaking stopped and the words falling on your ears disappeared and there was nothing resounding within, then you would have no awareness.

That is why a few thinkers go to the extent of saying – and their statement is correct ninety-nine times out of a hundred – they say that nothing like consciousness exists; your consciousness is only the echo within of the presence of other things.

This third state of sleeping, becoming unconscious, discloses great mysteries. The first revelation is that we are in the great illusion that we already have consciousness. We have no consciousness. That is why sleep will immediately take over when you are unoccupied. It seems very difficult to remain awake while unoccupied. If you are not busy sleep will immediately start descending on you, so it is necessary to be busy. There is another side to it too: when you become too busy, sleep will not come in spite of your best efforts. It is night, you are lying on your bed, but your thoughts keep rushing everywhere nonstop and sleep does not come, because when your thoughts go on rushing about you have to be alert, you cannot sleep; the object is present, although it is not of the outside world.

If someone is playing the drums close to you, you cannot sleep. Why is that? Because that beat of the drum keeps your consciousness alert, it doesn't allow you to sleep. But even if there are no drums being played and you are lying with your eyes closed, many thoughts will be rushing through your mind, fantasies will be going on in your mind, then also sleep will not come. Even if you are thinking about sleep, trying to sleep, you cannot. When you are thinking about how you can make yourself fall asleep, what you can do in order to fall asleep, sleep will not happen, because you will remain conscious as long as there is an object. And then, as soon as the object disappears, you will immediately drown in unconsciousness.

So your consciousness is dependent on objects, you are not its master. If we understand it rightly, then deep down this is the bondage. We can remain awake if someone or something keeps us awake; if nothing keeps us awake, we immediately fall asleep. That is why man invents new sensations every day, otherwise life becomes boring. The same wife! – and life begins to lose its excitement; so the husband wants to find a new woman. The same house! – and life begins to lose excitement; so another house is needed. Only one type of food! – life begins to lose excitement; so every day one wants something new and different to eat. This desire for change is to keep ourselves awake, otherwise we will go to sleep – if there is no change we will fall asleep. Hence all methods to induce sleep use only one technique.

All methods created to help people who cannot sleep use the simplest technique of repeating something. After a little while they get so bored because of the absence of anything new that there is no reason to be awake. Even if you repeat "Rama, Rama, Rama, Rama, Rama, Rama, Rama, Rama," you will fall asleep. That is why people who repeat mantras fall asleep and worshippers in temples get sleepy. There is simply no novelty, hence no challenge; there is no point in staying awake.

The mother pats the forehead of the child five or ten times – the same patting…the same patting…the same patting – and the child goes to sleep. There is nothing unusual in the patting; the child just gets bored. There's nothing new happening, so the child goes to sleep.

That is why you fall asleep more easily in your own room; in a strange room it takes time because a strange room is unfamiliar. You fall asleep quite quickly on your own pillow or bed but it takes a long time to fall asleep in someone else's bed; there is something new which keeps you awake. Hence, everyone has his own sleeping ritual.

A small child, feeling uneasy, puts his thumb in his mouth. In a few moments, because there is nothing new happening, he gets bored and falls asleep. There is not much difference between children and adults. Someone cannot sleep unless he smokes a cigarette at night. He smokes a cigarette – that is his substitute for sucking his thumb – then he goes to sleep. The daily routine makes one feel bored immediately. Sleep is also difficult in a new place, among new people, in a new house, because there are a lot of things around you which keep you awake demanding your attention, your awareness – because something is new.

Sleep has been disturbed in the West for the simple reason that the West is changing so fast that there is always something new. The East is at ease as far as sleep is concerned, but that will not last much longer. A villager will sleep deeply; someone living in a city cannot sleep so deeply. There is no particular reason for it except that the villager lives in old patterns, lives in boredom, there is nothing new to keep him awake. For someone in the city, every day there is something new: there are new films showing, a new newspaper is printed, there are new people to meet, new commodities are arriving on the market, shop windows are being decorated with new displays, there are new fashions, everything is new every day. The effect of all this novelty is that he is constantly awake and it is difficult to sleep. In the village everything is old; the same village, the same streets, the same people, everything is the same.

If I go back to my village after one or two years I find that everything has remained the same. When I enter my village I know exactly which porter I will see at the railway station and he always meets me – he is the only porter. I know which *tongawalla* will meet me and what he will talk about, because for years whenever I have gone there he has said the same things. And when the tonga goes through the village streets I know who will be sleeping outside his house and coughing. I know what will be going on in the village; everything is predictable. I know already what will be happening, almost nothing has changed. Sometimes something does happen: someone in the village dies, someone is born – sometimes. Everything else goes on as usual.

The East has had no problems about sleep, because everything was static. The West is in trouble; everything is changing, and is changing so fast that after five years it is difficult to say whether your town is the same town because everything has changed so much. The ability to sleep has been disturbed. If no object excites you sleep comes naturally; if there is excitement, you stay awake.

This is a strange definition of sushupti, the sleeping state: that we have no awareness, no self-awareness; we have no self-consciousness, we are only conscious of others. If others keep us awake we remain awake, if others stimulate us then we remain awake; if others create some challenge, maintain some struggle or friction for us, then we stay awake. And if nobody keeps us awake we fall asleep at once, we disappear into the depths of sleep.

Once I was staying in a village when a man was bitten by a snake. There was no physician in that village so he had to be taken to another. The elders of the village suggested to keep him awake, not to allow him to fall asleep, because if he fell asleep perhaps it would be impossible to revive him. So people took him to the next village keeping him awake, not allowing him to sleep, sprinkling water on him, making him sit up, shaking him so that he would not fall asleep.

I also traveled with them for a while on that day in the same train, and suddenly it occurred to me that this man may have been bitten by a snake, but that all of us are also in the same condition. If people around us don't keep us awake, we will also be lost and fall asleep. Someone continuously keeps us awake, a new sensation keeps us alert. That is why when a war starts peoples' eyes become brighter and a freshness comes to their faces – something new is happening. In the morning they get the daily newspapers, and even those people who usually never get up early, wake up early and wait for the newspaper. What happens? It is surprising, you would think that war would bring sadness but it brings happiness, that war would bring anguish but it brings freshness. Even dead nations begin to throb with life; blood starts circulating faster. Why?

Psychologists say that, as man is, he has to continue to fight or he becomes totally lethargic and he has no taste for life. Something must continue to happen somewhere, some sort of trouble, or we will just fall asleep. We are all bitten by snakes.

This third state, the state of sleep, happens when no object excites us – neither within nor from the outside, neither in the world of thoughts nor in the world of objects. We are still alive, but unconscious.

And the fourth state is called *turiya*. When someone has

broken through the third state, then even if the whole external world vanishes still his consciousness will be there, awake. Even if the stars and the moon cool down and the earth disappears and everything is destroyed, nothing is left – if only I am, left all alone – even then I remain awake, I remain conscious. All around emptiness prevails, everything becomes insubstantial – I alone remain. Nothing to know, only the knower is left. No sounds to be heard, only the listener is left. Nothing to see, only the capacity to see remains. When all else is not and still I can remain in awareness, Indian seers have called this state the fourth state, the real state, the *turiya*. He who attains to this state attains to everything; he who has not attained to this state only goes on accumulating objects or ideas and remains deluded, remains under the illusion that "I know who I am." But if you take away his objects and thoughts he will be lost in his sleep and nothing will be left of him.

If a man is very rich and someone steals his money, his agony is not only due to the loss of the money, but also to the fact that with the money a part of his soul is taken away, because he has no real soul as such; it is only in relation to the money. When we take away a palace from someone, it is not only the palace, his soul is also taken, because he has no real soul as such; he has just an illusion of a soul in proportion to the size and grandeur of his palace. Now that his palace has been taken, his soul is lost in the same proportion.

That is why for thousands of years on this earth, in this land, sannyas – the renunciation of "the world" – has been a unique experiment. I will explain that experiment in this context to you. In fact sannyas is not a matter of renunciation, it is actually an effort to see whether, after having renounced everything, one still remains behind.

It is not a question of renouncing the world because it is evil, and it is not a question of renouncing your home because there is something wrong with it, or of renouncing your wife because sex is a sin. Primarily the unique experiment of sannyas has been done to see whether you will remain when you have renounced everything. If you don't remain, then you were not in the first place – "I was an illusion." And if you do remain even after renouncing everything – when you have found the wife is not "mine," the son is not "mine," the friend is not "mine," the house is not "mine," the money is not "mine" – when you stand totally naked, alone on the street, do you still exist? "If I exist, I have a soul; if I do not, I should seek a soul."

The purpose of renunciation was not because possessions are evil, its purpose was to see whether you are just the sum total of your possessions or whether you exist independently, because it is difficult to get a clear understanding while surrounded by possessions.

The seeker would go to the forest not because the city is evil, not because the truth is impossible to attain in the town, not because God is afraid to come to town – no, he can come there too! The seeker used to go into seclusion just to see whether he would remain conscious in aloneness or whether he would fall asleep, whether the awareness would remain or would he lose consciousness? When he had renounced everything, did something still remain or not? If something did remain, only then he has some small measure of a soul. If he does not have, he should now set out on the search for it; if he does have a soul, he should develop it.

That is why when a Buddha or a Mahavira attains the truth, his soul, he comes back into the marketplace; now there is no fear, now there is nothing to worry about, now he knows his reality.

We do not exist independent of things at all, that is why we are so attached to objects; that attachment is not to the objects – they have become our souls. When someone takes your shirt, he is not only taking the shirt, he is almost taking your life. It is not only the shirt! If it had only been a shirt there would be no reason to suffer so much.

Jesus said to his followers that if someone takes your coat, to give him the shirt too. Who knows, he may be in need but is hesitating to take it. That was not the reason why he said this, but so that you should not be so attached to your shirt that it becomes your soul. And if someone asks you to carry a load for one mile, then to carry it for two miles, so that you can feel that your body does not only belong to you, it belongs to the other as well.

Consciousness manifests with the transcendence of sushupti.

I have mentioned Gurdjieff. Gurdjieff used to tell his seekers: "Focus your eyes on the watch, on its second hand which is moving, and do a small experiment: be aware of the second hand and keep watching it, and remain aware, simultaneously, that you are aware of it."

This is a small experiment, but not so small – if you do it, you will know that it is very difficult. It is easier to climb Everest; this small experiment is very arduous. The second hand will complete its circle within one minute. Gurdjieff used to say that if you could be aware of it for the entire minute you have a little bit of soul. Even this much, for one minute...that the second hand is moving, and being aware at the same time that you are aware of it – a double-arrowed consciousness, a double-ended arrow – watching the hand and also watching yourself watching it.

You will be surprised that it is not possible even for four seconds; you get lost in between. It does not even last for four seconds – either the hand is forgotten or you forget yourself; you forget one of the two.

It is difficult for you to remember for a single minute that "I am." Your sleep must be very deep! If the second hand is forgotten, that means you have fallen asleep. When do you forget the second hand? – you forget it when some other thought comes to you and your attention is diverted. If the second hand is not forgotten and you are putting your attention forcibly on it, you lose the focus that you were directing on yourself.

The condition of man seems to be very pitiable – that even for a whole minute man cannot remember that he exists. But there is a reason for it. The reason is that we have never been outside the current of sleep; deep down we are continuously asleep. At the most a slight uneasiness can be felt from the outside, as when a man is sleeping and you pull his legs, then he turns over, opens his eyes a little, mutters something and falls asleep again – that is all. Our waking state is similar to that.

Man is helpless; he feels hunger, so he has to get up in the morning. He is helpless; he has to attend to his jobs, feed the children, he has to go to the office – moving automatically, as if someone is pulling his legs in his sleep. And as soon as there is a gap he falls asleep.

If you are given the chance to sleep for twenty-four hours, would you then want to be awake? If someone arranged for you to sleep for twenty-four hours, would you then want to stay awake? No, you stay awake out of compulsion. That is why those who can afford it, they even induce sleep by taking alcohol; now they are not obliged to keep awake. Those who have more choices drown themselves in LSD, marijuana, mescaline...

Whenever a society is able to gather even a little affluence, the first thing it spends excess money on is alcohol. Forget about the society: any man who can afford some luxury first spends his money on alcohol. Why? Why is there such a keen desire to be unconscious? Is consciousness so painful? The consciousness which we know is very painful. It is like somebody is forcibly shaking you the whole time to keep you awake, but as soon as there is even the slightest let-up you drown in sleep.

We are filled with layers of sleep, we are stuffed with sleep. This is the third state and the seeker must know it rightly, because there is no way to reach to the fourth without shattering this third state.

The sage says:

When there is inactivity
and rest of the fourteen instruments,
there is a lack of perception,

and gross objects, such as sound and touch,
are not experienced.
This state is called sushupti,
the sleeping state of the soul.
The eternally witnessing consciousness
which knows the presence or absence of the three
states,
and which is itself beyond presence or absence,
is turiya.
This is the fourth.

These are the three states – waking, dreaming and sleeping – but to whom do these states belong? Who is it that goes through all these three states? Who is it? Who is awake? Who sees the dreams? Who falls asleep? Certainly he must be separate from all these.

You pass through one railway station, then through the second, then through the third – these are three stations; certainly the one who is traveling must be separate from these. You are not the station, otherwise how could you reach the second station? You are not the second station because you reach the third; and you are not the third because you come back to the second and to the first.

Man wakes up, dreams and sleeps; then again he falls asleep, wakes up and dreams – he moves through all three. So the sage says that the one who moves through these three is the fourth, he cannot be one of these three.

What can we do? How is it possible? – how to shatter this *sushupti*? Sleep is surrounding us everywhere. We walk sleepily, we stand sleepily, we sit sleepily...whatever we are doing, we do it sleepily.

Buddha was walking on a path. This is an incident from before he was enlightened. A friend was walking beside him, and a fly came and sat on Buddha's shoulder. Buddha continued his conversation with the friend, kept walking on the path, and waved away the fly with his hand. Then he stood still. The friend asked, "Did the fly bite you?" But Buddha closed his eyes, did not reply to his friend, raised his hand, moved the hand to where the fly had been sitting, brushed away the fly – which was not there – and brought his hand down. The friend asked, "Have you gone mad? The fly flew away the first time, what are you brushing away now?"

Buddha said, "Now I have brushed away the fly as I should have done it before. I had brushed it away unconsciously. The hand moved as if in sleep. I was not awake, I was occupied in conversation with you. The hand moved and brushed the fly away, and then I became aware that the fly had flown away and I had done it unconsciously. I was doing it in my sleep. To disrupt my unconsciousness I then did it the way I should have done it the first time. This hand was raised and with it arose the consciousness; this hand then touched the shoulder consciously and brushed the fly away.

"When I brushed away this second fly, I was aware of what I was doing and I was also aware of my awareness of what I was doing. This is double-arrowed consciousness." Buddha said, "If a fly sits on me again, I will brush it away like this. It was just a little practice; let us go on."

If we look at our lives from this angle, all our activities appear to be done in sleep. Can a man who does not even remove a fly unconsciously be angry? Can he abuse someone? Can he be jealous? Can he be hateful? All these things happen only in sleep; with consciousness they begin to drop.

Ananda was with Buddha for many years. One day he asked Buddha, "Everything is okay, but there is one thing I don't understand: do you sleep in the night or not?"

Buddha said, "You know that I go to sleep daily."

Ananda said, "I do see that, but wherever you put your foot, it remains there for the whole night, and wherever you put your hand, it stays there. Last night I kept awake just to see whether you moved your hands or not, whether you changed sides, but everything remained in the same place. Do you take care not to move the whole night? How do you sleep? Do you really sleep?"

Buddha replied, "Once it did happen that I changed sides without awareness. But then, since that day I have not changed sides; I have stopped changing sides altogether. What is the need to associate with such things? I sleep, but I am awake inside. The hand should remain there where I have put it; it is mine, and if it moves without my permission I become a slave, I cease to be the master."

So start becoming alert in the waking state. Start waking up in this state which we call "being awake." Go on becoming alert. Try: make the effort and wake up. Slowly, slowly, when full alertness has happened in the waking state, then you can move further. One who has become alert in the waking state suddenly becomes aware of his dreams while he is dreaming. And as soon as he is aware of this the dreams disappear, because dreams cannot take place when you are aware; unawareness is a must for dreams.

And when your dreams disappear, the awakening enters into the third state; the arrow of awakening enters into sushupti, and then one is also aware when one is asleep. It means that one knows that the body is relaxing, that is all. Sleep is a relaxation for such a person, whereas your way of sleeping is just hard work.

Look at a sleeping man then you will know. He is working even harder in his sleep than he did the whole day – throwing his hands around, banging his head, making faces, and what not. People have been filmed while they were asleep and these films have been later shown to them. They were shocked and said, "Do I do all this? It's impossible; there must be some cheating, some trick." If you were filmed while asleep during the night and it was shown to you in the morning, you would know that you also do this. So much, so much disturbance even in sleep! No peace even in sleep?

Even our sleep is an exertion, whereas for the aware person even the waking state is a relaxation. We are tired when we get up after sleeping because we have been doing so much the whole night that it is beyond imagination. I am not exaggerating. We get up tired even after sleeping the whole night, and this is a daily routine: we fall asleep exhausted after the day's tiring work, and get up in the morning exhausted from the night.

Our life is a long fatigue, a burden which we go on carrying. We could never get rid of it if there were no death. Death comes and takes away the burden forcibly. But we are so full of lust and we are so attached to the burden that as soon as we die, our consciousness sets out for a new birth – in search of a new burden, in search of new diseases, new troubles. As soon as the arrow of consciousness enters into the sleeping state, it transcends our deep sleep, then sleep remains only as rest for the body.

Krishna has said in the Gita that a yogi does not sleep even in his sleep. He did not say that the yogi stands all night with open eyes as some madmen do. This is madness! This is another madness. Some madmen are unable to sleep even with closed eyes, some madmen stand with open eyes to avoid sleeping, because Krishna said that a yogi does not sleep even in his sleep – but they have not understood. He has not said to stand open-eyed. But there are people…

Sometime ago I happened to be in a village. There is a Khade Shri Baba, "Standing Baba" there. The people asked me whether I knew about Khade Shri Baba. "What happened to him?" I asked.

"He is called Khade Shri Baba because he has been standing for ten years."

I told them, "Take him to a doctor – what can I do? Try to make him sit somehow, put him to sleep."

But now he cannot be seated, his legs are swollen due to

elephantitis. His legs have stored excessive blood, all the veins have become stiff; now he cannot sit. I told the people, "Do something, make him now Baithe Shri Baba, 'Sitting Baba.' Don't hesitate. His intelligence is totally lost. It is bound to be; all the blood has gone to his legs and nothing is left for the brain. Look at his eyes, they are as dead as stone. This man is suffering death while he is alive."

Why is he standing? Man can do anything for the ego. People are bowing their heads at his feet, offering flowers, offering money, temples are being constructed in his name! The exchange is not costly, it is cheap; he gets so many temples, so many flowers and so many bowing heads! As I see him, he is utterly stupid. He can try hard for fifty lifetimes and he won't be able to make a single temple through his own creativity. So this deal costs him nothing. And by now the practice is strong, now a tremendous amount of massage would be needed to reverse the practice. It is very difficult; it is unlikely that his legs will ever bend again. He is just standing like an idiot.

Somewhere, if Krishna happens to meet him, he will sue Krishna: "Why did you say in the Gita that a yogi does not sleep even in the sleeping state?" Krishna used to sleep normally. *He* never slept standing! But still we don't see the true message in the Gita. No intelligent person has remained standing. Those who bow to the feet of this yogi don't even ask him, "Krishna didn't do this practice, Buddha never did this practice, Christ never did it – are you trying to go ahead of them all?" But this does not occur to us.

This awareness which does not sleep even during the sleeping state... When the body falls asleep, when all its fibers and nerves fall asleep, when everything sleeps, the flame of awareness remains burning within. The sun remains with its sunlight even when surrounded by the clouds.

When this sushupti is transcended, *turiya*, the fourth state, is attained. It is called a "state" for the sake of language; otherwise it is not a state, it is our nature. We are already "that." It is not that first we are in illusion and then we are changed. No, our illusion is just like when a stick is immersed in water. In the water it looks deformed, but it is not deformed, it only looks that way. Take it out, and again it is straight – it does not become straight, it was straight already. When it looked deformed, even then it was straight. When it is taken out, it looks straight. Water only creates the illusion in its appearance, not in its being.

So when the consciousness is in the three lower states – in sushupti, in dreams and in the waking state – it appears to be lost, but it is never lost, not in the least; it only appears to be so. When consciousness is reclaimed it only appears as if it is attained – it has not been attained, it was already there. But this illusion does happen. And without shattering this illusion that consciousness is to be attained, no glimpse of bliss is possible in life; without shattering this illusion there can be no taste of the nectar of bliss; without shattering this illusion there is no possibility of realizing the truth.

If illusion has to be shattered, understanding is necessary but not enough, understanding is essential but still not enough. One has to move, one has to travel. We have already made a journey, now we have to come back. We have moved far away from our home, now it has to be searched for again. There can be thousands of paths for this search; take any single path and you can reach there.

But generally I see that there are three types of people. There are a few who are afraid of doing anything – so they call all this nonsense and nonexistent. They say that these things do not exist. I know many people who deny the existence of God – not because they have some enmity with God, not because they know that God does not exist, not because they are atheists, but because they are simply lethargic. If God does exist they will have to move, it will be troublesome. It is better to deny God from the very beginning. This makes them free from uncertainty and they settle happily into their lethargy. Why search for that which doesn't exist? If it does exist, you will start feeling anxious even though you don't search. If God is and you remain lying on your bed, you will begin to feel anxious. Somewhere within you a call will vibrate to search for that which is.

Thus, many times I see religious people having a cover of irreligiousness – just so that they need not move, need not go anywhere or do anything. Their lethargy becomes their atheism. There are others who do not make their lethargy atheism. They are more clever; they make their lethargy theism. They remain settled in their laziness and only *talk* about God.

It is very easy to become an expert in talking about God. It is not so easy to talk about other things because you may land yourself in trouble. If you make a statement about a stone, you will have to prove it in the laboratory. But regarding God you may say what you like; it can neither be proved nor disproved. There is no way to prove it, either right or wrong. That is why talk about God is so interesting and even the dullest person can take part in it, hence those who do nothing indulge in talking about God.

If they make some statement about the earth they will have to face troubles; but about heaven – no trouble. If you draw a map of this place, Matheran, you will have to prove it right, you will have to take measurements, and there will be a thousand other problems. Why create trouble? Draw the map of *Satyakhand*, "The Realm of Truth," or draw the map of *Brahmlok*, "The World of the Absolute," then nobody on earth can challenge you because you are out of the range of challenge. People are sitting in their armchairs and talking about God. They don't even move from there. They regard themselves as theists, but they are not. Theism is not satisfied with just talking, it demands experience.

So there are a few who deny all this, and for them there is nowhere to go. There are others who accept all this and say it is already known to them, and for them also there is nowhere to go, "Whatever exists, it is all in the scriptures. Saints and sages have already said these things" – so now there is no need for them to search.

Remember it, this is the basic difference between religion and science: in science, once a thing is discovered others don't need to discover it again; but in religion, if a thing is discovered, don't be mistaken that it has been discovered forever and you don't need to search for it anymore. Religion is an individual search; every individual has to search for it again and again. And this is the beauty; this is why religion is always fresh, it is never stale. Science becomes stale. Today, Newton is totally stale, but this Sarvasar Upanishad is still fresh – because the search is to be made again and again.

Religion is like love. You don't say, "Look, Majnu has loved, Farhad has already loved, so why should I take the trouble? Everything has been written about love – we will read about it, learn about it, write poetry about it, why take the trouble of being in love?"

No, someone may have loved a lot, Farhad may have loved a lot, but this cannot satisfy you, you will have to fall in love yourself. You will not be contented until you yourself are in love. Love is an individual experience. Millions and millions of people may have loved, it makes no difference. It is never stale. You have to love again, and when you do love you know it; prior to that you do not know.

There is no way to know about love from Farhad, or from Buddha either. Religion is like love, this search is like a love affair: it is to be discovered again and again.

The fourth, out of which the three states are born – sleep comes, dreams arise and waking happens, then all three again dissolve back into this fourth – this fourth is neither born out of anything nor dissolves into anything. It is the eternal principle of life, it is the basis of life; this is the very beginning and this is the very end, and he who has not known it wanders in the middle, in the cycle of life and death.

Enough for today.

Now prepare for the experiment. A few words about the experiment: yesterday the dust created so much trouble for you, so today those who want to do it vigorously should remain on the raised area, and others can spread out all over the ground.

Revolutionary results can come during this experiment, but for that you have to put your total energy into it. That is why I have scheduled it for the night. The morning and afternoon experiments will encourage you and make you able to put your total energy at stake in this night experiment.

After this you will go to sleep, so don't worry about tiredness. At the most you will become tired! There is no harm in it. You will go into deep sleep, nothing else will happen.

So it is essential to put your total energy into it.

6

The Physical and Energy Bodies

The assemblage of cells created by food
is the annamay kosh, the physical body.
When the fourteen different winds,
such as the prana wind, act in the physical body,
they form the pranamay kosh, the energy body.

Man as a whole is made up of many layers, and a right understanding of all these layers is necessary in order to go beyond them. It is essential to know that which we have to transcend, it is essential to recognize that which we have to get rid of. How a man appears from outside is not his complete body, it is only the first layer of his many bodies. When we look at a person, what we see at first glance the sages have called *annamay kosh*, the physical body.

This body is inherited from the parents, it is not yours; this layer is not you, this layer has a long tradition behind it. Thousands of bodies have created your body. The first cell you inherit from your parents contains the complete inbuilt processes of your body; all the potentialities of its growth are hidden in it.

Now the scientists say that whatever is manifested in your body throughout the whole of your life is all hidden in that first seed cell – apart from this cell nothing new can happen. The color of your eyes, the color of your hair, the color of your skin, your life span, whatever will blossom in your personality, all this is hidden in that cell. But that is not you. That body has had its own long journey: you received it from your parents, they received it from their parents – it has had a long journey, a long journey of millions of years.

If we trace back in the body we will find that the whole history of the universe is hidden in each man's body. Something of your body must have been present on the day when this world came into existence for the first time; by and by that same part has developed to become your present body. The whole story of existence is hidden in this small seed cell. It is not yours, it has a long tradition. That cell has traveled up to you through many human beings, many animals, innumerable plants and minerals. That is your first layer; that layer the sages call *annamay kosh*, the physical body. It is called *annamay kosh* because the process of its creation is through food, it is created by food.

The whole of the human body changes every seven years; everything changes – bones, flesh, marrow – everything is changed. If a man lives for seventy years his body has been renewed ten times. The food you take in daily creates your body, and every day you throw out the dead cells from your body. When we say that someone has died, it refers to his final death, when his soul departs from the body. Otherwise, man is dying every day, his body is dying continuously. When you cut your nails you don't feel any pain because the nails are dead parts of your body. When you cut your hair there is no pain because it consists of the dead cells of your body. If the hair was a living part of your body, then you would feel pain when you cut it.

Your body is renewing itself daily. It is surprising that often the hair and nails of dead persons grow in the grave. Because nails and hair have nothing to do with life, they can continue to grow on dead bodies; they are the dead parts, they can continue their growth.

Food is giving your body new cells daily, and the dead part is discarded by your body every day. This is a constant process. That is why the body is called *annamay kosh* – because it is created by the *anna*, the food.

Hence many things will depend on what type of food you eat. Many things depend on your food. Your food is not only supporting your life, it is also creating the first layer of your personality. And whether you can begin on your inner journey or not depends a lot on this layer, because all food is not the same. There are some types of food which will not allow you to go within, they will keep you tied to the outer world; some types of food will not allow the growth of consciousness within you because they will keep you unconscious. Some types of food will not allow you peace and tranquility because the process of digestion itself creates a disturbance in your body, disease. There are unhealthy foods, healthy foods, pure foods and impure foods.

Pure food is that which does not create difficulties for the inner journey – that is all, there is no other criterion. Pure food only means that it will not create a body that will be an obstacle on your inner journey.

Someone may build the walls of his house with solid stones, another may build the walls with only glass. Glass is transparent; standing outside, you can look inside. A solid stone wall will not allow you to look inside from the outside.

The body can also be as transparent as glass. Food is considered to be pure when it makes the body transparent – so that it gives you glimpses of the inner even while you are moving outside. You can also make this body such a dense wall that the inner journey is totally forgotten and glimpses of the inner being can never occur.

The purpose of *satvik* and *asatvik* food, pure and impure food, is that your physical body, the first layer, can become transparent. Only then the inward journey begins. Only when the first layer has become transparent can the second be known, not otherwise. We may never know that there is another body within this body. This is the reason for the emphasis on *satvik* food. The meditator knows that another body exists inside this physical body, because his first layer has become transparent and glimpses of the second layer have begun.

Then there are ways to make the second layer transparent, and then glimpses of the third body begin to come. The third body can also be made transparent, and then comes the fourth. When the fourth has become transparent, the fifth is there. And when the fifth becomes transparent, glimpses of that which is bodiless, beyond all the bodies, begin to come. So you can make your body as solid as a stone wall or as transparent as glass.

The sage, therefore, begins with the first: the physical body. This body around you is certainly created by food; there is nothing in it which is derived from any other source. It may be that your father ate *that* food, or your grandfather ate *that* food, it makes no difference; there is nothing in this body except food. When analyzed, the human sperm and egg which creates the first cell shows nothing except the elements of food. The essence of the food is contained in the seed.

Wise ones have done great experiments in relation to this. For thousands of years, generation after generation, a few families dared to live only on vegetarian food. No transformation can happen in the body within one day; the body has a long, complex history. But if a family has lived on vegetarian food for thousands of generations, there is radical change in the body. The same happens with nonvegetarian food, then too the body radically changes. Through constant refinement, becoming purer and purer over a long, long period of time, the very seed cell is altered. And only when the seed cell is altered, does transparency happen.

To transform the whole body by changing the food eaten was a unique experiment. Now scientists also agree that whatever we take in changes the body.

The difference between the male body and the female body is only a few hormones and nothing else. The difference is very small. These hormones are also created by food. If we take just a few hormones out of the female body it will start changing into a male body. If we take just a few hormones out of the male body it will start changing into a female body. It will not be long before a person born as a man will be able to choose to become a woman, or someone born as a woman will be able to choose to become a man, because the difference is of only a few hormones – only a few – and hormones are food. Hormones are the essence created by food. A small hormonal difference creates the difference between a man and a woman.

A little change in your food can also make the intelligence sharp or dull, because if the nutrients that are needed do not reach the brain through food, the intelligence becomes dull. Then, in spite of your potential, intelligence will not flower, because this flowering needs the help of the physical body which is then not available. Then the intelligence becomes totally dull because the substance at the third eye center in the pineal gland is not produced. In fact, when a man drinks alcohol it is not the intelligence which is affected – alcohol does not affect consciousness – but the pineal gland stops producing its fluid and intelligence is lost. Alcohol does not directly affect intelligence, but it affects that part in the physical body which is related to intelligence and it then becomes inactive.

A madness has started spreading all over the world from the West: the use of things like LSD. Scientists say that lysergic acid, or mescaline, or things like that also affect the pineal gland, and the fluid secreted by the pineal gland, which in turn obstructs intelligence. So it will not be surprising if the new generation in the West which uses LSD brings down the whole of the Western civilization because it is sure to harm the intelligence which is its very foundation.

Certainly if man's intelligence falls he is free from a kind of bond-age, because intelligence also brings its own kind of limitations and he becomes free from them. It is a great mistake to think that freedom from those limitations is freedom, because freedom comes in two ways: it can come by going beyond limitations, or it can come by falling below the limitations. The freedom that goes below is just madness, and the freedom attained by going beyond the limitations is the ultimate state. So they are purchasing cheap liberation through chemicals.

But even that is only a chemical, a food.

This body, our first layer, is the layer of food. Hence the right choice of food is significant – it is not only a superstition. To be a pure vegetarian gives a flexibility to the body which is not available to the nonvegetarian. The physical body layer of a nonvegetarian slowly, slowly becomes like an animal body.

It is amazing that you don't realize that the meat you eat is the creation of those animals, it is an organic part of those animals. You take that meat directly into your body and thus slowly you start making your own organic system animal-like. That system will affect you. That system will make your body a solid stone wall. Perhaps the reason why animals could not grow in intelligence is mostly because of their physical body. The intelligence which has evolved within you will slowly be reversed with the accumulation of animal flesh in your body. And very small things can make revolutionary changes – so small that we cannot even comprehend that they could do so.

Scientists say that the growth of intelligence in the human brain was possible because he stood up on his hind legs; had he been moving on his hands and feet his brain could not have evolved. It is such a small thing that it is amazing that it has made so much difference, such as the difference in intelligence between a monkey and a man, a man and a dog – what a tremendous difference there is between an Einstein and a monkey! And scientists say that this difference is due to such a small thing: standing up on our hind legs. How could it happen? It happened because the flow of blood to the brain was reduced; blood now had to be pumped upward to the brain. When the flow was reduced the brain could grow tender tissues, subtle nerves. If the flow is fast, the subtle nerves are destroyed. Animals have a constant large flow of blood toward the brain: that is why subtle nerves do not grow. It is like a river flowing very fast and not allowing the tiny plants to grow; not even the tiny pebbles can stay. They are all flushed away, thrown away.

The only reason so much evolution of human intelligence

became possible is that the brain received less blood. This is also why when you get up in the morning after a night's sleep your intelligence is fresh. Using your intelligence the whole day, by nighttime you get so tired you fall asleep, and during sleep more blood reaches to your brain.

So there is not much difference between our sleep and an animal's sleep. The difference is in the waking states. Howsoever you look, you can't tell the difference between a sleeping man and a sleeping animal, or can you? No, all the differences begin in the waking state of a man and an animal.

A sage is asleep and a sinner is asleep – in deep sleep, can you tell the difference? You may surgically analyze their brains, but can you differentiate through this as to who is the sage and who is the sinner? No difference can be found during deep sleep. In fact, no difference remains in sleep; all the difference lies in the waking state. The differences begin when we stand up on our hind legs. One is an enlightened being, one is an Einstein and one is an idiot. But all this difference is in the waking state: when no large flow of blood reaches to the brain then these differences of subtle nerves arise.

Have you ever noticed that for a good sleep you need pillows under your head? Remove the pillow and sleep becomes difficult, because when you remove the pillow the blood rushes to the brain. In fact the structure of the human head is such that if one sleeps without a pillow the head becomes a basin. In sleep, compared to the whole body the head is at the lowest level, and the flow of blood runs fast toward the head. The flow is so fast that it does not allow the tissues to relax, then it becomes difficult to sleep. That is why, as the intelligence of man grows, more pillows are also required. There is a reason for this: as the tender tissues grow within they need to be protected otherwise there will be no sleep; the tender tissues will vibrate so fast that sleep will not be possible.

This is such a small thing, but scientists say that it radically changed man. I am telling you this small incident just as an example so that you understand that food might not be such a small issue. Small things can make a great difference.

Scientists say that because man stood erect, families could come into existence; otherwise they would never have happened. Who would have thought that there could be a relationship between man standing erect and the birth of the family? And when there is no family, there can be no civilization or culture either, because culture and civilization are the expansion of the family. But could you have ever imagined that standing erect might have anything to do with the existence of the family?

Scientists say that the phenomenon of love was born because man stood erect, otherwise it could not have come into existence. You cannot imagine that standing erect has anything to do with love, but this is how it happened. And researchers are unanimous about it. While animals make love they don't face each other – they can't. While animals make love they don't face each other because they approach from behind. Scientists say it is because man stood erect and stopped approaching from behind, when having sex man could face his partner – copulation took the face-to-face position – and when we can see someone's face only then the idea of the person's personality occurs, otherwise it does not. So when a man makes love with a woman face to face, a relationship between their faces, between them, is soon established.

It is interesting to note that all bodies are so similar. There is not much difference, only faces differ. And it is the faces which carry personality. If you were all beheaded, your bodies would be difficult to recognize. But faces can be recognized because they have individuality, the expression of your personality is in your face. Human beings could see each other's faces during lovemaking, so sexual desire was transformed into love…and personal relationships grew, families began to come into existence, and slowly the rest of the body became secondary and the face became important. For animals the face is not important at all. A deep relationship with the face never developed. Scientists say that because man stood erect the family, love, culture and civilization could then come into existence – that such a small thing could be so significant!

So food is not a small thing; it is a big thing, immensely important, because it creates our whole body. Whatever we take into our bodies has its own quality and that quality will become the quality of our bodies in a few days' time. If we suddenly ask someone who is always pouring alcohol into his body to stop drinking, he will not be able to stop abruptly. Why is that? Because now it is not he who is drinking, but rather each and every cell of his body that drinks – each and every cell! It is out of his control; now every pore in his body has started drinking – every cell. There are millions and millions of cells in a human body, and each and every cell has started drinking; every cell has become a drunkard. This is called addiction. There is no other reason for addiction.

When we say that someone is addicted, that means that it is not he who is drinking, but each and every cell in his whole body is saying, "Drink now, otherwise you won't be able to function – you can't walk, you can't stand, you can't sit." Now it is very difficult to drop it, because millions of lives within you are asking you to drink – millions and millions of living cells! You are a big crowd, a big city; you are not alone, you are living in that big city.

Hence we chose the word *purush* for the soul. *Purush* means, the resident of the big city, the dweller in the big city, *purush*. Every person has a big city within their body – a big city! It is not a small town. You have millions and millions of lives around you, and when all of them make demands you are in a great difficulty, you will have to fulfill their demands. You cannot get out of this situation even if you wanted to.

So what you take as food creates these millions of cells and their subsequent demands. And then you have to live in a bondage with them, and these bonds become a barrier to the inner journey.

We call that food *satvik* which does not create addiction –

food which only gives the body energy and does not intoxicate it. You have to understand this distinction clearly: *satvik* is that food which gives the body energy but does not intoxicate it, that food which supplies the needs of the body but does not create madness in the body, that food which fulfills the needs of the body but does not become just an indulgence for it.

To whatever extent something intoxicates your body, the body will be polluted to the same degree. But we don't think about this, we don't consider it; we don't care about what we eat, we don't care about what we drink, we go on doing the same as the crowd is doing.

India, more than any other country, has made great advances in researching the principles of food. Perhaps it was first realized in India that for the inner journey, for the journey within, first the body has to be transformed. This body as it is at present is not fit for the journey.

Pavlov was doing experiments on dogs – great experiments; he worked hard on it for some fifty years. He discovered if you remove just a small gland from a dog, even from a ferocious dog who was a killer just a moment before, that now however hard you try the dog will not get angry even if he is beaten or tortured, because this small poisoned gland has been removed. What happened? Only a little poison was taken out, and that poison had come from the dog's food. So without removing the poison, but simply by changing the dog's food to something which does not produce this poison, he will not be vicious anymore.

Violence in man comes from the poisons produced within his body. If those poisons are removed from his body he will not be violent again, so a large number of physiologists say that it is nonsense to call murderers criminals, they are only ill. A particular poison is produced in their bodies. What can they do? So to punish them or to hang them is totally mad. If B.F. Skinner, a great American thinker and psychologist, were to succeed in getting the world to agree that the criminals should be operated on – that they are not criminals, that it would only be necessary to remove a few glands and they would not be able to murder or be violent again.

But if a scientist or a laboratory, a society or a state were to remove your glands, you would become a slave. If you are unable to get angry, then what is the value of your compassion? Impotence is not nonviolence; to be impotent does not mean to be nonviolent. Scientists can operate on you... You don't even have to alter your diet, you can go on eating whatever you eat, but your glands can be removed, the system which creates the poisons can be destroyed – then you will not be able to get angry, you will not be able to be violent, to murder. But that will not be due to any virtue on your part and it will not take you on your inner journey. You will have only become impotent.

But another process has been discovered, and that process does not put pressure on you from the outside or cripple some part of your body, that process allows your body to remain as it is – it is for you to voluntarily change the quality of the food you eat for an inner transformation to take place. Then slowly, slowly your body can become free of those poisons which lead you to crime and wrongdoing, and free you from those stimuli which lead you to focus only on the external.

And just the opposite is also possible. This is only one half of the coin – the negative half – which produces the poisons within you which are responsible for your anger. Is it also possible to produce that nectar in you which makes you compassionate? Skinner has no knowledge of it as yet. If you have a gland which makes you male or female and which creates in you the lust for the opposite sex, might it not also be possible to produce something within you which could set you free from this attraction?

Of course, you can be freed from this attraction by means of an operation, but that is falling below; then you are only becoming impotent. But if your whole capacity of being male or female remains and along with it that nectar starts flowing within you which takes you beyond the attraction for the opposite sex –

where even the thought of being a man or a woman is forgotten – then you are rising up, the energy is moving upward.

The physical body is the first thing.

The second layer of the body, this second layer the sages have called *pranamay kosh,* the vital body. You will know it as soon as the first body becomes transparent, otherwise it will remain only hypothetical. Hidden beneath this first body is the vital body. The *prana* body means the energy body, the vital body.

This is the difference between a stone and a living being: a stone has only one body – the physical body. A plant has one more body within – the *pranamay* body. A plant has two bodies, a stone has only one body. A plant has two bodies, so a plant is not just a stone; there is something in it similar to a stone, surrounding it on the outside, but inside there flows a life-stream. Even a plant is young at one time and then becomes old; when it is full of life's juices it is joyous, when its life is diminished it is sad.

In the morning when the sun rises a stone remains as a stone, and at night the stone also remains as a stone. But a plant is one thing at night and something else in the morning; a stream of life exists within it, an energy body which becomes blissful with the rising sun. This energy that it receives from the sun goes to its energy body. The stone remains a stone during the night and it is still a stone in the morning; a stone is not affected by the sun.

When I say a stone, notice that I am not saying a mountain, because a mountain *is* affected; a mountain is alive. A few mountains are young – for example the Himalayan range is still young, is still growing. The Vindhyachal range has grown old.

There is a lovely story, that Vindhyachal bowed its head to say good-bye to a sage who was setting out on a journey and the sage did not return, so it remains with its head bowed. The truth is something else. The Vindhya range is an ancient range – the oldest on earth – the Himalayan range is just a child; Vindhya is the oldest. Long ago it bowed its head and its neck became weak, it became old.

That story is mythology, but it is lovely. The myth says that now the mountain range has become so old that it can't hold its head up. Now, even if the sage were to return, it could not raise its head. But the Himalayan range is still rising, growing every day. It is difficult to say how much more it will grow.

It is interesting that the Rigveda does not mention the Himalayas. Yet it is impossible that something like the Himalayas should be missing from it. It is impossible that a mountain range like the Himalayas, with the peaks of Everest and Mount Kailash shining in the sky, that they would be there and the sage not sing a song of their glory – it is impossible. In fact when the sage sang his song the Himalayas had not yet been born. There appears to be no other logical reason, because the sage did not miss even the minutest thing, so how could he have missed the Himalayas? There can be only one reason, that when the sage composed his song the Himalayas had not yet come into existence, or even if they had, they must have been such small hills that they could have been overlooked.

The Rigveda mentions journeys and places which are not in India, places which are in Central Asia. It talks about nights which occur only at the North Pole and never in this region. The Rigveda mentions a place which has daylight for six months and night for six months. But the Himalayas have not been mentioned! It seems that the Himalayas were absent. And it appears that either the sage resided at the North Pole, or there was a straight pathway between the North Pole and India without the Himalayas in between, without any hindrance.

Scholars who believe that the Aryans migrated to India have difficulty because they cannot find any mention of hardship in crossing the Himalayas. If they did migrate into India, it is impossible that they would not mention the terrible difficulties in crossing the Himalayas because so many other things are mentioned. It would have been the deepest memory of the race – so many people would have died, so many people would have been lost, possibly only ten out of a thousand would have arrived – but there is no mention of it. The Himalayas did not exist. It is not a very old mountain range.

When I talk of a stone I do not mean a mountain, even a mountain has a vital body. Wherever there is growth, there is a vital body. All growth happens in *prana*, in the vital energy, not in matter. Growth always happens in *prana*, not in matter. So sometimes it happens that a large man seems to be quite lifeless, he has a heavy body but no vital energy. And sometimes a lean, thin body shows an oceanic vital energy.

This energy body is created by *prana* and the physical body is created by matter, created by food. This energy is received from the sun, the air, and from infinite subtle vibrations.

So sometimes it can also happen that a person can learn the art of being nourished directly from this *prana*, this energy. Then he can become free from eating food, or reduce the quantity of food he requires. This person can use this life-energy directly and can assimilate it. That art exists. Sometimes it happens accidentally…

There are still a few people alive on earth today who have not eaten food for years. They have not lost any weight – and they should have. It appears that somehow their system understands the method of changing energy directly into matter. And now, after Einstein, it is clear that matter and energy are not two things; matter is just energy, energy is just matter – two states of one thing.

Einstein's greatest formula states only this, that energy and matter are not two things, they are one; they are two states of one and the same thing. So matter can become energy and energy can become matter. The atom bomb was developed according to this formula. The explosion of the atom bomb is a declaration that matter converts into energy; one atom is split and it becomes energy. The opposite is also possible. The process is reversed when a person lives without food and the body is not in need of food: energy from the energy body converts into matter.

This energy body is an inner layer; we are not aware of it. Sometimes, in some moments it is felt – occasionally. One day you are standing on the seashore and suddenly you find a wave of energy running within you. That wave is not happening in the physical body, it cannot; that wave is an energy phenomenon. Energy waves don't affect matter, they can't affect stone: they are energy. When you fall in love suddenly vibrations, waves of energy arise in you. Those waves do not arise in your physical body, although the body feels the sensation, the thrill, the excitement.

Housman, a great Western thinker has written: "I call that poetry, poetry which makes your hair stand on end." The influence of poetry is not on the physical body, it is on the energy body. A real poet is one who enters into your energy body so that you can feel the waves inside.

A song which does not make you dance is not really a song – your ears may have heard it but your energy body has not. But when a song does reach the energy body then it becomes a dance. Sometimes when hearing a song, when hearing the notes of a veena, or being with the waves of the ocean, in moments of love, looking at the moon in the sky, watching the rising sun, feeling a rush of wind, watching a flower blossoming, you vibrate blissfully. That is not your physical body, that is your energy body.

Scientists now acknowledge the vital energy within; they call it bioenergy. They call it the body electricity. Some people have more body electricity and some have less. This is the reason why some people have a hypnotic effect on you. You go to a person and without reason you suddenly feel his influence – it is because of the energy body. This person has developed the energy body, and it is possible only when the first body is transparent, otherwise not.

If he has developed the energy body, you can immediately feel the waves within your energy body, one energy touching another energy. It can be touched from a faraway distance, the distance does not matter. For the physical body distance matters; for the energy body it does not matter. Then something within you is moved, something vibrates, your energy body aligns with it, it becomes enveloped by it.

The most significant part of the energy body which is visible in the physical body is the eyes. That is why nothing seems to be more alive in the body than the eyes; the rest of the body appears to be dead. In fact the eyes are functioning in two ways. Eyes are those places in your physical body from where your energy body peeps out, hence the eyes are so alive and vibrating. That is why the energy waves immediately rush into the eyes. It takes time for anger to come into your hands: you will clench your fist, your blood will rush and then you will run to attack; but the eyes show anger within moments. Love will take time to reach to the body, you will have to wait; but eyes fall in love at once.

Your eyes are the language of your energy body. Everything about your energy body can be seen in your eyes if they are thoroughly examined. Your eyes are continuously broadcasting what is going on inside you. Eyes are very expressive, vibrant.

This energy body also needs purification. This energy body needs transparency. All the exercises of *pranayama*, breathing exercises, are to make the vital body transparent. The more oxygen that enters the physical body, the cleaner and purer the vital body becomes; the more carbon dioxide enters it, the more impure, polluted and gross the vital body becomes.

That is why it is difficult to sleep during the day and it is easy at night, because during the night on earth the oxygen level is reduced and the carbon dioxide level is increased. During the day there is more oxygen and less carbon dioxide. Hence those who rise in *brahmamuhurt*, the early dawn, believe that it is natural to get up early, because if your energy body is not influenced by the rising sun you have made it very insensitive, dead. When the sun is rising even plants feel the influence, even birds begin to sing songs, but your energy body is unmoved. You just turn over onto the other side in your bed! You have become a stone.

This energy body, since it is energy, is affected by energized air. So the deeper your breathing is, the healthier it will be. Your breathing should be natural. Don't breathe superficially. The deeper your breathing, the stronger your energy will be; the deeper your breathing, the sharper your intelligence will be.

If women lag behind men in intelligence, one of the reasons is that many have a bad habit of breathing superficially. Among animals it is not so often seen that there is much of a difference between male and female intelligence – there seems to be no difference. But there is a vast difference to be seen among human beings. There are thousands of reasons for it, but one is the superficial breathing. The reason why women breathe superficially is that they are constantly self-conscious about their breasts. If you want large breasts, a superficial way of breathing is helpful. If there is deep breathing, breasts will remain small. In any case, big breasts are not needed.

It is interesting that, except in human females, all female animals have large breasts only when they are required, when the babies need milk; after that they become small. Only women have developed breasts which remain large even when no milk is needed. This is due to superficial breathing. If the breathing goes deep down into the belly the breasts will remain as the body requires them to be. If they are to be kept large, the belly has to be contracted and the breath should not be allowed to go down into the belly.

The wrestler does not breathe down into the belly just so that his chest remains expanded. That is why most wrestlers are not intelligent – they can't be. They can't be! I have not yet heard of a single wrestler who is intelligent, because intelligence cannot grow if the energy body is dense. The wrestler also keeps his belly contracted and breathes up into his chest.

Have you seen a baby breathing? The way a baby breathes is the right way to breathe. The baby's belly rises and falls, not the chest, because the baby has not yet been spoiled. The baby neither needs to become a wrestler nor to have big breasts; he does not have such problems yet. The baby breathes as nature requires him to breathe. His belly rises and falls.

You must have been surprised to see the statues of Buddha: Indian statues have large chests and small bellies, but Japanese and Chinese statues have small chests and big bellies. This looks a little ugly but there is a reason for it. Even though this was not factual – it is not true that Buddha had a big belly – but in China and Japan they made such statues knowingly because they say that the attention should be on the belly and not on the chest. If the attention remains on the chest, the breathing is within the chest. So one of the reasons why many women are less intelligent is that they breathe superficially, so that the energy body remains shrunken, not vitalized.

The more vital air that is available to the energy body, the purer this body becomes. This energy body also uses other more subtle foods. Particular vibrations or waves are available at particular places: there are many kinds of vibrations – pure vibrations and impure vibrations.

Satsang, the heart to heart communion with a master, is useful: you go to a sage and just sit near him without any conversation…just sitting there – for what? In this silence his vibrations become available to your energy body.

A unique thing which has come into existence in India is *darshan*, "seeing." In the West nobody can understand what *darshan* might mean – "Going for *darshan*, to see someone?" It is conceivable that you might go to meet someone, to talk with him, to discuss with him, to understand something…but going only to *see* him? What madness! What is this *darshan*? What will *darshan* do? *Darshan* does something…does a lot. Often something which cannot happen in conversation happens.

Darshan only means that you go to a place where there is an energy body, very much alive with an atmosphere around it full of energy, and by sitting there even for only a few moments your energy body is moved, your vital body is vibrated.

Seekers used to go away to the mountains, away from human

civilization, to escape the vibrations which emanate from large numbers of people. Energy vibrations can be either pure or polluted. A crowd is very tiring. Have you ever noticed that when you return from being in a crowd your energy is a little reduced, your energy has gone down a bit? Have you ever noticed that the crowd reduces your intelligence? In fact, if you have to get something done which is very idiotic and you cannot get it done by a single person alone, then you can get it done by a crowd. If a mosque is to be set on fire or a temple is to be demolished, only a crowd can get it done, not individuals.

It is surprising that if you asked a single individual in that crowd to do such a stupid thing he would not agree. What is the point in setting a mosque on fire? But when he is in the crowd his intelligence goes down and he thinks, "I am not responsible for it," because in a crowd intelligence and responsibility are lost. He thinks, "I will not be held responsible for this. There are so many people doing it, and I am just going with them." Everybody thinks that way. That is why crowds have committed greater crimes than individuals. Individuals only commit small crimes.

When the seekers used to go far away from the crowd it was only to gain the pure vital energy, not the energy given by the crowd.

Moses went to the mountains of Sinai, Mohammed climbed the mountains, Buddha and Mahavira roamed about in the forest, Christ remained unknown for thirty years.

Christians have no record of his first thirty years. The whole story about Jesus covers only about three years, and that too the three years before his death. Where was he for the rest of the time? There is one mention of his seventh year, when he was only seven years old, and then again when he was thirty. Nobody knows about the other twenty-three years when he was away from the crowd. These twenty-three years were for the growth of his energy body, of his vital energy.

We will talk about the third body during the night session.

Now let us do some work.

When I tell you to breathe deeply and fast, deep and fast breathing, I am trying to activate your energy body. Don't be a miser, put your total energy into it. When I tell you to go mad and to throw everything out that is being suppressed inside, it is for your purification – throw it out! When I tell you to do the "Hoo, Hoo," it is in order to hit your energy body.

Let us enter into the experiment. Spread out and stand far apart. Nothing less than madness will do. Put your intellect aside. Anyway you don't have much intellect, so it shouldn't be a problem! Nothing less than madness will do.

7

The Mental Body and the Bodies of Awareness and Bliss

When the soul,
in collaboration with the two bodies,
and through the medium of the fourteen
instruments,
conceives objects such as words,
it is called manomay kosh, the mental body.
When the soul,
in collaboration with the three bodies,
becomes conscious of all perceptions,
it is called vigyanamay kosh, the awareness body.
When the soul,
in collaboration with the four bodies,
remains in the innocence of its cause,
like the seed of the banyan tree,
it is called anandamay kosh, the bliss body.

The first body is the gross body – physical, and made of food. The second is the energy body. We talked about these two in the morning. One who purifies the energy body awakens toward the third body; when one layer becomes transparent, glimpses of the next layer start coming.

As we have understood, the first body is made of food, the second body is made of vital energy, and the third is made of thought waves. Thoughts are also food. Thoughts are also things. Thoughts are also energy.

Buddha has said: "As you think so you become. You are the result of your own thinking." This is true up to the level of the mental body. Buddha's statement is true because those people he was speaking to knew nothing beyond the mind. But we never regard thoughts as food – thoughts are also food, thoughts also enter within and create a body. Try to understand this.

In 1900, in Calcutta, a boy child disappeared. After seven years he was tracked down in the jungle and was brought back by a hunter. He had been carried off by a wolf. Tremendous efforts were made to make the boy human, but it was very difficult. The boy walked on all fours just like a wolf and he made sounds like a wolf. He had become as ferocious as a wolf, he ran as fast as one, and it was difficult to try to get him to stand upright. The boy died because of these excessive attempts. His mind had not developed because the mind had not received food.

This has happened three or four times. In Uttar Pradesh, some ten years ago, a boy of fourteen was brought back after having lived among wolves. But by the age of fourteen it was too late because he could not speak even a word. After six months he had only been taught to say "Ram." They had named the boy Ram; after six months it had only been possible to teach him this much. He also died. He was a healthy boy but he could not be saved in spite of the best of efforts. Now it had become too difficult to develop his mind and to make him a human being because the mental body had not been developed.

You speak a particular language; this is the food you have been given from childhood. If you had been in another family you would have spoken a different language. Language creates a deep layer.

One of my friends left India in his childhood and spent twenty years in Germany. His mother tongue was Marathi, but he forgot it. After speaking German for twenty years he had no memory of Marathi – he could not read it, he could not even speak it, let alone understand it. Then suddenly, due to an accident, he fell ill. His brother went to Germany from India. The hospital staff requested him to stay in the hospital with his sick brother even though it was against the hospital rules to stay overnight. But he had to stay, because whatever language the brother spoke in his unconscious state was unknown to the hospital staff. It was only when he was conscious that he would speak German. And his brother was amazed that when the sick brother was unconscious he spoke Marathi; when conscious he could not even understand Marathi, but while unconscious he spoke only Marathi and could not speak a single word of German. In the unconscious state he could not understand any German at all.

The food which creates the very first layer of the mental body is the deepest. So one may later learn another language but it cannot have the depth of one's mother tongue. It is impossible, there just is no way, because the first layer created in the mental body will always remain the first, all other layers will be created afterward.

Language, words, thoughts, all these create a body within us. The more cultured and well-educated someone is, the bigger this mental body is. But this body is not visible to us as a body; hence we go on throwing all kinds of thoughts into the mental body without caring. A man reading his newspaper in the morning doesn't understand that this newspaper is also creating his mental body. Walking along the street reading the posters on the walls, he cannot even conceive that these words are entering him and creating his mind.

We are totally unaware how we are creating our minds, hence our life is a chaos. If we were as unaware in creating our physical bodies as we are about creating our minds, even the physical body would become a problem. We do not choose to eat gravel and pebbles, but as far as the mind is concerned what we eat is much worse than that. It all creates the mind, whatever enters into the mind knowingly or unknowingly becomes a part of it. But we are not aware that our mental body is being created every moment; whatever we hear, whatever we read, whatever we think, whatever words resound within us create our mental body. If your neighbor tells you something meaningless you never say, "Please, don't put all this garbage into me." Although you may or may not be aware just how easy it is to absorb it, nevertheless it is very difficult to throw it out.

If I have put a word into you, it is not so easy to throw it out. Try it and you will know. I can say the word *Ram* to you; now however you try, you will not be able to get rid of it all night, instead it will go even deeper and settle inside because the more you try to get rid of it the more you will remember it. That which we want to forget first has to be remembered in order to forget it. And every time we remember it, we strengthen it.

That's why when you want to forget someone it becomes impossible. You may forget about someone, that is another thing, but it is very difficult to consciously forget someone, and even then that forgetting will just be superficial, it will not be erased from within. The mind doesn't lose anything, it is a great collector. The mental body goes on collecting in very subtle ways. Whatever it has received as a thought wave, even in past lives, is collected. It is essential to understand this mental body – because only then can it be transcended.

Remember two things. Firstly, I told you that the physical body is a gross body; behind it exists the energy body, and behind that exists the mental body. The energy body is the bridge between the physical and the mental body. *Prana,* the breath, is the connecting link between the two. That is why when breathing stops the physical body is left here and the mental body starts on a new journey. In death only the physical body disintegrates, not the mental body. Only when a person is enlightened is the mental body dissolved. When a man dies only his physical body dies, not his mental body; and that mental body starts on a new journey with all its old patterns. The mind searches for a new body and again finds a womb, and it receives the new body in the same way and creates almost the same old structure.

The connecting link between the two is the vital breath. Hence when a man becomes unconscious, we don't pronounce him dead – even if he remains in a coma for months we don't say that he is dead. But if the breathing stops we immediately regard him as dead because the connection between the body and the mind is broken.

And remember, with breathing the relationship between mind and the body changes every moment. When you are angry the rhythm of your breathing changes immediately; when you have a sexual desire the rhythm of your breathing changes; when you are relaxed the rhythm of your breathing changes. If your mind is disturbed, then too the rhythm of your breathing changes; if your body is disturbed, then too the rhythm of your breathing changes. The rhythm of your breathing is changing continuously with changes in the body or mind. That is why those who can truly master the rhythm of breathing achieve a profound mastery over mind and body.

In Japan, small babies are taught to relax their breathing whenever anger arises, because anger cannot be relaxed directly. You can suppress it but you cannot relax it, and the anger which is suppressed will again erupt some day, today or tomorrow, and perhaps with more venom in it. In Japan, children are told to relax their breathing if they feel angry, because when the breathing becomes relaxed the anger that has arisen in the mind does not reach to the physical body; without the bridge of the breathing that is impossible. And if it does not reach the physical body, then neither suppression nor expression is needed. If it remains in the mind it will slowly dissipate, if it reaches the physical body it is beyond your control. There are ways to dissipate it in the mind. But the physical body is a very gross thing. If it catches something, then it can only be either suppressed or expressed. If you express it that creates a problem, if you suppress it then it creates complexes within the body.

A great American psychologist named Wilhelm Reich died some time ago. After lifelong experiments on his patients, he found that when one attempts to suppress anger, the anger settles in the physical body in the form of knots. And strangely enough he discovered that he could make someone angry just by pressing those knots. After a lifelong study of patients' bodies, if he felt that the disease they had was due to suppressed anger, he would press those parts in the body where he thought the anger might have accumulated and the person would become immediately enraged. Someone else might never become angry if these same places were pressed, but that particular patient would burn with anger for no reason; there was no provocation from outside, and no apparent reason.

When you suppress feelings, knots are created in the physical body, complexes are formed. Ninety percent of diseases are the result of suppressed emotions. That's why the physician can only change them, not cure them. Today there is one disease, and the physician represses it, controls it, but tomorrow it will start appearing in another form. The physician only transfers the disease somewhere else. The patient feels a little relieved. One disease is cured, another will take a little time to erupt.

The complexes created within, the poisons accumulated inside which have become subtle knots, need to be thrown out. If they have not yet affected the physical body, there are ways in which they can be made to dissolve from the mind.

Breathing is the bridge. Whatever is conveyed to the body is conveyed through breathing. If your mind is full of sexual desire and your breathing remains undisturbed, it is difficult for this desire to reach the physical body; it is only through the breathing that it will reach the body.

There was a great Russian film director, Stanislavski, one of the most intelligent directors of the twentieth century. Stanislavski made some very profound discoveries about acting, and those discoveries are very useful, useful for everyone. His most profound discovery was the use of different rhythms of breathing, which he taught to his actors. He said: "If you have to be angry, don't bother about trying to be angry, adopt a particular rhythm of breathing and anger will come on its own. If you have to express love, don't try to express it, because that very effort makes it inauthentic and destroys the acting. Arrange the breathing within yourself and then breathe in that rhythm – the love you want will soon appear on your face. And this will appear to be quite close to reality, it will not look like acting."

Stanislavski used to say that an actor must be the master of both his physical and energy bodies – he must especially be a master of his energy body, only then can he become an expert in acting, not otherwise.

Nijinsky was a Russian dancer. When Nijinsky danced everyone felt that they were seeing an illusion – and that was partially the case. Although there were many great dancers of the same caliber, it is said there has never been and perhaps never will be a dancer like Nijinsky. The strange thing was that when he was dancing and he made a leap, it took him an unusually long time to come down. No other dancer took as long; it was as if gravitation had less effect on him. When he made a leap, it looked as if he was just floating in the air and taking his own time to come back down. Others who had leaped with him had already touched the floor again, long before he did.

What was the secret behind it? Investigations showed that there was a particular quality in the rhythm of his breathing that was quite different from that of others. It was uncommon.

During the last fifty years, there have been reports of people levitating. For example, there is one woman in Bolivia who rises four to five feet above the ground some four or five times a year. She was investigated scientifically, filmed, a lot of work was done, and now there is no doubt about it. It was discovered that the rhythm of her breathing was the same as Nijinsky's. She breathed in the same way.

Several rhythms of breathing have been discovered in the field of *pranayama*, the science of the vital breath. When these different rhythms are used changes occur in the mind and in the physical body. Breathing is the bridge between the mental body and the physical body: the physical body exists on this side and the mental body on the other side.

Thoughts are the most subtle things in our experience, but even thoughts actually exist. The idea that thoughts have no material existence has now been proved wrong. They do have a material existence.

Eddington has written in his autobiography: "Many times I am overwhelmed with the concept that thoughts are things." At that time it was just an idea, there was no proof, but now scientific evidence is available. In the last ten years machines have been developed which can pick up your thought waves. If you stand in front of such a machine and concentrate on a thought, it registers that you are concentrating – you only have to stand in front of the machine the same way in which you stand in front of an X-ray machine. If you relax and let go of the thought, the machine indicates that you have relaxed.

There is a man in America called Ted Serios. Perhaps in today's world his is the greatest evidence on earth proving that thoughts are matter. A peculiar power suddenly appeared in Ted Serios. He would concentrate on some thought, and the image of that thought would appear in his eyes and this image could be photographed by a camera. For example, if he was peacefully concentrating on a thought of the Taj Mahal its image would appear in his eyes, and even though he has never actually seen the Taj Mahal and it would emerge only in his imagination, it could be photographed. Ted was photographed at least ten thousand times. Often very interesting observations were made; and the photographs have been published. Hundreds of researchers worked hard using various approaches trying to detect any deception. But that was actually impossible, because while the researcher could see the Taj Mahal in his eyes and although he may have been deceived, it is very difficult to deceive a camera. What did the picture in the camera prove? It proved that if a thought can become dense and take on the form of the Taj Mahal in the eyes, then it is not only thought, it is a thing too; it is matter, it is material, because only matter can be photographed, a thought cannot. Only matter can be photographed. A thing which can be photographed is more substantial, more material.

Often really amazing things happened. Once, when Ted Serios was trying to bring the Taj Mahal into his eyes, he closed his eyes and confirmed that he had caught the image and asked for the camera to be kept ready. Then he opened his eyes, the camera clicked, and Ted said, "Sorry, I missed it. Now I caught the Hilton Hotel – the thought changed inside. Sorry, forgive me." Astonishingly enough the camera did not catch the photograph of the Taj Mahal, instead it caught one of the Hilton Hotel. It happened a few times that the Hilton Hotel was superimposed on the Taj Mahal, both were caught – the Taj Mahal going out, and the Hilton Hotel coming in.

Thoughts are also substantial, although very subtle. And we are "eating" them too, we are taking them in every moment. These thoughts are creating a body within us. It is a house built of the bricks of thoughts. Hence the type of thoughts you take in create the type of mental body you will have.

Man is very vulnerable in this way. At least in this century he has become very vulnerable. Radio is putting ideas in your head, newspapers, politicians, advertisers are all putting ideas into you; man is being fed with thoughts from everywhere. And you still think that you are making your own decisions? – you are mistaken.

Vance Packard has written a book entitled *The Hidden Persuaders*. When you go to a shop and ask for Berkeley cigarettes – do you think the choice is yours? You are mistaken. There are hidden persuaders all around you, telling you through newspapers, through signs on shops, on walls, television, radio – wherever you look – telling you to "Buy Berkeley cigarettes." "Berkeley" has been implanted in your mind.

American advertisers say: "Whatever anyone buys, we have created ninety percent of his decision to buy. The remaining ten percent is not his choice either, it is only because of the incompletely developed art of advertising. The individual has no freedom in it. As we develop it to one hundred percent, we will know in advance what we will make him purchase, we will know what he will purchase."

It is necessary to be aware of this, otherwise you are not free. If others are creating your mind you are not free. Your parents pass on their religion to you; your teachers give you knowledge in schools; advertisers, newspapers and the marketing net give you suggestions to buy things. You are being manipulated by these suggestions all your life.

Now, in America, while the production of cars has increased, the demand has decreased because almost everyone already has a car. The manufacturers were worried what to do. So for the past five years a new idea has been promoted: that you are rich if you own *two* cars. Now people are starting to own two cars. Owning one car shows a man's poverty, having only one car proves that you are poor. And once you have connected owning only one car with poverty, then life is hell without two. A rich man must have two houses – one in the city and another at the beach or in the mountains – only a poor man owns one house. Just plant an idea and people go crazy for it – and they always believe that it is they who are deciding. They are living in an illusion.

The mental body is a creation of words. You all know much about the chanting of God's name, and you must have seen others doing it, but are you aware that it is simply a protective measure and nothing else? Chanting is a safety device. If you are engaged in chanting while you are walking on the road no other words will enter into you, because some space is needed in order for words to be able to enter.

If someone is chanting "Rama, Rama" twenty-four hours a day, whether engaged in sweeping or eating or at a shop or talking to some-one else, always chanting "Rama, Rama" to himself, this is a protective measure; now you cannot force anything onto him. Now a thick layer, a wall of Rama has been erected within, and it is not easy to penetrate this wall of Rama. Such a person is trying to give a particular form and characteristics to his mental body.

And it is very interesting that if anything is to penetrate this wall of Rama, it can only penetrate if it is in accord with the concept of Rama, not otherwise. An affinity with Rama is required in order for it to penetrate. For example, if someone shouts "Ravana" near this person, the word will bounce back off the wall, but if someone says "Sita" it will penetrate. This layer is then a protection against the undesirable and is open to the desirable. In a sense, this man will start becoming master of his mental body; he is allowing those thoughts which he wants and rejecting those which he does not want.

And if we are not even masters of our own minds, what are we masters of? Our minds are almost mad because we simultaneously accept quite contradictory things – thousands of contradictory things. People complain how their mind is restless, perplexed, confused. It is amazing that they think that this is a disease to be cured. No, this is your own creation, you are practicing it twenty-four hours a day; you are taking in all kinds of contradictory things. You take in one thought, then you grasp another quite contradictory thought. This creates uneasiness. There is a polarization between these two thoughts; they fight and struggle with each other and you have to suffer.

It is not you that is struggling, but the thoughts within you. There are infinite thoughts within you, and they are all conflicting. Some thoughts want to move eastward, some want to go westward, some don't want to move at all, and all of them are in tremendous conflict, as if you have yoked the oxen of your cart in all four directions simultaneously. Such is your condition. Sometimes the cart moves a little eastward, sometimes westward. Sometimes the oxen in one direction are stronger, sometimes the oxen of some other direction are lethargic – but the struggle continues and the cart reaches nowhere. Ultimately it will shatter and will get you nowhere. We are all in this same predicament. There is an inner confusion, an inner conflict.

A man came to me and said, "I want contentment in my life, I want satisfaction in my life, but I cannot trust anybody so I have come to you – even though I have no faith in you at all, please tell me the way to find contentment."

I told him, "I will tell you the way, but you will not trust the method. Drop this search for contentment, because in fact you are searching for discontentment. A person who does not trust anybody cannot experience contentment" – because whoever does not trust has to be alert; he is always afraid, always in danger. Because he distrusts everyone around him he has no trust at all. If this man's distrust grows stronger he will not be able to stay in his house because, who knows? – the house may collapse any time. And he will not be able to stay outside either because some accident may happen. If his distrust continues to grow, eventually he will end up distrusting himself also.

Once I knew a university professor who was in fact a very intelligent man. Ultimately he reached a state where he could not trust even himself. He never kept a knife or a fork in his room during the night because he might at any time cut himself. He had no faith, no trust in himself. This meant that someone had to stay with him in his room at night – but he could not trust them either. Or someone had to stay just outside, but then nothing dangerous could be left inside the room because he had no trust in himself.

In fact, for someone who has no trust in others, a day comes when he also loses trust in himself. The fact is that he cannot trust at all; the main question is of trust; it is not a question of trusting others or himself. Then contentment is impossible. Contentment comes to the one who keeps his trust alive in spite of the contrary condition, in spite of the no-trust situation.

A boy is walking along with his father, holding the father's hand; he is totally relaxed, in trust. However, there is no certainty that the father might not push him down, it is not certain that the father himself will not fall down, and it is also possible that the father is holding the hand of the son for his own support. But the boy is satisfied.

I have heard:

Mulla Nasruddin asked his son to climb up a ladder. The boy was about ten years old. Mulla stood at the bottom of the ladder spreading his arms out, and told his son to jump down.

The boy hesitated: "What if I fall down?"

Nasruddin said, "You fool! Your father is here to catch you in his arms, so why should you fall?"

"I am afraid," said the son.

Nasruddin told him, "Why be afraid when I am standing here?"

The son hesitated, but the father persuaded him and the boy jumped. Nasruddin moved away. The son fell down and hurt his knees.

He asked his father, "Why did you do that?"

Nasruddin said, "I have given you a lesson about life: don't trust even your father. This world is not to be trusted; only deceitful persons live in this world and no one else."

Contentment is not possible with such a mentality. Contentment is possible only in a certain state of mind, and that state is an attitude full of trust. Discontentment is an attitude of doubt. If you want both, then trouble arises.

A friend came and said, "I am deeply afraid of death, and I have no trust in the existence of the soul."

I said, "If the soul doesn't exist, then why fear death? Then you are already dead; what is left to die? And if you have trust that the soul does exist, then there is no need to fear because it will not die. Choose one of the two. If you are certain that the soul does not exist, then the fear of death is total madness – how can something die which does not exist? Then you are only an assemblage and you will just disintegrate. Who will feel the pain of disintegration? – no one. Who is there to feel pain when a watch is disassembled? – no one. It was just an assemblage which is now disassembled. No one is left to feel the pain. Make sure that the soul does not exist, and then you have no reason to fear death."

He asked, "And what if the soul does exist?"

If! *If* the soul exists! – that is meaningless. It only means that you wish to sustain your fear of death.

If the soul exists! He wants the fear of death to remain. If a denial of the soul dispels the fear, then he is willing even to accept the existence of the soul – but then again what to do with the fear? I said, "If the soul does exist, then there is no need to fear because then the existence of the soul means that death does not exist."

But what is his problem? His problem is that deep down he wants to survive and to live eternally, but that he also has no faith that eternal life is possible. He contradicts himself. Such a person goes on contradicting himself. Mind becomes a mess because we collect all these contradictory thoughts. If the mental body is to be purified there is only one way, and that is that thoughts should have a coordination, a rhythm, a harmony. Then the mental body is purified and one enters within.

The fourth body is *vigyanamay kosh*, the awareness body. The third is created by thoughts, the fourth is created by consciousness, by awareness; that is the awareness body. When we become able to watch our thoughts the way we watch white clouds floating in the sky, or a line of cranes flying, when we are able to watch our thoughts from a distance, to see them flying in the sky of consciousness – then we are able to know the fourth body.

But we are so strongly attached to the first body that even the second body is not known. And then we are so captured by the third body, so thoroughly drowned in the mind, that we can't even conceive of transcending it.

Bodhidharma went to China about fourteen hundred years

ago. Wu, the emperor of China, asked him, "My mind is very restless. Is there some way to find release from it?"

Bodhidharma said, "You say your mind is not quiet, but have you ever known a quiet mind?"

Wu was surprised. He said, "No, I have never known a quiet mind."

Bodhidharma said, "Then why do you say 'restless mind'? In truth, mind *is* restlessness. 'Restless mind' – why do you use two words? Restlessness *is* mind, and you want to quiet the mind? You will go mad, but the mind itself can never be quiet."

Wu said, "Does that mean that I will die with this restlessness?"

Bodhidharma said, "No, you can go beyond this mind, and beyond this mind there is peace. You cannot pacify the mind, but if you go beyond the mind then what exists is peace; and if that is achieved, then the mind becomes quiet."

In fact "mind" as such disappears. As soon as the fourth body grows, the third begins withering away. And as soon as the fourth body has grown, the third, the mental body, remains as a thing of utility only.

The one who has developed his fourth body is not surrounded by thoughts; when it is needed he uses the thought process – just like with our feet: when we need them we use them. You don't say, "I will go on walking, moving my feet even while I am sitting in a chair." Although some people even do that. Some people do it because if they don't keep moving their feet while they are sitting down, then how are they going to walk? – they have to continue practicing! Or is it that they are not aware of it? Mostly the chances are that they are not aware that their feet are moving. When the master is absent, who is going to be aware? If the feet wish to move, they move; if the head wishes to wander, it wanders. Whichever part wishes to do something, it does it of its own accord; all are slaves with no one as a master. And no one part is ready to obey, to listen to anyone else.

With the experience of the fourth body, thoughts only have

a utilitarian function – when you need to think you think, when it is not needed you don't. If you are thinking when you don't need to, it will be difficult to experience the fourth body. It will be difficult because your thinking will continue, it will not obey your command to stop.

There is a reason. Have you ever noticed that thoughts don't stop, they don't cease in spite of your best efforts? But you are not aware that even your desire to stop your thoughts is a thought; otherwise they would stop immediately. One thought cannot stop another, they both have the same strength. Rather, when one thought tries to stop another, the other will assert itself more forcefully: "Who are you to stop me?" If one slave asks another to stop, the other will say, "I want to run. Who are you to stop me? I am the master." Your very effort to stop the thought is merely a thought. One thought cannot stop another.

In fact it only works when the command comes from a higher level, not otherwise. When the command to stop thinking comes from the *vigyanamay kosh*, the awareness body, then no thought will dare to move an inch, it stops there and then. But the order must come from a higher level, it will not work if it comes from the same level.

This is the fourth body – you will become aware of it only if you allow its growth. Then it will not be difficult to stop your thoughts. It is as if the master has come back and the servants immediately bow down to his feet, line up and wait for the master's order. Just a little while before they were claiming to be the master, but with the return of the master, they are standing with their hands folded waiting for his orders.

As soon as the awareness body has properly grown, thoughts wait like slaves – doing their work when called for, otherwise ignored. They lie stored in the memory, and do not drive you crazy twenty-four hours of the day so that by the evening you are begging them, "Please forgive me. Stop now, allow me to sleep a little." But they don't listen to you at all. Right now *you* are not present, so who are they to listen to? You will begin to be present when you start to have glimpses of the awareness body.

If you want to transcend the mind, don't try to stop it. You cannot stop it, but you can make it harmonious, you can make it rhythmic. Mind itself is confused; but it is in your hands, you can make it healthy. And as soon as the mind becomes healthy you will begin to see the layer behind it – or you can attempt to create the fourth layer. So don't ask the mind to stop. Do something which *causes* the mind to stop.

Meditation is the way to awaken the fourth body because meditation increases consciousness, meditation increases understanding, meditation increases awareness. So meditation is a way to increase, to develop this fourth body.

I told you: the fourth body is awareness; meditation is its nourishment. Thoughts are food for the third body, and meditation is the food of the fourth body. Meditation too is an energy, meditation too is a force; it is a force like other forces, but very subtle. You can understand it by doing a small experiment. Feel your pulse sometime, check its speed. Then close your eyes and meditate over your pulse for five minutes. Just be aware – and check it again. You will find a change in the pulse beat, it is not the same as it was before. What has meditating done? The energy of meditation flows toward the pulse beat and speeds it up. Meditation is an energy.

A man is walking...follow him, focus your awareness on his neck, stare at the back of his neck; don't do anything else, just concentrate. Within seconds you will find that he is feeling uneasy. There is a ninety percent chance that within two minutes he will look back to see what is the matter. You did nothing, but only with awareness, only with meditation, a very subtle energy came out of your body and touched him.

Meditation is the subtlest energy. In Russia they are interested in meditation because they will have to take it into consideration as their space travel expands – for scientific reasons, because machines are unreliable.

Recently some astronauts died because of some mechanical

failures. If radio communication breaks down, then the astronauts can neither communicate with us nor can we give them any news. And if their spacecraft is lost in outer space we will never know where it has gone, whether they are alive or not. We will not be able to say anything about them.

An American insurance company has advertised insurance for space travelers, with the condition that the payment will be made only upon certain proof of death. Otherwise they could be lost, but alive. Payment will be made only on certain proof of death. But if a space-ship is lost and their radio signals are out of order, there will not be any news as to whether they are dead or alive.

Russia is working hard on the possibilities of meditation so that machines can be supported by an alternative measure – and to a certain extent these attempts have been successful. The idea is that one astronaut should be a meditator, so that he can communicate via the energy of meditation if radio signals go out of order. And they have been largely successful – communication is possible through the energy of meditation. And the surprising fact is that whenever this type of communication is possible it is one hundred percent reliable, without any errors; and if it is not possible, it is not possible at all.

Meditation is also an energy, possibly the subtlest energy. Even physicists feel that meditation must be a form of energy. Not only physiologists and psychologists but even physicists feel that meditation is an energy, because it is slowly becoming clear that if we look at something meditatively the object is transformed; just by observing the object it becomes transformed.

If we observe an atom, the atom does not behave the same way as it does when it is not observed; our observation changes its behavior. For instance, if a man is walking alone on the street he walks in a particular way, and if suddenly someone else comes along the street, then his gait changes immediately. The change may be subtle but it is there.

You are taking a bath in your bathroom and if suddenly you

find someone peeping through the keyhole, your behavior changes. What has happened? This change in the behavior of human beings is understandable, but scientists say that change even takes place in objects; even objects move differently.

Experiments with meditation have been done on flowers in the de la Barr laboratory of Oxford. Someone lovingly meditates on one flower, while another flower of the same kind is left unattended. No one meditates on the second flower; although the flower is watered, the sun shines on it, every other arrangement is the same, but because of meditation the first flower grows and blooms much more and the second flower remains a dwarf. Seeds sown meditatively sprout faster than seeds sown without meditation. What has made the difference to the seeds? Is the flower influenced by the energy of meditation? There is no obvious connection, but there is definitely some energy working at some level.

Meditation is the food for the fourth body. The meditation we are doing is an attempt to awaken the fourth body. Beyond these four bodies exists the fifth body, which the sages call the bliss body. When one reaches to the awareness body and purifies it with meditation, then the most transparent body emerges.

The physical body can never be transparent because the very matter it is made of is so gross; howsoever you purify it, by its very nature it cannot become totally transparent. *Prana* energy is more transparent, but not totally. The mental body can be made more transparent than the energy body, but still not totally. The most transparent is the awareness body – completely transparent. It is so transparent that you cannot only see through it, you can even walk through it. It is so transparent that it has no resistance.

Meditation is the purest energy, the most purified energy possible. If you pass through it you will not even feel it – no resistance, no obstruction. If you are in the purest energy of awareness, then you will not even know the fourth body. And it is interesting that as soon as you enter the awareness body you don't feel this body, you feel the bliss body.

Try to understand this. The fourth body is so pure that it is not visible separately as the fourth. It is like the clearest glass, which seems to be invisible. If it is visible, that means there is still some impurity; if it is pure, only then is it totally invisible. But even glass is matter; it may not be visible, creating no obstruction for the eyes, but if you walk through it you will collide with it.

But awareness is the purest energy ever known, ever recognized. The subtlest energy available through yoga, through meditation is awareness, consciousness. So when you awaken totally you are not aware of this awakening, you become aware of being blissful; beyond the awareness body is the bliss body – only the bliss body is experienced. The fifth is the bliss body. And the sages have also called it a body; this is not the self, this is also a body. The sages say bliss is also a body.

Try to understand a few things about this. Firstly, as I told you, the fourth is the purest body, but it can also be impure; though it is the purest, it can become impure. In us it is impure, it is totally impure. It is purified through meditation, it becomes impure due to unawareness; it becomes pure by being conscious, it becomes impure due to unconsciousness. So all intoxicants basically harm the awareness body. They may harm the other bodies too, but that is another thing. It is also possible that intoxicants may be beneficial for the other bodies, but they are harmful for the awareness body. Alcohol may sometimes prove beneficial for the physical body, to some extent. And it can also happen that alcohol can strongly activate your vital energy. So often the joy and strength you feel after drinking alcohol belongs to your vital energy.

Alcohol can be beneficial to the thinking process too in some ways. It appears to be a help to people who live in thoughts – poets, writers, painters, sculptors – people who live by imagination, giving form to their thoughts, here it may be beneficial to some extent. But it certainly harms the fourth body and is never beneficial for it, because unconsciousness is the impurity, and consciousness is the purity for the fourth body. Every kind of unconsciousness is harmful to it. The fourth body can be the purest of all, but it can become impure as well; both possibilities exist.

The special thing about the fifth body is that it is the purest. It cannot become impure. That is why there is no word as an opposite to bliss. Joy is opposite to sorrow, peace is opposite to disturbance, love is opposite to hate, consciousness is opposite to unconsciousness; but bliss has no opposite. Bliss is the only word which has no opposite. If someone were to say "no-bliss," that would only be the absence of bliss, it is not the opposite of bliss. "No-bliss" has no form, no place, no existence.

There is no energy opposite to bliss; hence, the fifth body *is* pure. So nothing needs to be done with the fifth body. When the fourth is purified, the fifth is available. The fifth is always present. And that is why everyone feels that bliss is his birthright, that you must have bliss – that's why you seek it. Nobody asks why one seeks bliss: "What need is there for bliss? What is the purpose of it?" Every search can be questioned with, "What's the point?" The search for bliss is the only thing which cannot be questioned. Questioning seems meaningless.

People come and ask me, "Why should we seek God? Why seek the truth? What is the aim of life?" But nobody comes and asks me, "Why should I seek bliss? What is the aim of bliss?" Bliss is taken for granted. Even the search for the divine is ultimately the search for bliss: there is no other purpose. The search for truth is ultimately the search for bliss. If you knew for certain that there was no bliss after attaining the truth you would sink in sorrow, you would stop your search at once. You would have nothing to do with such a futile search.

Nietzsche raised a question. He often raised profound questions which even a buddha would have had trouble in answering. Nietzsche asked: "If bliss is the goal of life, and if you are feeling happiness while lying, in being untrue, then what is bad about it?

If bliss is the aim of life, and if you are finding it in your dreams, then why seek any further for truth or reality? If bliss is the aim of life, then put God aside. If bliss is attained through illusions, then what is there to worry about? There is just one decision to make: whether or not bliss is the aim of life."

Moralists and theologians are at a loss to give an answer to Nietzsche's question. And Nietzsche asked: "Can you be sure that the truth will not bring sorrow? *How* can you be sure that truth will not bring sorrow?" "Because," Nietzsche says, "our experience says that the truth is very bitter and that it creates a lot of trouble. Have you totally decided that delusion will always bring trouble and suffering? Our daily experience is that delusion is very pleasant! Why are you trying to destroy people's dreams? – because these dreams can also be beautiful and pleasant. Of course there are nightmares, but you can always get rid of nightmares and make your joyful dreams eternal, never to be broken. Then what would be the need for any search?"

This creates problems for theologians – theologians, not the man of wisdom. The man of wisdom says: "Dreams are things which can never be made eternal. Where there are pleasures they will be followed by sorrow, they are interlinked. If you sometimes get joy from the false, it is because the false gives you the illusion of being the reality. If you sometimes get glimpses of happiness from the false, it is because the false claims to be true. That is the reason why no liar admits to being a liar, he will always claim to be truthful. In fact only a liar claims to be truthful, while truth needs no claim." Lies have to use the mask of truth. If dreams are to survive, then they have to create the illusion of being the reality and claim that they are not dreams.

Bliss is not joy, because joy is essentially connected with sorrow. Bliss is not a dream, because dreams are bound to be disturbed. And that which can be disturbed is not bliss, because there is no opposite to bliss which could disturb the bliss. Bliss is non-dual and alone. Hence, the search for bliss exists because it is our ultimate body – but it is still a body.

The search of the sages is so subtle that it has no comparison. They even call bliss a body. Why? They say: "Until you know bliss, you have not attained that which is worth attaining; and as long as you are conscious of your knowing, the duality continues to be present – the knower is still separate from the known."

You say, "I am blissful." Now two things are obvious: the one who feels, and the object of feeling itself. So this bliss is also a sheath around you and you are standing at the center, aware of this bliss. As soon as this awakening comes – and this awakening is more subtle and difficult than the first awakening... I have told you that meditation is the food for the awareness body; freedom from the mind comes through awareness. If someone becomes aware of the bliss body, he also transcends bliss and attains that which he is. Then he is not the body, he is the self.

But awakening from the mind – although very difficult – is still easy in comparison to awakening from bliss. There is an intrinsic difficulty in awakening from bliss, because we do not desire to awaken from it. Who wants to awaken from bliss? Bliss was our whole life's aspiration – for several lives. Who will wish to part with bliss? One may want to drop their fetters, their iron chains, but no one wants to drop golden chains. And bliss does not appear to be a chain, it appears to be an ornament set with precious stones. But the sages say that even this is a chain. And remember that the iron chain is not as strong as the golden chain set with precious stones, because the prisoner himself does not want to drop this golden chain. It is this that makes the golden chain stronger.

The bliss body is the last thing. Hence when people asked Buddha, "What will happen in nirvana? Will there at least be bliss in nirvana?" Buddha answered, "You will not be there, so how could bliss be there? Neither you nor bliss will be there."

This is very interesting, that a duality is needed in order to feel bliss, that there needs to be someone inside to experience the bliss. Every experience is outside – *every* experience; the one who experiences is within. But can we then talk about "an experiencer" when there is an absence of the experience? When there is no experience, then how can you call someone an experiencer? So Buddha says, "Both disappear – something remains, but not you; something remains, but not bliss."

If the bliss body remains, then one is reborn in bliss – but one is born again, life does not end. One is reborn blissfully. Life is a dance, life is bliss – but life is there. Nirvana comes with the annihilation of the bliss body.

How to awaken from bliss? Right now we do not know bliss, and it is difficult to understand the renunciation of that which we do not know. How do we let go of that which we do not have? It is like asking a beggar to renounce a throne. The beggar will ask, "Where is the throne that I have to renounce? We can talk about renunciation later on, first tell me where the throne is. First I want to enjoy it, I want to sit on it."

But to talk about discarding this bliss right from the beginning is useful in a way. If you are aware even before attaining the throne that it will have to be renounced, then the throne will not have a hypnotizing charm. After all, it will have to be renounced.

Bayazid was a Sufi mystic. He used to tell his disciples, "Always remember this mantra: that you have to renounce every experience, whatever it may be."

Hassan, a disciple of Bayazid, asked him, "Even if it is the experience of God?"

Bayazid answered, "Remember, even that has to be renounced. You have to go on renouncing everything until nothing remains, don't stop until nothing is left, because I can say to you that where nothing is left, there godliness is. Before that, God must be your own creation. Go on renouncing everything."

The world exists as long as there are experiences. Every experience, even the subtlest experience, belongs to the world. The experience of bliss is also a part of the world.

The sage makes very wonderful statements. It is amazing to realize that such courageous people have lived in this world. These courageous people were describing such revolutionary experiences – and a strange thing happened: the non-revolutionary people gathered around them! It is strange, because it appears that they have not even understood.

The sage says:

When the soul,
in collaboration with the four bodies,
remains in the innocence of its cause,
like the seed of the banyan tree...

That innocence of any inherent cause is called the bliss body. This has been called the basic innocence. The banyan tree is hidden in the seed, and until the seed is broken the tree will not be born. Similarly, the layer closest to the self, the deepest and the first, is the bliss body. But they are amazing, the people who say "...remains in the innocence of its cause" – and that innocence is called the bliss body.

This bliss body is the shell of the self, like the shell of a seed. And until that bliss is transcended, the soul, the self is not attained; until the seed is broken, there can be no tree. Those who think that the wise men of India are seeking bliss are mistaken. Wise men in India are seeking that state where bliss too has been discarded as a worthless thing, is not needed anymore. As long as bliss is needed, as long as there is a desire for bliss, as long as bliss interests you, your poverty continues. You are the emperor only when you renounce bliss the way a seed renounces its shell.

These are the five bodies. To attain to the fifth is transcendence, because as soon as you attain to the fifth you are standing so close to the existence that you are pulled in. Then nothing is to be done. It is like when a flower is floating near a whirlpool: slowly, slowly it comes closer to it, and as it touches the first layer or the circumference of the whirlpool it is pulled into the pool, it sinks deep and is drowned.

Human effort is needed to attain up to the fifth body, but no effort is required to go beyond that. Hence if the one who is making his effort to reach to the fifth body remembers that it is the grace, the benevolence, the kindness and the compassion of existence which will pull him in from that point onward, from the fifth body onward, this person will be helped by grace. But if in his effort to attain to the fifth someone starts thinking that he can do it by himself, then from the start it will already be difficult to even reach it. And even if he does reach to the fifth, in his vanity he may stand there thinking, "If I have done so much, then I can also go beyond the fifth. If I can get this far, what do I need the grace of existence, of the divine?" Then it is possible that he may be standing just on the threshold and yet the gravitational force may not touch him, may not work on him, because his receptivity is essential for it to work – he must be ready to be pulled in; only then does it function.

Hence we do not call it gravitation, we call it grace. There is a reason for this. Gravitation is quite mechanical, attraction is quite mechanical. A magnet does not have to ready itself before a bigger magnet will pull it. No readiness is needed on the part of the small magnet. A stone may not wish to be pulled down, but if you drop it the earth will pull it down.

Hence we have called this force grace; it is not mechanical.

A preparation is needed to receive this grace; one's hands should be open, held out to receive; only then this grace can happen.

This realization of grace is the key to transcending the fifth body, to enter the bodiless self.

Enough for today.

Now we should try to reach to the fifth. Remember the grace of the divine. It is possible that you may fall within the gravitational field and be pulled in.

Those who want to participate vigorously may come up on the raised area and those who go slowly should stand off to the sides. No lazy ones should remain on the raised area. If you want to go slow, even slightly, then stand off to the sides.

8

Going beyond the Senses

According to one's inclination toward pleasure or
pain, when one focuses on the pleasant
it is the happiness-oriented mind,
and when one focuses on the unpleasant
it is the misery-oriented mind.
The doer is that which arises from the actions
of the embodied soul in its efforts
to achieve happiness and to avoid misery.
The senses – sound, touch, sight, taste, smell –
are the causes of both happiness and misery.
When the soul is identified with its karmically
acquired body, this is a diseased embodied soul.

In order to reach your innermost emptiness that is enclosed by the five bodies, your being that is bound by these layers of bodies, it is essential to understand the nature of happiness and of misery which cause this bondage.

The body does not bind you, it cannot. It is your idea that the body can give you happiness that binds you. If you have the idea that a prison can deliver happiness, you become bound even to the prison.

Here it is necessary to understand that it is not the same as when someone else locks you up in a prison; this prison we are talking about is of your own choosing and no one else is responsible for putting you there. So to become free from this bondage is very difficult but also very easy. It is difficult because you yourself have created this bondage and therefore you must be enjoying it, otherwise there would be no reason for you to stay this way. If someone else had tied you up, you would not be enjoying it. But you have bound yourself, hence the difficulty. It is also easy to break free from this bondage because you put these chains on yourself, so whenever you choose they can also be broken. If someone else had bound you, just wanting to be free would not have been enough; a struggle would have been needed to break the chains, strength would have been the deciding factor. And if the other had been stronger than you, your freedom would not have been certain.

If we have chained ourselves, then we must be enjoying it in some way; it cannot be altogether painful. Maybe this happiness is only an illusion, maybe it only appears to exist – yet still it is. Maybe it is dreamlike – maybe it is like a mirage, where there is no water, it only appears to be there. When you are thirsty, even something that just appears to be water is enough. A thirsty man cannot afford the luxury of thinking about whether the water seen in the distance really exists or not, he will simply run toward it.

All our striving is centered around happiness and misery; therefore it is essential to understand the real nature of happiness and misery. Maybe it is just because there is the possibility of being either happy or miserable that this becomes the cause of our bondage.

What is happiness and what is misery? They look contradictory, quite opposite to each other, but it is not so. They are two sides of the same coin. We do not notice it, but a strange thing happens: what we call happiness today becomes our misery tomorrow, what we call misery today may become our happiness tomorrow. In fact tomorrow is too far away – just within moments our happiness can become misery. It is possible also that even as we are calling it happiness it has already become misery.

Those who have studied the human mind deeply assert that

as soon as someone says, "This is happiness," it has already converted into misery – because if it is happiness, then there is no space even to say "This is happiness." You only have this space when it is already disappearing.

The first thing to be understood is that happiness and misery are not contradictory, they are interchangeable, like waves – sometimes washing up on this shore and sometimes on the other shore. We all know this, and we have seen our happiness changing into misery, but we never learn from it. We don't allow the mind to learn its lesson; as soon as one happiness changes into misery, we immediately rush off in search of another source of happiness. We don't stay to see that what we knew as happiness yesterday has become misery today – and maybe it is always like that, that whatever we come to know as happiness will necessarily change into misery. The mind will say that this might actually have been misery in the first place; there must have been some mistake – it must have already been misery, it was just an illusion to perceive it as happiness.

That is why it is amazing that the greater the happiness you can imagine, the greater the misery you are in when it changes. If you don't get much happiness from something, the misery is also diminished in the same proportion when it changes. The proportion will be just the same.

For example, if a man has an arranged marriage settled by his parents he has not much expectation of happiness. As a result he is not very miserable. An arranged marriage does not bring as much misery as a love marriage, because there is not that much expectation for happiness through an arranged marriage. What is there to be broken? What is there to be damaged or shattered? There will be no great misery when it breaks up – of love withering away, of splitting up. The greater the expectation, the greater the misery that follows.

For the last one hundred years the West has believed that to marry for love would bring much happiness to their lives. And they were right. But what they did not know was the other side, that a love marriage would also bring much misery, that it would come in equal measures. The greater the expectation of happiness, the greater the misery when it changes.

Eastern people were wise in a way, their approach was different. They tried not to expect too much happiness so that when the inevitable change came it would not bring too much misery.

An arranged marriage gives neither too much happiness nor too much misery. So arranged marriages work, while a love marriage does not work because when things change after the expectation of so much happiness, it brings a lot of misery. When the peak is desired and the abyss happens, the break is certain.

Man can only walk on even ground where there are neither too many abysses nor too many peaks. He cannot walk for very long where a fall from the peak into the abyss is inevitable. This is why, after the experience of only a hundred years, the West is shifting from love marriages to no marriage at all.

For five thousand years, arranged marriages without love have worked in the East. Marriage without love is like flat ground – neither the deep abyss, nor the high peaks. But the West could not maintain the concept of marrying for love for even a hundred years. Now the intelligent man is discarding the whole institution of marriage; there seems to be no need to continue with it. For the sake of greater happiness people are choosing to remain free, the institution of marriage is being discarded.

But this is the same mistake. It was thought that arranged marriages should be abandoned for the sake of attaining more happiness, which would supposedly be more available in a love marriage. Love marriage does give more happiness, but only for a little while, and then it leaves an abyss of misery behind. And this abyss of misery seems to be much deeper compared to the momentary happiness.

The Western intelligentsia is again repeating the same mistake by doing away with marriage in the hope of achieving more happiness. What they don't understand is that more happiness will also be followed by more misery. The mistake is natural, because we only know happiness and misery as opposites, not as they really are – a flowing, interchanging reality. They are changing all the time, without even a moment's break in continuity.

Based on this understanding, the East has carried out another experiment – that if happiness converts into misery, then why can't misery be converted into happiness? This understanding gave birth to the principle of *tapa*, purification through austerities. This principle of purification through austere disciplines is unique. It came out of the understanding that if happiness converts into misery, then there should be no difficulty in converting misery into happiness. In fact in the East it has been found that misery *can* be converted into happiness – if you accept your misery, then it starts turning into happiness. If you get settled in your happiness, it starts turning into misery.

Change comes through your acceptance. Whenever you accept a situation, it becomes ready to change. As soon as you accept it, the change begins. As soon as you say, "This is happiness, I want to live only in this happiness, I don't want it to change," it has already started changing. If you are able to say this, even in misery: "I accept it and no change is needed" – then you would be following this principle of self-purification. And it is very interesting to note that misery turns into happiness.

If you have to choose between the two, it would be wiser to choose the art of changing misery into happiness than the art of changing happiness into misery. Why is that so? –because the happiness of one who has managed to change his misery into happiness does not then revert back into misery. If he can even change misery into happiness, how then can his happiness ever change into misery? When one can change even misery into happiness, then happiness no longer has any power over him and therefore a change to its opposite does not happen.

In fact someone who can change his misery into happiness has already dropped the desire for happiness, that's why he could change it. And when there is no desire for happiness, happiness loses its capacity to change itself into misery. It is the desire that gives it that capacity. Experiment with it and you will be surprised.

Acceptance is the deepest alchemy for transformation within human nature. Accept misery when it comes to you. It is because of the rejection that it is misery, it is because of the denial that it is misery. Accept whatever comes wholeheartedly, agree to whatever comes – embrace it, live with it, do not desire to get rid of it – and suddenly you will find that everything has changed. What you originally felt was misery has turned into happiness through your acceptance.

Happiness can change into misery, misery into happiness – why? Because they are two faces of the same coin. And why do they change? What is the reason for this change? In fact when a man lives in happiness, he can even get bored with this happiness. Long association breeds boredom – it is natural. Even happiness can become boring.

You love someone and want his company for twenty-four hours of the day, but if you have his company all the time eventually you will be wishing you could get rid of him, at least for a little while. You will want to be alone for a while. This is very natural. Now, the separation from the same person whose company once gave you happiness, brings happiness.

One becomes bored. The mind gets tired. In fact the mind gets tired of whatever you get to know well. The mind will get tired of anything that it knows well. Then it will start searching for something new. Even a tasty thing can soon become tasteless. Do not repeat the food tomorrow that you enjoyed today – even by mistake – or the day after that; otherwise you will lose your taste for it. The sage says:

...when one focuses on the pleasant
it is the happiness-oriented mind,
and when one focuses on the unpleasant
it is the misery-oriented mind.

To imagine something as pleasing is happiness, and to imagine something as not pleasing is misery. And the pleasant changes into the unpleasant and the unpleasant into the pleasant.

Alcoholics say that in the beginning alcohol doesn't taste good; they say that you have to develop a taste for it. Those who know say that actually the sense of taste has to be ruined, it has to be destroyed. When you start drinking coffee it doesn't taste good, but coffee drinkers say, "Don't worry, practice will make it taste better. You have to develop a taste for it."

Man somehow develops a taste for anything! You start smoking; on the first day it is really unpleasant, but you imagine that it must be a pleasure because everyone else is enjoying it, and they can't all be fools. The new smoker sees that even those people who prohibit smoking are smoking. They are saying, "We are addicted; don't you also start to smoke." The new smoker feels there must be some deep secret, something hidden, some pleasure to enjoy which is being denied him. When he smokes for the first time it is so unpleasant that it hardly appears to be a pleasure. Inhaling the smoke it tastes bitter, there is nothing pleasant about it – making him cough and feel uneasiness, his head gets hot – but he is hoping for some pleasure and goes on imagining that happiness will happen. Slowly this misery changes into pleasure. Slowly this discomfort changes into happiness.

Practice turns misery into pleasure and pleasure into misery. If you go on tolerating misery, your sensitivity decreases and you become accustomed to it. Misery becomes a habit. If you are continually happy it creates boredom, it creates uneasiness, and you want to get rid of it also.

If we can understand what is pleasant and what is not pleasant then we can understand how happiness turns into suffering. What is pleasant? What do you call pleasant? The sage has said: What is favorable to and in accord with the senses is pleasing – in harmony with the senses, not you – and what is not favorable to and in accord with the senses is unpleasing.

Music is pleasing when the musical vibrations are in harmony with your ears – then it does not disturb you, then the music does not trouble you but instead it helps to pacify the turmoil within. But this is not always so. For a man who is in deep silence even music is unpleasant, because even music is a disturbance.

A great Western musician, Schubert, used to say this about music: Music is a composition of sounds which are the least unpleasant, the least disturbing. But there is disturbance, because, after all, music too is an outcome of friction. The ultimate music is silence, and for someone who knows that silence, music is not a joy to his ear.

Hui-Hai was a great Chinese musician. The deeper his music went, the more silent his musical instrument became. Then one day he threw his instrument away. His fame had spread far and wide, people used to come to hear him from distant places. But the next day, in the morning, when new visitors came to listen to him and they saw him sitting under a tree without his instrument, they asked him where it was.

Hui-Hai answered, "Now this instrument has become a disturbance to the music. When the music becomes complete the veena, the musical instrument, has to be discarded."

And there is a reason for it. If we understand it rightly, then musical sounds are enchanting to our ears because there are so many unpleasant sounds within us, there is so much disturbance and so much chaos within us. In that chaos, these enchanting sounds are like tranquilizers. They feel pleasant, they are consoling, and they create a kind of silence. But if the music is chaotic, only a frantic noise, it becomes distasteful and painful to the ears because it creates uneasiness and there is no tranquility achieved.

Within our physical system, the senses are the doors that allow the happenings which occur in the outer world to enter inside. Whatever makes them feel calm and quiet is pleasant to them, whatever makes them uneasy is unpleasant to them. That is all that "pleasant" and "unpleasant" mean, nothing more than this. But what pacifies the senses today may disturb them tomorrow, because the senses themselves are like a flowing river, changing from moment to moment.

For example, a new employee goes to work on the Indian railways; he lies down to sleep on the railway station platform but he can get no sleep at all because of the noise of the trains coming and going, the engines shunting and whistling, and many other disturbances that don't allow him to sleep. The ears are bombarded with noise, but sleep is a basic need, so after a while this uneasiness drops away and sleep descends. But now what happens is that this man cannot sleep at home because all the noise and commotion has become a part of his sleep. He can only sleep when all of these disturbances are going on, not otherwise. It has become a part of the sleeping process. That disturbance has become a necessity.

Many people come to me complaining of disturbance, uneasiness, troubles, and I know well that if they were to be deprived of these disturbances they would pray to God to get them back. They don't understand; they don't know that these are their rituals, that they cannot live without these troubles. If they were sent into seclusion they would be wanting to return within four days because they would be feeling vacant, empty, meaningless. Meaning only exists for them when all their troubles are present. Why is this?

If you go on feeding the senses unpleasant things they will adapt to them within a few days because they have to, they are helpless, and when they have become adapted, those things which were once unpleasant are now pleasurable. Or, if you are continually eating delicious food, your sensitivity will decrease and so the taste will decrease, and what was once delicious then becomes distasteful.

A famous poet had come to meet me, and we were talking. A little later a musician also came in. The musician requested the poet to recite a few poems. The poet said, "Excuse me, but

I am really fed up with poetry. Let us talk about anything else, but not about poetry." He was a famous poet, but bored with poetry. But it is natural. And that is why, amazingly enough, it can happen that many times in his life a man will take a leap – a quantum leap.

Sometimes very intelligent people will start indulging in very unintelligent things just for the sake of change; the change is needed because they are bored. Hence you might come across a chief justice of some high court sitting at the feet of a very ordinary villager who has no experience, no depth, no value. What has happened to this chief justice? He has become fed up with his intellect, he has had enough of it. He cannot get rid of the burden of his intellect until he does something unintelligent. Seeing him, and knowing him to be an intellectual man, many stupid people will follow suit. He has paved the way for unintelligent people to follow him, people who are not even aware that he is simply bored with his own intellect – utterly bored.

What is pleasant now will not always stay pleasant. There are a lot of reasons for this. You are changing every moment. The child enjoys his toys, but after a certain age he will not enjoy them anymore because a child does not remain a child, he has to throw away the toys. And these are the same toys which, if they had been broken earlier, would have been like the death of a loved one for the child. But one day he will leave these toys behind him because his consciousness is always growing. What was interesting yesterday becomes uninteresting today. The child will run after new toys, not understanding that these are also toys.

Yesterday he dressed up his doll, today he will dress up his woman. But it is the same idea. Yesterday he wanted his doll to be admired, today he wants his wife to be admired. But the doll was just a doll; one day he discarded it without any difficulty – it is not so easy to discard a wife. In just a few days his mind will be fed up with her and he will be in anguish, then old promises and assurances will create problems. Man finds himself bound by his own creations: "I created all this, I said all that, and now it is difficult to turn from it." Now the charm has been lost, the infatuation is gone and he has no interest left in her.

We are continuously changing. When this same man was young he did not like to go to the temple. He would pass by the temple thinking that people had to be mad to go there. Then, the brothel was the place that was more to his liking and more pleasing, the temple was a place for fools. But the temple was soon to become meaningful.

Karl Gustav Jung wrote in his memoirs that most of the patients who came to be treated by him were over forty years of age. Their only problem was that they had forgotten where the gates of the temple were, the only trouble with them was that they did not even know about the existence of the temple. After the age of forty the gates of the temple start becoming meaningful – but even that is a toy.

There are toys for children, for young people and for old people, and until the day you become fed up with all of it, unless and until you become free of all your toys, your troubles will persist, even though they will change.

So someone who has become fed up with decorating his woman now decorates his statue of Lord Rama and parades his statue of his god. But he does not understand that this too will not last. How long can this new fad continue? How long can one go on changing dolls? But he can't conceive that what is a pleasure today will become stale tomorrow. What can we do? Let us try to understand the nature of liking and disliking.

Whatsoever appears pleasing to the senses in that moment, whatsoever appears to be soothing and rhythmic, is called happiness, and whatsoever goes against them is called misery. "I like happiness and I dislike misery; I want happiness to come in abundance and misery to stay away." This desire is the reason for the attachment to the body because the body's senses are the doors for happiness; and it is right there that misery can also be stopped. For this reason the consciousness identifies with the body and is trapped, and unless one transcends both happiness and misery by understanding their nature correctly, one cannot go beyond the body. That is why, after explaining about the five bodies, the sage immediately starts talking about happiness and misery.

Talking about happiness and misery is meaningful, because talking about the five bodies alone won't help unless we know the reasons for our identification with the body. The state through which we can break with this identification is what is called purification through austerities.

Don't desire happiness, and don't have an aversion to misery; don't ask for happiness, and don't reject misery. Someone who asks only for happiness and avoids misery will remain attached to the body. Someone who does not ask for happiness and accepts misery when it comes, begins to get rid of his attachment to the body.

It is the expectation of happiness and the fear of misery that makes one an extrovert, and it is the no-expectation of happiness and a fearlessness toward misery that turns one within. This is the difference between indulgence and purification through austerities.

If you ask for happiness you will have to fight for it, so as to hold on to it and to avoid any misery. A fierce struggle is inevitable. Hence the consciousness will always have to be engaged outside in all the external things like property, power, money, other people and so on.

Purification through austerity means that "No, I have no desire for happiness. I have known many experiences of happiness and have seen them all turning into misery so many times. Now I have no desire for happiness anymore, nor is there any desire to avoid misery." You have avoided misery again and again but it never ends, it only becomes more persistent and instead you experience more misery in trying to avoid it – it comes back with a vengeance. So you must neither avoid misery nor ask for happiness, now just accept whatsoever comes. Now the inner journey begins and the external struggle no longer exists. And it is this inner journey which can free you from the bondage of the body.

A person who does something to create happiness or to avoid misery, the sage calls a doer. But the person to whom happiness and misery make no difference, who accepts every situation, does not continue to be a doer, he becomes a non-doer. And once you have become a non-doer, existence itself becomes the doer. This state gave birth to the precious concept of destiny.

Destiny has nothing to do with astrology, it is concerned with spirituality; it has nothing to do with the lines of the palm, it is not related to the future, it has nothing to do with the street astrologer. The idea of destiny is born when you cease to be the doer and things begin to happen on their own. You remain a doer as long as you are doing something to attain happiness and to avoid misery; you are the doer as long as you continue to struggle. But when you cease to be the doer, accepting whatever comes – not bothering about the result, whether it be happiness or misery – slowly the differences disappear and it even becomes difficult to recognize happiness and misery as such. You become indifferent toward both.

In this indifference the doer will disappear, because there is nothing left to do. And what was it that you had to do? There was only one thing – to work out how to obtain happiness and how to avoid misery. That was your only activity. Now no action is needed and still things will go on happening. When man is not the doer existence becomes the doer, and when existence is the doer this state is called destiny, fate.

Then if such a man is going to be beheaded he can say, "This is how it was meant to be." He does not even blame the executioner, because now he trusts that no one is the doer. For him the doer has disappeared – it was meant to happen. And if such a person is poisoned he says, "It was meant to happen, I had to drink the poison." And if someone who at the time of taking poison recognizes it as a happening, he cannot feel anger even for a moment toward the one who gives him the poison, because now he knows that no one is the doer. He does not accuse anyone and no one else is responsible; whatever is happening is the ultimate destiny, it has nothing to do with others. It is not surprising if such a person attains to ultimate peace and the ultimate contentment.

One who chooses between happiness and misery will never attain contentment, the one who distinguishes between happiness and misery will never find satisfaction. But the one who abandons all the distinctions between happiness and misery is contented.

Sometimes valuable ideas become the bases for foolish concepts. People who say, "Happiness lies in contentment" are mad, they do not know what contentment is and they are still connecting contentment with happiness. They are teaching you that if you want happiness, just be content. And yet if you are striving for happiness you cannot be contented, because the desire for happiness is the very root cause of discontent. Whoever strives for happiness will also be trying to avoid misery, otherwise he cannot be desiring happiness. So how can he be contented?

Happiness is not contentment, contentment is not happiness. Contentment is beyond both happiness and misery, and only the one who abandons the distinction between happiness and misery is contented. Contentment transcends both. If you are choosing contentment for happiness you are in an illusion and your contentment is a mere deception.

Destiny, fate and fortune are great spiritual words. They denote a state of egolessness, a state where there is no ego, no complaint, where whatsoever comes is totally accepted – and there is no reason for it to be any other way, it could not have been otherwise. Desire for anything different no longer exists. The dream that something different should have happened does not arise.

If this total acceptance, this devotion to suchness, pacifies all the waves of thoughts inside you, is there any surprise in it? Is it surprising if all the waves in you disappear? And with this disappearance of the waves, you will go on sinking deeper and deeper within yourself.

The senses are the cause of both happiness and misery.

The senses – sound, touch, sight, taste, smell –
are the causes of both happiness and misery.
When the soul is identified with its karmically
acquired body, this is a diseased embodied soul.

You dwell in the body but you are not the body. To dwell in the body and to be identified with the body are two different things. The one who knows that he is in the body is the soul, and the one who thinks that he is the body is the embodied soul – and this embodied soul is diseased, it has fallen into illusion. It really does not know that which it is, it knows itself as that which it is not.

Why does this identification with the body happen? – because of happiness and misery! As long as we desire happiness and avoid misery, then we identify ourselves with whatever seems to accomplish that. The lover says to his beloved, "There is no distinction between you and me anymore; we have become one" – although this oneness can never happen. But he says "We have become one" – why? Because we want to identify with that which brings us happiness, and any distance which might lessen this happiness is not bearable. Even a little distance is unacceptable; the smallest separation has to be eliminated. We want to get so close that no space is left between us because any distance may be a hindrance to our happiness.

Hence we identify with that which gives us happiness, and we create a distance from that which causes pain. We avoid it, we don't want to look at it, and we don't want to go near it. We want to keep completely away from it. We will even think of killing someone who causes us pain, the very fact that he is alive feels to be a kind of nearness. He may be living anywhere – in the Himalayas, in Tibet – but if he is alive it feels that "He is breathing the same air I am breathing," or "He is under the same sky that I am." We do not want to tolerate even this much of him, we want to eliminate him; he should not live, he should not exist, only then will we be at ease. The distance between us should become as vast as it is between the dead and the living. So whosoever causes us misery we wish to keep him far away, and whosoever is a cause of happiness we wish to keep close.

Now the amazing thing is that whenever we experience happiness we think that we are getting it from our body, but whenever we experience misery we think that we are getting it from somebody else. This is really quite amazing! It is a mystery that whenever we are experiencing happiness we think it is coming from our body, that no one else is responsible for this happiness, that we ourselves are responsible for it. But as far as pain is concerned, we always feel that someone else is responsible.

If someone loves you, you simply think that you are worthy of love, that this is how it should be, there is no reason even to feel grateful: "I am worthy to be loved." But if somebody gets angry with you, then you think that this person is a scoundrel and that he is just full of anger. Then you do not consider yourself to be worthy of this anger at all.

Both of these things are together. Any division is a fabrication, a deception. Either you accept both or you accept neither of them. As long as you choose one of these two, your journey toward truth becomes easy. One can choose either way. Either you are both worthy of love and worthy of hate – and if this is your choice, then one will negate the other because it is not possible to be both at the same time; or if your choice is that you are neither this nor that, neither worthy of love nor worthy of hate – then too you become empty.

But it is a trick we play that we take it for granted that we deserve all the happiness that comes our way. If misery comes it is a gift from someone else, someone else is always the cause of it.

That is why no one ever asks why such a thing as happiness exists in the world. But people ask me, "Why does so much misery exist in the world?" I have not met a single person who has asked why happiness exists. They take it for granted that they deserve happiness, so there is nothing to question, that this is how it should be. The real question is: "Why is there misery?"

No one ever asks me, "Why is man alive?" They ask me, "Why does man die? Why is there death?" Life is taken for granted. But why is there death? Life appears to be within us, but death comes from somewhere outside. A strange idea! And we think that death is far away, coming from the outside to kill us. Life is ours, but death is an outsider which sometimes comes in the disguise of an illness, in the form of a bacteria or a virus, in the shape of an enemy – but it always comes from the outside, it comes to kill us. So your question remains, "How to avoid it?" And yet you go on thinking that you are life itself!

It is always our method that whatever is a happiness to us and whatever gives us joy, we connect it with ourselves; and whatever is miserable, painful, we connect it with someone else. That is why the religions had to conceive of the existence of Satan along with the existence of God. All this trouble! It seems very difficult to understand life without the existence of Satan. It is conceivable that God is compassionate – but then a child dies of cancer. What is the explanation? And this child has not yet committed a single sin – no theft, no murder, nothing of that kind – and even so he died, or he was born dead. But if it was meant to happen in this way, then why did God create him in the first place? If he was to be born dead, then why this nonsense of going through birth? At least God should have known that the child was going to be born dead. Then why did he go to so much trouble?

So we have had to invent another personality to project onto, because we want to identify ourselves with God. But if even God gives cancer to a child, while old men wishing to die continue to live and cannot die, and millions of people are hungry, and wars are waged in which millions die… If all this occurs in spite of the existence of God, how can we identify with God? That is why we have to keep God's image completely virtuous and good. But how will we deal with evil? Who is causing it? For this another god has to be created, and we call him the Devil. The Devil is the god of evil, he is to blame; the Devil is the cause behind all evil.

Hinduism is the only religion on earth which has dared to accept both attributes in God – and it is only because of this that I hold that no other religion has been able to understand truth as deeply as Hinduism. Hindus have attributed both aspects to their God – Mahadeva, or Shiva – who is both the creator and the destroyer; he is the lord of poison and nectar both. It is a daring statement! And to be with such a God is a great revolution because all logic has to fall away. All our logic of identifying ourselves with good and putting the evil aside will fail; that if you steal the Devil has provoked you, if you pray it is your doing. Strange idea! If you give to charity it is your doing, but if you steal there are evil forces that are doing the stealing through you!

So we want to be identified with good but not with evil. But the world is a combination of both. Either refuse both or accept both; in either case you will be liberated from both.

Our bondage with the body is because we say that the body is the source of all happiness and any misery is inflicted by others. And so you avoid others, or change the others – or else be with others until they start causing you pain, and when they do cause you pain you move away from them. Marriage and divorce doesn't only exist between a husband and a wife, it exists in all relationships.

A friend who used to visit me always asked, "How can my intelligence grow, how can an alert intelligence be awakened in me?"

I would console him that, "It will grow, the possibility of growth exists. Make an effort."

He would happily go away thinking of this possibility. Intelligence does not awaken because of a possibility, it awakens through your effort, but he would go away happily, and he was very pleased. He would come for such consolation once or twice a month. In this way, he would get enough momentum to last for ten or fifteen days, living as usual with the consolation of this possibility. This would continue for some fifteen days, and then whenever he would run out of fuel he would again come to me, and again go away with some reassurance. This went on for a while, and then I thought that no possibility could become a reality in this way, so the next time he came I said, "Now there is no longer any possibility."

He was taken aback. At first he could not get the point: "What do you mean, no possibility?"

I said, "There is no possibility. There is no intelligence in you which can grow, and wakeful intelligence is not so easily acquired. It is beyond your capacity, just drop the very idea."

His face became pale, and he went away very sad. Now he is against me, and he says, "This man is not right."

I was the right man as long as I kept assuring him of some possibility, and he could leave happily and radiant with joy. But now I am the wrong man. He tells other people, "Don't go to him, he is not the right man to go to."

This is very strange. I was right while I pleased him, and as long as I pleased him, he thought of himself as great because of this possibility. But now I have become a source of pain to him because I said that there was no way for him to grow, and that his hell was certain.

We want to identify with all that is pleasing to us, we want to be with it; and we want to separate ourselves from that which is painful. And so we are attached to our bodies because we think that the body is the source of our happiness. The sages have called this identification with the body "the disease," the *only* disease – the illusion of thinking that the soul, the self is the body.

The only way to get rid of this disease is to realize the fact that the body is the source of happiness and misery both. They will negate each other, and then you will have to search for that which is the source of bliss – which is neither happiness nor misery.

Bliss is neither happiness nor misery, it is the absence of both. That is what we have to search for.

Enough for today.

Now let us try to recede from the body, try to withdraw from the body.

9

You Are Your Prison

Mind, life-current, desire,
piety and virtue are the five basic knots.
When the embodied soul is identified
with the nature of these five knots,
it cannot become free of them
without self-realization.
As these five afflict the soul like subtle diseases,
then the soul is known as ling sharir,
the identification body.
This is the knot in the heart.
That which illuminates there as the consciousness
is kshetragya, the knower field.

Man's bondage does not come from outside of himself, his prison is within – it is created by him within himself. It appears to us that we live only on the outside; it appears that happiness exists on the outside, that misery exists on the outside, that all achievement is outside, all defeat and victory are outside, all success and failure are outside – but it only appears to be this way. In fact everything is within: all striving is within, all attainment is also within; our failure is within, the happiness which seems to be on the outside is experienced within and the source of misery which seems to be coming from the outside is also hidden within.

Your beloved may seem to be on the outside but the center

of love is within. If the center of love within is destroyed, then no beloved can be seen outside. Gold is outside but the greed for it is within. If there is no greed, then what is the difference between gold and dust? The difference is because of this greed. The expanse of objects is outside, but the seed is within.

The sage describes five basic knots; man's inner disease has been divided into five categories, as five knots. Try to understand each and every category.

The first knot is the mind and its whole creation. The mind has been called an entanglement, a disease, a sickness. Why?

If we stand on the seashore and there is a storm with high waves and a mighty wind blowing, the ocean itself cannot be seen, the only thing visible is the wild dance of the roaring waves. The ocean is also within these waves and these waves are also a form of the ocean – they are born out of the ocean, they are a shape of the ocean – but still these waves are not the ocean, because the ocean can be without waves. After the storm the sea is tranquil; the waves have gone, but the sea remains.

The opposite can never happen – it is not possible for the ocean to disappear while the waves remain. The waves can disappear but the ocean will remain. The disappearance of the waves doesn't disturb the existence of the ocean, but if the ocean disappears it won't be possible to save the waves. So the ocean is the source; the waves appear and disappear.

The ocean of human consciousness is just like that: thoughts are the waves, the patterns rising in it. That is why I told you yesterday that there is no such thing as a peaceful mind. Have you ever seen a peaceful storm? It is meaningless to say "peaceful storm." If it is a storm it cannot be peaceful, if it is peaceful it cannot be a storm. But we say "silent mind" – it is a linguistic error. As long as the mind is there the disturbance continues, restlessness persists.

Disturbance is another word for the mind. Existentially, disturbance and mind are synonymous – but not in the dictionary. If you look in the dictionary you will not find anywhere the word *disturbance* meaning mind, or *mind* meaning disturbance. It is not necessary for etymologists to know existence. Those who do know existence don't create language because they say, "It is difficult to express it in language."

The existential experience is: where there is disturbance, there is mind. Mind means disturbance, so the words *peaceful mind* are contradictory; such a state cannot exist. Just as there is no such thing as a healthy disease or a calm storm, so there is also nothing like a peaceful mind.

A diseased person can become healthy, remember it, but the disease itself can never be healthy. The diseased man can become healthy because the disease is not the diseased; it is separate from him, it comes and it goes. It is very interesting to note that the sick man can be without the disease, but the disease cannot exist without the sick man. Consciousness can exist without mind, but mind cannot exist without consciousness.

Mind is a disease. The sage sees it as *granthi* – a knot, a bondage, a disease, an illness. Mind is a disease. Mind is a disturbed state of consciousness – agitated, unstable and full of waves. When peace is achieved mind disappears, it ceases; when peace disappears, mind appears.

If we go deep into it, there is a reason why we describe it as a knot. Understand the word *granthi*, because it is a valuable word in yoga terminology. It is so valuable that when Mahavira became enlightened the Jainas called him *nirgrantha* – free of all the *granthis*, knots – he who has no knot within. Try to understand this concept of a knot.

A knot is a strange thing. You must have seen many knots but had never noticed this: that when you tie a knot in a rope, is there any change in the rope, in its nature, in its existence? Does it weigh more? Is there any qualitative change? What happens to the rope? Nothing happens to the rope – but even then, a lot happens. Nothing happens to the rope, nothing is added to it and nothing is taken away; it remains as it is, but still it is not the same; it is knotted, entangled. The rope's nature is not changed a bit, but a knot can arise without any change in its nature. Actually nothing is changed in the rope, yet everything is changed. The rope is of no more use; now you cannot tie anything with it because it itself is entangled. Now it is of no use, but there is no qualitative change, no existential change to it. It has not changed at all.

And what is this knot? Is it an object? Try to understand it correctly. Is the knot an object? Had it been an object it would have existed without the rope, the knot could have been put aside. But the knot cannot be separated from the rope. It does not mean that the rope cannot be freed from the knot, it can be. The rope can be freed from the knot, but the knot cannot be separated from the rope. You cannot separate the knot and the rope into two things.

So a knot is not an object. It doesn't have substance, it has no independent existence; it is just a form – just a shape, just a form without any substance – only a form and nothing of itself in it. Inside the knot is the rope, but a knot itself has nothing inside it. A knot is nothing in itself – just a form without any substance. Hence it can be understood like this: that a knot has no substantial existence, it is just form, it only has a form.

That is why the sages have called this world *namrup*, which means a name and form with no substantial existence of its own – just like a knot. The knot exists in name and is recognizable in form, it creates an obstruction and it can be undone, yet it does not exist. The knot is *maya*, illusion. Those who know say that the world is a knot of name and form – just a knot. And this applies to man in the same way as it applies to the world.

Man too is just a knot of name and form. If the knot is untangled, untied, what remains is called the universal self. Man is just a knot; if untied, man disappears – the name and form disappear, the one who was saying I disappears. The I disappears – I is just the sum total of all the knots. We will talk of the *panchvargas*, the five categories; I is the name of the sum of these five knots.

The sage calls the mind the first knot because mind has no

existence, it only appears to exist, it is only a form. When consciousness is disturbed mind is created – it is only a form. A dream in the night has no existence but has a form. You go to see a film: a film has no existence in reality but has a form on the screen, it only appears to exist. And it is strange that even the so-called intelligent people can be seen wiping their eyes and drying their tears at the cinema. Even an intelligent person cries and laughs at a film, although they know perfectly well that nothing exists on the screen.

But the form creates an illusion – the illusion of existence. And for a moment, when we are overwhelmed by the form and forget the self, then the form becomes very real. If you can remember, next time when you go to see a film, do an experiment – try to remember yourself continuously and watch the film at the same time. Then tears will be impossible. Tears are possible only if you forget yourself – when you forget yourself as the watcher, when you become so identified that you forget that you have come to see the film – then only the film which you are watching exists and you are not. When the thing you are watching becomes everything and the one who is watching is forgotten then you can cry, the mind can become sad, the mind can become happy; everything can happen in the mind, although there is nothing real on the screen.

Mind is form. But the watcher inside, the knower within, has forgotten his own existence. That is all. Only this much forgetfulness and the film becomes everything; then the knot is formed. It is formed and it becomes stronger. And for many lives we have been sitting in this cinema called the mind. The knot has continued to become more and more entangled, making the forms thicker and thicker.

Why do we call a man "mad"? We call him mad because he has a bigger mind than we have, there is no other reason. We only see the images within ourselves, but he is seeing the images in the outer world also – he has a mind more capable of seeing than you. You also talk within yourself to the ones you love, the madman talks out loud to his dear ones who are not present because his mind has grown more in that dimension, it is bigger then yours. You do it too, but secretly, within yourself. His capacity to project is greater than yours, he is more skilled; he starts talking to a nonexistent person sitting opposite him on a chair. Then we say, "This man has gone mad."

Is there any qualitative difference between him and us? We also talk to our loved ones as if they were sitting in front of us, but we do it inside ourselves. Our projecting mechanism is weaker and his is more efficient than ours. His projector is so efficient that even if you enter into the room – and you are real – he will not be bothered about you, he will only be concerned with the nonexistent figure sitting on the chair.

So many poets have written along such lines as: "My beloved, the whole audience may be present but if you leave that gathering, then nobody else exists for me; and when you are present, then no one else may be there and yet the whole world is present for me."

The poet is a little crazy, that is why he sees that which we can't see, he senses that which we can't sense, he creates that which we can't create. Hence there is some similarity between the poet and a madman. Perhaps the poet is a madman with some method, while the madman is a poet without any method, he does not know any order. But one quality is common to both of them – a capacity to see that which is not.

The mind is a machine which can see that which is not there, so the mind is a mechanism which can drive one mad. The mind is an expansion of dreaming. This is the first knot. The one who is entangled in the mind can never attain to his real self, because the only way to become entangled in the mind is through forgetting your self. You cannot know the self and retain your mind at the same time. Forgetting your self is essential for the mind to exist – mind is not possible without the forgetfulness of the real self – and if you remember the self, then mind will disappear. With an awareness of the self, with the awakening of the watcher, all images start fading away, becoming only name and form for you. No substance is left in them, they lose their hold. So what to do?

This mind is the first knot. If we can awaken our awareness to this knot, it will open. To open any knot, the device to use is to bring in the watcher, the awareness; witnessing is the device to undo any knot. We all want to untangle our knots, but an interesting thing happens. We all want to untangle our entanglements, all of us – it is difficult to find a person who does not want to – yet why does nothing get untangled?

It is often observed that those trying to untangle themselves get even more and more tangled. The effort to undo the knot doesn't work – instead, the entanglement gets worse and worse, although everyone wants to get untangled. We must be making a basic mistake somewhere. We all want to become disentangled without awakening the witness.

We want to disentangle the mind using the mind – this is the mistake! The mind is an entanglement, hence the mind cannot unknot itself. And trying to undo the knot of the mind through the mind is like trying to grab one's own hand with the same hand, trying to hold a pair of tongs with those same tongs, searching for one's spectacles with those very spectacles on one's nose. Some people do that – it is not unusual – and we are all doing the same as far as the mind is concerned.

Have you ever seen a dog chasing his own tail? A dog is sitting in the street; the morning sun is rising, he is sitting idly with his tail lying close to him – his own tail – and the dog pounces on it to try to catch this tail. The tail moves away. Naturally, the dog gets angry – it becomes a challenge – there is a limit! It is only a little tail and yet it escapes him. The dog jumps with more strength and the tail moves more quickly. A deep enmity emerges. The tail is his own, and the dog himself is the catcher; it will never be caught and the dog will get tired. He does not know that his jump is also a jump for the tail – that they are not two different things.

The mind which you are using to undo the knot is itself the mechanism that creates it – so whatever you do with the mind, it goes on becoming more and more knotted.

Hence you should be aware that as the human mind develops the number of insane people will also increase; the more undeveloped the mind is, the less insanity there is. Primitive societies produce very few insane people. Sociologists say that in prehistoric times the society rarely produced a single insane person, and that this person was not called insane, he was revered because he was rare, he was special. So in a primitive society someone who was insane could become a messiah, he was revered because he had a quality which no one else had.

Today mad people are in trouble: now no one is ready to accept them as messiahs and instead many are ready to consider a messiah to be mad. The situation has totally changed. Slowly, slowly insanity is becoming such a usual thing that just as very rich people in India say with pride that such and such a renowned physician is their private physician, a rich American says, "Such and such a great psychiatrist is my private psychiatrist." Only poor people remain wretched; they can't say that they have their own private psychiatrist. They have to visit hospitals where they need to wait in line with other ordinary people to see the psychiatrist.

Once it was inconceivable that the time would come when people would tell each other such a thing with pride. Now the situation in the West is such that people ask each other whether they have or have not gone through psychoanalysis. Whosoever hasn't feels miserable because it means he cannot afford it. Psychoanalysis is an expensive business – it can take two, three or even five years, and involves spending thousands of dollars. So the super-rich announce that they have gone through psychoanalysis not only once but twice, three times. The extremely rich people go regularly. They have regular appointments twice a week to visit the psychiatrist for psychoanalysis.

In the past it could never have been conceived that mental disease would become so common. But there is a reason for it.

When you educate people, give them the capacity to think, culture, civilization, give them so much knowledge, then the mind develops more and the knots become more complex. And as the mind grows, its capacity to project increases. These capacities can increase to such an extent that you become dissatisfied with your mind as it is and you begin to look for other help for it. Such things as LSD and marijuana are things which make your mind more capable to project. Under the influence of LSD you start seeing colors which you have never seen before, a beauty which you have never seen before starts spreading around you.

Huxley has written in his memoirs: "When I took mescaline for the first time, in a few moments the chair in front of me became seven-colored" – more than any rainbow. The chair! – in a short while rays started to emanate from it!

Van Gogh, a great Western painter, once painted a picture of a chair. But no one was prepared to recognize this chair as a chair until Huxley wrote about it in his memoirs. Van Gogh painted it one hundred and fifty years ago. The chair was more colorful than ever ordinarily happens – he painted it like a rainbow. People thought it was just his imagination: "A chair never looks like that." But Aldous Huxley wrote in his memoirs: "Under the influence of mescaline that chair before me disappeared and a colorful, heavenly and transparent chair appeared. Had I died at that moment I would have felt complete." The experience of this chair was so strong and so deep for him. After this experience of the chair, it was believed that if an intelligent man like Huxley could see these colors in a chair under the influence of mescaline, then it was not surprising that a painter like van Gogh had been able to see these colors in a chair without mescaline. But van Gogh died insane because his mind went into chaos. He started seeing that which was not, he started seeing not what was really outside but that which had come from within him and was then being manifested outside, projected outside.

We all engage in this phenomenon on a small scale. When a

lover of money has money in his hand he sees more in it than you do. Don't think that what you see is everything: someone who has not loved money can't see what a lover of money sees in it.

I know one gentleman: when he holds a currency note in his hand which does not even belong to him, he holds it as no lover holds his beloved. No poet regards a flower as lovingly as he does when he looks at the note. Greed is dripping from his face, he looks at it with such fascination; he establishes an unimaginable connection with the note. Now people call him a miser because he will not spend his money; spending his money is impossible. But we do not understand his fascination, the poetic world he lives in. His condition is like that of a poet.

We are prepared to respect a poet but not this man, and the reason for it is that a poet takes nothing from us, while this man appears to take money away from us; otherwise there is no difference between the two. We allow the poet to have his pipe dreams, we regard them as harmless because he is not snatching another's dreams. This miser also has dreams but they are about money, so people are annoyed by him. Hence society condemns him, is angry with him, and calls him a wicked person – in fact considers him to be a sinner. But there is no difference between him and the poet. It is just that the miser makes money the object of his poetry; his romance is with money.

That is why he who loves money cannot love anyone else. He needs no other love. His is such a great love that a wife, a son, literature, religion – all become secondary. Mind becomes the knot, because the watcher is forgotten in this mental projection. When this man is looking at a rupee it is impossible to believe that he is still a human being; he becomes the rupee. He is not a witness, he does not remain a watcher, watching the rupee as separate from him. This man becomes the rupee itself.

Mind means that whenever the consciousness has forgotten the watcher, the witness, then consciousness wavers and becomes diseased – this is the first knot.

The life-current, *prana*, is the second knot. We are utterly pulled, driven by our lust for life, the survival instinct. Lust for life means the yearning, the desire to live, to live at any cost – and without even asking why. Nobody asks why to go on living. Just to live…as if living is enough in itself.

A man is begging on the street with broken knees, decaying limbs, lying in the gutter, rotting, infested with worms, but if you ask him if he wants to die he will look at you with anger. And he is not wrong. His body may have decayed, but his lust for life never decays and it is the same as yours. It may even be more than yours, because the dying flame burns luminously, the night is darker before the dawn. Feeling death so close at hand he puts all his energy into clinging to life, which you may have never done. You have tomorrow to wait for, but he has not; he has to live at any cost. And it is surprising that a man agrees to live at any cost. This is why so many cruelties have happened in the world, otherwise they could not have been tolerated.

For five thousand years we have made sudras, the fourth and the lowest class among Hindus, creep like insects on the earth. And it would not have been possible except that their lust for life is so deep, so strong that they are prepared to live in any situation.

Millions of people in the world have been enslaved like animals. The responsibility for this is not only on the wicked and cunning people who enslaved them; a deeper reason is their lust for life, that they want to survive under any conditions. This drive is so strong that even if a man is forced to creep and crawl on his hands and knees for the rest of his life he will agree to it, because it is better than death. Anything is better than death.

The lust for life holds that anything is better than death. One is prepared to live under any circumstances. But if a person has too great a drive to survive, then the inner journey becomes impossible. He will be attached to the body, to the mind, to his life-current, and the attachment will be so strong that he won't be able to let go. He will hold on to everything so tightly that nothing can slip out of his grasp – for fear he may become lost.

People come to me to meditate. During meditation a moment certainly comes when one experiences death – the moment is inevitable. The feeling of death is so acute – a near-death experience. They come to me and they say, "We have come to meditate, not to die. What is this that is happening inside? We are afraid we may die."

I tell them, "That is such a precious moment, to die within. Don't be afraid to die. Accept this death, then you will never die."

But they ask, "Is there no other way? This going within, this annihilation – is there no easier way?"

No, there is no other way. Meditation is the experience of death – a voluntary death. Your death does come eventually, but then there will be no experience of meditation. Death has come to us many times – we have died so many times! Even in the future we will die so many times. We will go on dying because of this lust for life – life and death...life and death...life and death. The lust for life exhausts us, our life never comes to a fulfillment, life is never experienced and the body comes to an end. But the lust for life never ends, it finds another body. It goes on finding new bodies...and each time we have to die. Death keeps happening, but the lust for life never dies – it is so strong that it is reborn again and again.

What happens in death happens in meditation too, but in death it is a forced thing. People become unconscious at the time of death, and most die unconsciously. Another life is certain for those who die unconsciously, but there will not be another life for those who die consciously. Why do we die unconsciously? Unconsciousness is not a prerequisite for death. We die unconsciously because this is a protective measure of the body.

Sometimes people say that they are feeling unbearable pain. This is completely untrue, because no one can tolerate unbearable pain. Man becomes unconscious before unbearable pain begins – this is an inbuilt protective measure. When pain increases beyond the limit of tolerance one becomes unconscious. This unconscious state signifies that the pain threshold has been exceeded; to remain conscious and bear the pain is no longer possible, the only way to tolerate it is to become unconscious.

Hence we make use of the unconscious state at the time of an operation. A surgeon first anesthetizes the patient, because during an operation the pain is going to be unbearable and it is therefore humane and helpful to make him unconscious during that experience. Nature has its own internal surgical arrangements: whenever pain becomes unbearable we become unconscious. So nobody has ever experienced unbearable pain. Whatever pain you have felt it was bearable, otherwise you would have lost consciousness.

Death is the greatest surgical operation – consciousness is being removed from the entire body. All other operations are only partial – only a part is taken out. Sometimes a bone is taken out, sometimes a part, sometimes a piece of flesh and so on – but death separates the whole consciousness from the body, and that consciousness is actually identified with the body. That is why the possibility of unbearable pain exists. Only people like Buddha do not die unconsciously.

Another interesting thing that happens is that a person who dies consciously has a prior knowledge of his death – in a natural way. That too is an internal arrangement: he is not informed of his death, but his body mechanism itself becomes aware of the impending death. But you are not informed prior to your death, because if you come to know that you are going to die in seven days you will die even before that; these seven days will become a period of terrible death. So you are not to be trusted – even your body will not inform you, it will hide the secret from you. But someone who can die consciously, he comes to know.

The day that Buddha was to die he told his disciples, "Now, today, it is time to depart. If there is anything left to be asked, ask it!" But there was no question of asking him anything – they all began to cry, to weep, to scream. Buddha said, "Don't waste time! Don't be in such a hurry to cry, you can do that later on. My time is running out. Do you want to ask anything?" But they were so distressed that it was impossible to ask any questions. Asking questions is only possible when you are at ease. And what kind of man is this Buddha? Is this a time to ask questions?

Ananda said, "No question comes to my mind."

Buddha asked thrice and then said, "Okay, then you do your work, now let me do mine."

He went under a tree, sat in an appropriate posture with closed eyes – and the story goes that he began entering into death. The first step was complete.

Buddha has described the four steps of death. Those four steps belong to meditation also. He completed the first step, then the second. He was just going to complete the third when a man came running from the village and said, "I have heard that Buddha is going to die, but I have something to ask." They asked him to keep quiet saying, "You are too late and Buddha has already begun his final journey inward."

Death is just a journey for Buddha – a conscious journey. It is not that death is coming to Buddha, it is Buddha who himself is entering into death. Try to understand this difference correctly. Death comes to us; we go on struggling with it and it goes on overtaking us. Buddha himself approaches death, step by step.

So the disciples said that he was too late. But the man insisted, "I can't stop, I have to ask, because one never knows how many lives it will take to find a man like Buddha again. And my question..."

The disciples asked him, "You idiot, Buddha has been in this town for a long time. Where were you?"

He replied, "That doesn't matter. I knew that Buddha was passing through this town for thirty years, but then I was too busy with my customers in the shop, sometimes a child was sick at home, once there was my daughter's marriage – I kept postponing it for some suitable time but now there is no way. He is close to death."

Buddha came back from behind the tree and said, "Don't

stop him! I was still in the third stage, not in the fourth. I don't want to be remembered as someone who was still alive while a man with a question had to go away without an answer. Let him have his answer."

This is also a way of dying. But this way of dying is available only for one who has already learned the art of dying in meditation. The steps in meditation and death are the same because meditation disengages us from the body and takes us to the center of our consciousness, and death too takes us away from the body to the center of consciousness. But in death you are unconscious because it is against your will, while in meditation you are conscious because it is your own choice.

So the life-current, the lust for life, is the second knot. The third knot is desiring. Have you ever known a moment when you had no desire? If you can even for one moment come to a desireless state, in that very moment you become godly. People ask, "Where is God? We have a desire to search for him and find him." And it is because of this desire that you will not find him. Even this desire is not small – it is enough to prevent you.

Desire means: "I am not interested in what already is, I am interested in what I desire there should be." What does desire mean? What is it that we call desire? Desire means you are not interested in what is available. Your interest is in what should be available. But when it does become available you will not be interested in it anymore, because now it has become the present and your interest always lies in the future.

Desire always reaches out into the future and goes on missing the present. And yet whatever actually exists is here and now. Hence anyone who is obsessed with desire gets entangled with knots; the more desires the more knots, the deeper the desires, the more complicated the knots. We are just a collection of desires – all unfulfilled desires, because no desire is ever fulfilled. Desires and desires...we are just a collection of desires. We exist as demands – thousands of different types of beggars exist within us – and each and every desire demands a different kind of satisfaction. Nothing is ever achieved.

Within us there is only a stack of begging bowls and they are all empty, and we go on chasing after more. We go on collecting new begging bowls every day. Old desires remain unfulfilled and new desires are just added to them, because it is very easy to give birth to a desire and completely impossible to fulfill it. Whatever is seen around us becomes a desire in us to have this, to have that – but no desire is fulfilled, they just go on accumulating. We remain an empty bowl – a begging bowl, a beggar!

Buddha called his sannyasins, beggars. He was mocking us. This is ironical, and he said it only as a joke, but the joke is deep and penetrating.

Buddha went to a village to beg with his begging bowl, and the wealthiest man in the village said, "Why? Such a beautiful man like you…"

Buddha's whole body was so beautiful; perhaps at that time it was difficult to find another man as beautiful as him "…and you are a beggar, on the road with your begging bowl. You are worthy of being an emperor. I don't care who you are, what you are, what is your caste, your religion, your family. I will marry my daughter to you, and you will become the owner of all my riches, because my daughter is my only heir."

Buddha said, "I wish it were true that I was a beggar and that you were the master – but the fact is that when I saw that you are all beggars thinking you are masters, I took the begging bowl in my own hands. Seeing the situation, it did not feel right for me to call myself a master. You all call yourselves masters, and we are happy to call ourselves beggars! Because in a world where the beggars think they are the masters, it is right for the masters to show themselves as beggars."

This was a rare phenomenon, a rare happening on this earth. There have been very few emperors born in the world who were so great that they dared to become beggars. India is the only country – alone on the earth – where men like Buddha and Mahavira went out on the roads to beg. But this is indicative of some great inner mastery. And it is a great piece of satire, played on all of us – great satire!

People who only have begging bowls within live under the illusion that they are masters, and those who have no desire left at all walk the streets begging for alms. This is a psychodrama, a biting satire. But we cannot understand the satire of men like Buddha, and that creates the problem.

Desire and greed – demanding and demanding and demanding. And the one who goes on demanding will go on wandering on the outer journey, in the outer world. Only the one who ceases to demand enters the inner depths.

So desire is called the third knot.

Enough for today.

Two sutras remain. Those we will take up tomorrow morning.

10

We Are What We Do

The one who knows the birth
and the dissolution of the knower, the knowing,
and the objects of knowing,
yet is itself without birth or dissolution,
this self-illumined one is called sakshi,
the witness.
That which resides in the consciousness
of all living beings,
from Brahma, the god of creation,
to the smallest insect, and which remains
even when all gross and subtle bodies are no more,
is called kootastha, the indestructible one.
Just as a thread passes through each bead of a necklace,
the soul threads each cell of the body
in order that it may become aware of its true nature
from among the different characteristics.
This one is called antaryami,
the knower of all thoughts and feelings.

Indian wisdom has not regarded man, as he is, as any more than just a bundle of diseases; as man is, he is a disease. But this is not a depressing attitude toward life. This attitude is not pessimistic. As man is, he is regarded as a disease, because as long as he believes this state of disease to be his health he cannot attain to his intrinsic potential.

Man has infinite possibilities. If a diamond lying among the pebbles and stones accepts itself as an ordinary stone, then it stops the possibility of any growth; no possibility is left for any refinement, for any evolution. If we believe that as we are is all there is, then there is no possibility to grow. Growth is possible only if we do not take what we are to be our ultimate potential. Wherever there is the possibility of growth in any aspect, we must not believe ourselves to be already perfect in that aspect.

A unique thing has happened in the history of mankind. It is that the West has never considered its external conditions to be the ultimate state of perfection; hence the West has succeeded in changing these conditions to a great extent. If there was poverty, it did not accept it, if there was illness, it did not accept it, if there was just a small hut to live in, it did not accept it, it did not accept rugged and uneven roads, it did not accept a slow speed of movement. The West did not accept the external circumstances as they existed. That is why the West has totally changed them.

But the East has undertaken an even deeper experiment. The East does not accept the inner state of man as it is. An indication of this is given when it is said that as man is, he is a disease. He is worthy of transformation; he should transform himself. He can attain to his inner being, only if he changes. If he transforms, only then can he attain to the state where he can be peaceful, content and blissful.

Our anguish is the anguish of a seed. If a seed does not become a tree, the anguish is natural. And if a seed believes in remaining a seed, that it is perfect as it is, then there is no way for it to sprout.

Hence the sage is explaining these five groups of diseases. We talked about three last night, now the fourth. The fourth is *sattva*, piety, the feeling of being "good," and the fifth, *punya*, virtue.

The third was desire, lust, greed. Desire means the demand

for some object. A desire for money, a desire for reputation. Money and reputation exist outside oneself. There is even a more subtle desire which we do not normally understand. The sage calls it *sattva*.

A man has no desire for money, for reputation, but he wishes to be a good man – to be a saint, to be a sannyasin. This too is a desire. Although nothing will be added by it to you on the outside, yet this too is a lust – not for money but for religion. Desires are diseases. This desire, "I want to be saintly," included; even though it is concerned with the inner.

A friend came yesterday and said, "I want to be initiated into sannyas – but the inner sannyas, not the outer, because anything of the outside seems to be part of desire – even the outer sannyas." The inner sannyas does not look like a desire – but it is a very subtle desire. It too is a desire. Whenever you want to become something, desire is bound to be there.

The sage says that if you get tied even with the desire for sattva, it is also a disease; even the desire to be good, the desire for inner purification, perfection, is a disease. This is interesting. These diseases need to be understood so that the inner perfection may manifest.

Now one more thing to understand: I told you about the seed; this example works to some extent, but it does not go very far. No example goes very far, and to stretch it beyond its limit creates problems. If a seed is satisfied with being a seed it will never become a tree, this is true. But that inner reality that man is, is already there. If he mistakes himself for something else he will not be able to realize this reality, nevertheless it is already there. What he is within is not something that he will grow into in the future, it is already present right now.

For example, there is a beggar who has the key to a treasure in his pocket. That treasure is available right now, the key is available right now, but the beggar has forgotten about the key, doesn't remember it and continues to beg from dawn to dusk. He is so busy begging that he has no time to put his hands into his own pockets because his hands are always reaching out to other people. And hands which are reaching out to others can't be put into one's own pockets, they are always occupied in begging. His mind is always focused on others, so he finds no time to search within. Whatever time is available during the night he uses in counting and re-counting what he received from others. In the morning it is the same rush again. In the evening the same counting and re-counting.

Not only millionaires keep accounts, even beggars do it. And that is why the difference between a millionaire and a beggar is only quantitative, not qualitative; one has a small account and the other's account is a little bigger, but the begging is the same.

Life comes to an end and the beggar is still only keeping accounts; he has no time to look inside. And one thing is certain: the beggar believes that what he lacks, others have, and he has to get it from them. Constantly begging, he becomes settled in the idea that whatever is worth getting is with others: "I don't have it."

What I am saying is true about all of us. Whenever we find something to our liking, it belongs to others. The means to fulfill our desires are always with other people, always with the others. So we go on begging, begging, and this continuous begging forms a strong habit and leaves no way for us to look within ourselves.

So now the sage says that even those who may be trying to become superior not through money or through fame but through all the "good" intentions – through religious pursuits, through charitable behavior, through the search for truth, through this search for *sattva*, for serenity – things nobody considers to be bad…

A man accumulates riches; anybody can look down on his accumulation. Then a man accumulates religious knowledge, but nobody will look down upon this accumulation, although both of them are doing the same thing – fulfilling the desire to accumulate. People will say that the man who is accumulating wealth is piling up garbage; and yet the man who is piling up spiritual knowledge is appreciated for he is on a virtuous trip, a religious trip. But the worthless coins of spiritual knowledge are just as available on the outside as money is.

There are coins of knowledge also. A man memorizes the scriptures and becomes wise. But the scriptures are as much a part of the outer as money. He is not depositing this wealth in a safe but in his memory. The memory is also a safe. And in a way this man is more clever, more calculating, because a bank safe can be broken into, can be stolen from, but it is difficult to steal from the locker called memory. Unless a man like Mao rules over the society it is difficult to steal from it. But it is possible.

Efforts are now being made to interfere with your memory, so that you yourself do not remain the master of it. Brainwashing devices have been developed – your brain can be washed, cleaned out completely.

After the Korean War, China did some thorough brainwashing experiments on American prisoners of war and an interesting fact came to light, and the information is valuable. This fact is that only five percent of the people created any problem during the brainwashing. There was no problem with the remaining ninety-five percent, because this ninety-five percent were not the masters of their own memory, they could easily be brainwashed. Memory is erased by simple methods, and the person who has been brainwashed cannot notice the change that he has undergone – the forgetting of old concepts, beliefs and ideologies.

Stalin and Mao both did some significant experiments – dangerous, and against man's freedom, but significant because they revealed several things. A man who had not committed a murder can be made to confess that he had done it, and he will even state this in court. And the absurdity happened: the actual murderer was caught, and yet a brainwashed man had confessed to a crime which he had not committed and had been hanged for it. And he had not confessed under any pressure. What is new about it is that he was not beaten or forced to confess, he was simply brainwashed and then made to confess. Once brainwashed, it is easy to put anything into the memory.

If a man is kept awake for seven days and not allowed to sleep he will become deranged. He will not be clear about his states – whether he is dreaming or sleeping or waking. If he is not allowed to sleep or dream for seven days he will start dreaming with open eyes; then he will not be certain whether the wall in front of him actually exists or only appears to be there.

As soon as he is unable to distinguish between the dream and reality he becomes vulnerable, anything can be put into or taken out of his brain. At this vulnerable time recordings are being played giving him new ideas and erasing others. He is now suggestible, and will accept whatever you tell him; whatever you thrust upon him will go deep into his unconsciousness. He can even confess in a court that he has committed a murder because that thought has been put deep into his mind. He cannot negate it – it is beyond his control. He himself now believes that he has committed the crime, because his memory has been interfered with.

But until recently no one had been able to attack and break into the safe of the memory, so the wise men have written – they should not be called wise, they were only knowledgeable scholars – they wrote that money can be stolen, but not knowledge. But now it can be stolen, because it is also just an accumulation. The habit of accumulating is the same, it does not make any difference what one accumulates – postage stamps, wealth or knowledge – no difference. The joy of accumulating belongs to the outside.

That is why so much value is placed on non-possessiveness, on not accumulating. Non-possessiveness does not mean the renunciation of outer possessions it means the renouncing of the attitude and the desire to accumulate. Only then is the inner journey possible.

Sattva, piety, is also a kind of accumulation. Someone proudly says, "I have been on a fast for three months." He did not accumulate anything, not even the food which accumulates within the body. He did not even accumulate food within the body – in those three months his body lost weight; he lost something and accumulated nothing. But he accumulated a three-months-fast worth of religious merit! He has accumulated this. Now he wants to brag that he has fasted for three months. This is the same accumulating attitude.

Another man says, "I gave so much to charity." In giving to charity one is not accumulating; on the contrary, in giving to charity one is losing. One loses money but accumulates the pride of charity: "I gave so much to charity."

A man had come with his wife to meet me. The wife was already acquainted with me, and she had come to introduce her husband to me. At the time of the introduction she said that her husband had given one lakh rupees to charity. The husband interrupted, "No, no, it is one lakh and ten thousand." It has been given away, but the pride of giving is accumulating. We count not only what we possess, we also count what we give away. The counting continues.

We even accumulate piety – we remember whatever good we have done. But it is strange that we choose not to remember when we do something bad. So a sinner has not much recollection of his evil deeds. Others might call him bad, but he says, "What, me?" But the so-called good man has the accumulation of his good deeds. Surprisingly enough it often happens that a sinner takes the leap to go within himself sooner than the so-called good man. That is because, in a way the sinner is empty inside; he is not keeping any account of what he has done because the account is not pleasant. Whatever he has done, he himself doesn't like that he has done it, hence he keeps no account of it.

But a "good" man – he keeps an account of everything he has done. Perhaps he counts even that which he didn't do;

he inflates the account. Maybe several things are in his mind, but not in deed, but he counts even that. This accumulation is an obstruction.

It has happened so many times that even some Valmiki, some Angulimal – total criminals – attain to the truth within a moment. This is because the accumulation of good deeds is a bigger obstruction than crime. What can a criminal collect? He knows that he is nothing, has no standing – egolessness is possible. But with a "good" man there is too much ego.

The sage says that even sattva, the feeling of being "good," is a disease. This is a very daring statement. No religion outside of India would say that even goodness is a disease. Evil has been called a disease, sin has been called a disease, but goodness has never been called a disease. Certainly no religion born outside of India has been able to transcend the limitations of a moral code, hence none could become religious in the real sense.

When the West became acquainted with Eastern wisdom for the first time they were amazed because these statements appeared to be irreligious, they were very anarchic statements. If you tell a man that the accumulation of good deeds is also a disease, then you are allowing him to go astray. But it was a misunderstanding. Those who could say that even the accumulation of good deeds is a disease, of course they are implying that the accumulation of evil deeds is an even greater disease. The disease is the accumulating, so accumulate religious merit and it becomes a disease. Of course evil deeds are a disease; there is no need to even mention it, it is obvious. It does not need to be discussed.

To tell someone that stealing is sin only shows that society is so unevolved that such things still have to be stated. But to have the conceit of not being a thief is also a sin. And this statement is possible when the society has gone beyond a certain limit where stealing is naturally understood as being a sin. Then there would be no need to talk about it!

When Christians first studied the Upanishads they were amazed; there was nothing like the Ten Commandments in the Upanishads – do not steal, do not desire another's wife, do not commit adultery. They asked, "Where are the Ten Commandments? Where are the basic teachings?"

They were not aware that the writers of these sutras knew that to talk about Ten Commandments is childish; that this is only suitable for primitive societies where people need to be told that adultery should not be committed, that another's wife should not be desired; that this is evil. Such statements convey that the primary lessons are still being taught. The time has not yet come when the virtuous ego, the ego of one who does not desire another's woman, is also considered sinful. To be self-conscious of this goodness is also a sin, because this also strengthens the ego.

Sattva is also a disease – a "good" disease. It happens to good people; nevertheless it happens. Because of this disease it often turns out that good people prove worse than the bad people, because they have the vanity of being good and this creates domination; vanity creates a kind of dangerous slavery imposed on others.

It is not easy to be the son of a so-called "good" father. A pious father proves so heavy for the son that this itself can become the cause of the son turning evil. Too strong a drive for becoming good also becomes an attraction to turn to evil. And if the father is so good that his goodness cannot be transcended by the son there remains only one alternative, that is to transcend him through doing evil.

That is why so-called "good" fathers generally have no-good sons – the reason is very obvious: a repeated, routine goodness becomes boring. Goodness has a fault in it – that the other person can't even say to you that you are wrong. So your vanity cannot be challenged.

I have heard about Rinzai, a Zen master. Sometimes he would do things which were not good, although he was of the same caliber as Buddha. Those who knew him well asked many times, "Why do you do such petty deeds which bring unnecessary insult and defame your name?"

Rinzai used to reply, "Just to be human among humans, otherwise I become superhuman. If I become so good that I have no evil, I become quite superhuman; I become as heavy as a rock on people. Even my disciples criticize me and thus they feel light, and when they can laugh at me in my absence, I am saved from making them my enemy."

This is really amazing. He must have been a strange man, but he had a great insight into the human psyche.

A good teacher knows well that students must have occasion to laugh behind his back. This is a way to cathart the anger which they accumulate within the five or six hours of compulsory sitting before the teacher.

So the good people become very heavy, but it only happens if their sattva, goodness, is their disease, not their very nature.

When the sage says that sattva is also a disease, he is not saying that to be a *sattvik*, a person of goodness, is a disease. What he means is that the accumulation of goodness and good deeds and attaching it to the ego is the disease. The feeling that "I am good" is the disease; being good is not a disease. The really good man is so good that he can always even forgive the evil.

Bayazid, a Sufi mystic, was going on a pilgrimage during the days of Ramadan, the time of fasting. He had a hundred disciples with him. It was the first day of their fast and they were just entering the first town as some people came and told Bayazid that a man who loved him, who was a shoemaker, had sold his house just to arrange for food for Bayazid and for his disciples; that he had invited the whole town to eat because his master was coming to town. The man had sold everything, saying tomorrow would take care of tomorrow.

Bayazid accepted the invitation and arrived, and sat down to eat. The disciples were at a loss, they were really disturbed. They had one more excuse to feel sorry for wasting their lives with this greedy man, Bayazid, who was so obsessed with eating delicious food that he would break the vow of fasting. Bayazid started enjoying the food with great pleasure. When Bayazid was eating, the disciples also had to eat. But Bayazid took pleasure in it, while the disciples suffered for breaking their fast.

Later in the night, when everyone was gone, the disciples rushed to Bayazid and said to him, "There is a limit! We didn't expect this from you. Have you forgotten? Did you forget about the fast? Or did this food attract you so much?"

Bayazid replied, "It was not a question of the food – we can extend our fast for one day. But this poor man who had sold everything to arrange for our food would have felt hurt if we had talked about our fast. It would have been a crime. It was useless to talk about that; we can extend our fasting for one day, what is the harm in it? Why assert our saintliness so strongly? And beware! – there are occasions when one desires to assert one's saintliness."

This is very subtle. And it was a good opportunity – the whole town would have come to know that Bayazid was really a saint – but he let go of this opportunity to become known as a great saint. There was not even the slightest mention that they were on a fast.

This I call goodness, this I call being a *sattvik* – a man of goodness. When even piety has to be announced, has to be publicized, or expects respect, it becomes a disease.

The sage has called virtue the fifth disease. Sin is a disease in the whole world, virtue is a disease only in India. Even virtue is a sin, virtue is a disease, because the feeling that "I have done good" creates a subtle ego, and this feeling that "I can do good," creates the ego as a doer. In India it is understood that in this world nothing is a sin except the ego. That is why whatever creates the ego becomes a sin.

Bodhidharma went to China from India. Many other Buddhist *bhikkhus* had already gone to China – thousands and thousands of bhikkhus. Emperor Wu had spent millions to get the Buddhist scriptures translated, he had built hundreds of monasteries. Then the news came that Bodhidharma, the man of ultimate wisdom was coming, so Emperor Wu went to the border of his empire to welcome him. Just after the welcome, Emperor Wu asked Bodhidharma his first question: "I have built so many monasteries, so many guest houses, spending millions and millions; I have had Buddhist scriptures translated and I give food to thousands of bhikkhus daily. What will my reward for all this virtue be?"

Bodhidharma replied, "You will go to hell, directly to hell."

Wu asked him, "What are you saying? Hell? Are you joking?"

No bhikkhu had yet dared to say this, in fact every bhikkhu had said that he was a great and virtuous man. They must have been beggars, not bhikkhus. Telling him, "You are a great and a virtuous man," the beggars could manage to get their sustenance from him.

They all said, "You are a great and virtuous man; nobody ever gave so much to charity. Your nameplate will be inscribed in golden letters in heaven, your palace is already being prepared beside God himself."

Bodhidharma said, "You will go directly to hell."

Bodhidharma's statement did not appeal to Wu. It would not appeal to any virtuous man, that virtue is also a sin.

Wu said, "I cannot accept your statement."

Bodhidharma said, "Then I refuse to enter into your sinful empire, I am going back. I will stay outside of your empire. The day you know that even virtue is sin, I will enter."

Somehow this was all ignored and forgotten. Wu became against Bodhidharma, and the other monks also turned against him. They had pinned their hopes on him, that his arrival there would expand the work. The emperor was willing, but Bodhidharma had spoiled everything.

After ten years Wu was on his deathbed, and as fear gripped him he again remembered Bodhidharma. He could see that in spite of so many virtuous deeds death is the same for him as for a sinner; he was just as decrepit in old age as any sinner would be. After doing so many virtuous deeds there was no peace at the time of death, so how would it be possible after death? The emperor's mind was very disturbed.

He sent for Bodhidharma: "Call him back, I have wasted ten years. Today I also feel that I am going directly to hell."

But Bodhidharma had already died. However he had a message written on his grave, knowing that "If not today, then tomorrow, or at the time of death, Emperor Wu will remember me." Because to deceive oneself is easy while one is alive, when one is in high spirits and under the impact of the illusions of the so-called life. One realizes the real situation only when death is approaching.

Bodhidharma had said, "Wu will remember me at the time of his death. So this is my message for the emperor, write it on my grave: 'You performed good deeds all your life. If you can let go of those good deeds even now, at the time of death, the door of heaven is very near.'" Drop your attachment to being virtuous. You have dropped so many things in order to be virtuous, now drop even that virtue.

It is very difficult. It is very easy to drop iron chains, but it is very difficult to drop golden chains, they look like ornaments. And virtue! – what is more golden than virtue? It is pure gold, one doesn't dare to drop it. But someone who recognizes that chains are chains sees no distinction between iron chains and golden chains. Prison walls may be decorated like palace walls, it makes no difference. The ego is a prison, hence the sage has talked about five diseases.

Unless one has known the character of these five diseases, unless one has entered into the nature of these five diseases, one cannot be free of them. In fact there is no way to get rid of anything except by knowing it. Knowing alone is freedom, knowing alone is liberation. As soon as we know a thing in its totality we become free of it.

Ignorance is bondage, not knowing is bondage. Freedom happens with knowing. Anger possesses us while we do not know it. The day we know our anger, the day we enter into its layers, the day we see anger in its nakedness, we are free from anger.

After knowing, nothing needs to be done about freedom: try to understand this deep wisdom of the Eastern seers. It is not that first you need to know what anger is and then you have to do something to drop anger – no. The Eastern concept is that knowing is freedom, nothing needs to be done beyond knowing. If doing is needed even after knowing, it means that knowing is still incomplete.

Psychological diseases do not first require a diagnosis and then a cure. Their diagnosis itself is the cure. Why? Because psychological diseases are due to ignorance, they have no other cause.

For example, it is dark and in this darkness there are snakes and scorpions. Then you light a lamp. Now two steps have to occur. All the snakes and scorpions will now become visible, although they will not yet disappear because they were not just an effect of the darkness, the darkness was only the cause of their invisibility. But now it is not dark and the snakes are visible. However nobody can say that the snakes have disappeared just because the lamp was lit; the next step is that the snakes and scorpions have to be removed. So realization alone is not enough, something more needs to be done, one more step is involved.

But one more thing is happening. When the lamp is lit, do you also have to remove the darkness? Do you ever wonder: Okay, the lamp is lit, but now how will I remove the darkness? No, the cause of darkness is the absence of light.

Physical ailments require both a diagnosis and a cure. But for diseases of the consciousness the diagnosis itself is the cure: the lamp is lit and the darkness is gone. Disease of the consciousness is like this.

The sage says: *When the embodied soul is identified with the nature of these five knots, it cannot become free of them without self-realization.* What do *we* do? We become identified with them and we acquire their attributes. Doing virtuous acts we become virtuous, constantly doing good deeds we become good, performing evil deeds we become a sinner – whatsoever we do, we become one with it. This identification itself is your ignorance. If you want to know, it is necessary to stand at a distance. A little distance, a little gap is needed to know. In fact we can only know that which we see from a distance, otherwise we cannot know. Whatever we want to know first has to be placed before our eyes for observation.

If you want to know anger, it is not possible to know when you are identified with anger. Anger can only be known after separating the anger from oneself, by going beyond the anger to look at it neutrally, as we do with an object – like a scientist in his lab observing an object from a distance.

Meditation is a science of putting oneself at a distance. Looking at your own diseases of the mind from a distance, and entering fully into those knots, becomes the liberation.

As these five afflict the soul like subtle diseases,
then the soul is known as ling sharir,
the identification body.
This is the knot in the heart.

That is the basic disease of the heart. This disease is actually the one where we are stuck. These five diseases together produce one disease, and that disease is identification – we become one with what we do. Stealing, we become thieves; meditating, we become a spiritual man; we become one with what we do, we cannot remain separate from it.

If we understand this properly, this is the meaning of sannyas: while we are doing anything we are not to become the doer, we are just to remain the watcher. The basic meaning of sannyas is that we perform actions, but we are not to become involved with them any more than as an actor. We may play a part in a theatrical production, but as soon as we leave the stage we drop the role we were playing. An actor leaves his role behind. When he is lying on his bed he does not wonder about what might be happening now to his leading lady who was in trouble in the play. But sometimes such illusions do happen.

I have heard that trouble occurred once during the drama of the god Rama's life story.

The actor who was playing Ravana, the villain, played that role every year and the girl who was playing Sita, Rama's wife, had also played her role for several years. Every year he played Ravana, kidnapped Sita and kept her in his Ashoka Garden – the same mischievous game every year. But the actor fell in love with the girl.

The Ramaleela production happened again. When it came to the part of the ceremony in which Sita would choose her husband, Ravana had also come as a possible suitor in the ceremony. Then the messengers arrived with the news that a fire had broken out in Lanka, Ravana's golden capital. But Ravana replied, unexpectedly, "To hell with the fire! This time, I will not move without marrying her." He picked up the bow of Lord Shiva that was kept for the test to find the right suitor and broke it into pieces.

Janak, the father of Sita, was in a fix; this was not in the play, it was an unexpected problem. The public too was bewildered – what is going on? What was going to happen now? Would Sita marry Ravana? But Janak was an old and experienced man. He had played his role for many, many years so he could improvise. He called for his servants and shouted, "Why did you place here this toy bow and arrow meant for children? Bring in the real bow of Lord Shiva." The curtain dropped, and another actor was brought in to play Ravana – because the original actor was still shouting that he would not move without marrying Sita.

Now this poor man playing Ravana must not have been sleeping well at night. For him it had no longer remained a matter of only acting, it became something very real!

Sannyas means letting go of this subtle identification body. It means that the state that you have created by identifying yourself with your diseases, by identifying with *how* you appear to be, has to go.

That which illuminates there as the consciousness
is kshetragya, the knower field.

The knower, the knower field, perceives it all sitting within this identification body. But we are not aware of it at all; this knower is lost among all that which we know. To discover that knower is the science of religion.

The question has been asked: Who is *sakshi*, the witness? Who is *kootastha*, the one who resides deepest? Who is *antaryami*, the knower of all thoughts and feelings?

These three are the dimensions of the soul in three different contexts. It is like this: you are a father in relation to your son, a husband in relation to your wife, a son in relation to your father. Among friends you are none of these. In the office you are not even a friend, but in spite of all this you are one and the same.

Sakshi, *kootastha* and *antaryami* are the names of different situational dimensions of the soul. All three are nothing else but the soul, but these three words are used in three different contexts. Try to understand the contexts.

The one who knows the birth
and the dissolution of the knower, the knowing,
and the objects of knowing,
yet is itself without birth or dissolution,
this self-illumined one is called sakshi,
the witness.

If you enter into yourselves, whatsoever you will come to know you cannot be that. Remember this sutra: whatsoever you can know, you cannot be that, because you are always the knower. So it means that whatsoever you know, you are standing behind that knowledge, otherwise you would not know it. Whatsoever can be known, you cannot be that. The basic principle, the foundational, the seed mantra of *yoga sadhana*, meditation practice, is: you cannot be that which you know.

You can know when you close your eyes that your physical body exists around you. You can know, you can feel the pain of the thorn stuck in your foot; you can know your heart beating – you can know your heart is beating fast when you are anxious, you can also know the heartbeat is slowing down when you are peaceful. So the knower is different from the heartbeat, from the pain in the foot, from the form of this body, because a duality is needed in order to know.

A duality is a prerequisite for knowing, a gap is necessary in order to know. Knowing occurs because of that gap, otherwise there is no knowing. That is why when you look at your reflection in the mirror you have to keep a certain distance. If you come very close and you put your head on the mirror, it will be difficult to see your reflection in the mirror. You can see a little bit because there is still a gap, but the more you reduce the distance, the gap, the more difficult it is to see anything. If there is no gap between you and the mirror you won't be able to see anything. A certain distance is necessary for knowing, or seeing.

The sage says: All these things which are born, created and destroyed, all this is known by the one who dwells within.

In the night, when sleep starts descending, you would know it is descending. One thing is certain: you are not the sleep, otherwise who would know it? The one on whom the sleep is descending must be separate from it.

In the morning you are sitting at your door, the sun has arisen, spreading the sunshine; you know the sun is shining. Then the sun rises in the sky and the heat increases, then the sun is above your head, it is noon. You are neither the noon, nor the morning. Then in the evening the sun is setting, darkness is descending; you are aware of the descending darkness, which means you are not the darkness.

Morning happens, noon happens, then evening comes; you know the sun rising, when it is at its peak, and the setting sun. You cannot be one with the sun, you are separate from it. Similarly, whatever happens in your life is known by the one who dwells within. And the interesting thing is that you can never catch hold of this knower.

Try to understand. You have a pain in your foot. You know that there is pain in your foot, so the knower has become separate from the pain in the foot. Now you can also know that you know the pain in the foot. Now you have gone behind this knowing. Try to understand it correctly: you have pain in your foot, you know the pain in your foot, hence your knowing is separate from the pain in your foot. But you also know that you know of the pain in your foot. Then this second knowing has gone behind the first knowing.

You can know even this knowing, that will be the third knowing. And then even this knowing can be known – that will be the fourth knowing. One thing is certain, that whatever you know, you can move back from there; you will never be caught in any knowing, you will always remain the knower, not the knowable. This ultimate knower, this ultimate witnessing self behind every knowing, is very mysterious. It is very mysterious.

Perhaps this is the deepest mystery in life, that we cannot reduce ourselves into an object, the observed, by any means; we always remain the knower, the observer. That is why a man like Mahavira, a man who searched deeply for the ultimate witnessing self, said that it is meaningless to say that there remains a knower in the ultimate state of being, only a knowing exists there. Because even if we maintain that there is a knower, one who knows, we have come to know that knower, we have receded behind it. We should only say that there is simply knowing. So Mahavira called the ultimate state *keval gyan*, just knowing; not even the knower, not the known, just knowing – pure knowing. And this pure knowing goes on receding forever behind each knowing.

The one who knows this mystery, the experiencer of this mystery, has been called *sakshi*, the witnessing self. The self is a witness, because the knower, the known and the knowing, all three are born out of it and dissolve into it, but the witness always remains standing apart.

In English there is a word, a very precious word, *ecstasy*, which helps one to understand the concept of the witnessing self. *Ecstasy* at its root means to stand out. *Ecstasy* means to be apart from. Whatever way you try, there is no way for you to be within the experience; you are always apart from that which can be experienced. Wherever you stand, you "stand out."

That is why Western mystics use the word *ecstasy* for *samadhi*, the ultimate awakening. Ecstasy means the witnessing self. Ecstasy does not mean *samadhi*, it means witnessing. No matter what you do, however much you try, there is no way you can make the witnessing self other than itself, it remains only a witness.

This is one situational definition of the soul.

Every definition is of a particular dimension. That is why no one definition can convey the whole nature of the soul, and that is also why there are so many differences between religions. There are no fundamental reasons for these differences – one religion emphasizes one definition of the soul according to one dimension, while another religion emphasizes another definition of a different dimension. These definitions will appear to be different. In this sense the Upanishads are beyond all religions because they accept all definitions. This definition of the witnessing self is given by Jaina philosophy, the Jaina religion.

The second question is: What is *kootastha*, the indestructible one? The sage says:

That which resides in the consciousness
of all living beings,
from Brahma, the god of creation,
to the smallest insect, and which remains
even when all gross and subtle bodies are no more,
is called kootastha, the indestructible one.

The remaining… That which remains even after the destruction of all the bodies is called the *kootastha* soul – that which always remains. Do what you will, it remains.

Even science accepts that matter has a *kootastha* form because matter is indestructible, we cannot destroy it. We may change its forms, but that is not destruction – it is a transformation. The *kootastha* state of matter always remains, and the Upanishad says that consciousness too has a *kootastha* state which is eternal.

You may be a child, a young man, an old man; you may become a sinner or a virtuous person; you may abandon all your sins, renounce your religious merit, renounce the passions of youth, become old, remain in the body or leave the body – do whatsoever you wish – but after all this has been destroyed, that which still remains, which is indestructible, is *kootastha*.

This is the second definition of the soul. This too belongs to a specific context; this is from the aspect of what is destructible and what is indestructible; this is called the *kootastha*. In the dimension of knowledge it is *sakshi*, the witness, and in the dimension of the indestructible it is *kootastha*, the indestructible one.

Just as a thread passes through each bead of
a necklace,
the soul threads each cell of the body
in order that it may become aware of its
true nature
from among the different characteristics.
This one is called antaryami,

the knower of all thoughts and feelings.

The two earlier definitions are a bit too far away for you, because to be a witness is the ultimate state of knowing and to achieve the state of the indestructible one, you should be totally ready to die as you are.

To know the witness one has to go deep into the purity of ultimate knowing where no object remains and only the knower is left, where nothing remains to be known, only the knower remains. This is a very arduous process of elimination – to go on denying whatever you come to know, to throw away whatever becomes the object of knowledge.

It is interesting to note that although you have begun your journey in order to know, whatever you know will have to be thrown away, only then will ultimate knowing happen. Whatever becomes the experience, say, "It is useless." It is an arduous discipline! Whatever becomes part of your experience, declare it as useless. Even if the experience of the godliness happens, become aware that, "What I am is beyond it," because whatever can become an experience, "I am not that."

So Mahavira and Buddha simply denied the existence of God; they said whatever can be experienced is not it.

People say that they have experienced God, that they have seen God, that they have had a glimpse of God. If you have had a glimpse of God, one thing is certain: that you have not had even a glimpse of your own self, because whatever you can see becomes an object, the other, and you remain beyond it. So here you have even gone beyond God!

Certainly whatever you have glimpsed, experienced, must be your own imagination, not God. God is the eternal witness, the divine. He is known when all experiences dissolve. To talk about an experience of God is ignorance. There cannot be an experience of God. It is useless to even say so. It is the disappearance of all experiences.

So a man like Buddha becomes unintelligible to us because

he gives the ultimate statement. He denies the existence of God, soul and liberation – because whatever becomes known is useless. What words can he use, how can he give a name to that which is not known? So Buddha remains silent.

Whenever someone asked Buddha about that which really exists, he would reply, "If I say something it too becomes an object, hence I will not talk about it." He suggests to go on denying every experience and every object of knowledge. This way, one day you will arrive at a point where nothing remains.

It is difficult for this to be understood: we seek in order to attain something, and Buddha says that nothing remains. What does it mean? It doesn't mean that there is nothing, but that nothing remains to be known, nothing to be experienced, nothing to be recognized – no knowable object, no knower and no knowledge. The trio of knowing disappears, but what remains is all.

But these definitions are a bit distant for you. The third definition which may feel closer to you is: That which is living in each cell of the body, threaded through the five bodies like a thread through the beads in a necklace, drowned in the five diseases, entangled in the world...

Only the beads are of the world; the thread is always of the soul. Only the beads are of the bodies, of the diseases; the thread is always of the soul. The most important thing in a necklace is the thread. Beads cannot make a necklace without the thread; the beads would spill all over the place, the necklace would disperse. The thread is the link that keeps them together. But the thread is invisible, only the beads are visible. So whosoever has not seen a necklace being made will not understand the existence of the thread if a necklace is suddenly put in front of him; he will only see the beads because the thread is invisible, it is hidden within the beads.

We are in the same situation: the bodies are visible but the thread is not. Everything is visible but the thread, and we go on jumping from one bead to another.

These bodies are not possible without the soul – but the soul is not visible. One body is so close to the other, one bead is so close to the other, that you slip from one bead to the next, to the next, and go on missing the thread.

Whatsoever we are within all these bodies, all these diseases, there the soul is not only *kootastha* and *sakshi*, it is also *antaryami*, the knower of all thoughts and feelings. *Antaryami* means, it is *here* as well. *There*, in the ultimate state which we call the witness, it certainly is.

When we come to the point of the ultimate annihilation of all, what is left we call *kootastha*, the indestructible, because it still will remain; but *it is here as well*, within us as we are.

Here it is invisible, here it is hidden under the beads; there it will be without the beads covering it, there only the thread remains. Here there are many beads and it is within them, but nevertheless it is still here. Because that which exists there must be here also; otherwise there simply will be no way to arrive there. Hence it has been said:

Just as a thread passes through each bead of a necklace, the soul threads each cell of the body in order that it may become aware of its true nature from among the different characteristics. This one is called antaryami, the knower of all thoughts and feelings. Begin the journey from the knower of all thoughts and feelings, make witnessing the key of your spiritual endeavor, and that which is the indestructible will be the attainment. Begin at *antaryami*, practice *sakshi*, and *kootastha* is the attainment.

Enough for today.

11

What Is Eternal?

The soul, the ultimate reality,
is called twam, thou, when free of all descriptions
– truth, wisdom, the infinite, the abode of bliss –
just as gold when it is free of all form of bangle
or crown.
The soul is then revealed in its own self-nature,
perception and consciousness.
Brahman, the ultimate reality, is truth.
It is infinite and the abode of knowing.
Truth is indestructible.
What is not destroyed, even as the mediums
of space,
time and objects are destroyed,
is avinashi, the indestructible.

Innumerable ornaments can be made out of gold and many forms are possible – beautiful or ugly – but the form is not the gold. Nevertheless the form cannot appear without the gold, it cannot exist alone. A form has no independent existence, it appears only when it envelops something.

So gold can take many forms, but no form is the gold. Gold is free of all forms, that is why one form can change into another. If gold had a fixed form, then it could not take on another. However we have never seen gold without a form – whenever we see it, it has a form. But gold can also change its form – today it is a bangle, tomorrow it can be molded into some other form, and the day after tomorrow something else again. The form changes, but the intrinsic nature of gold is constant. So we may not have seen formless gold, and yet the gold is not the form.

The sage starts the talk with this example. He says: "Whatever we see in the world is all form. The base on which the form appears is without form, and the search for this formless is the search for truth. But in order to search for it, the form must be dropped. All form and all attributes need to be discarded, all limitations transcended, only then can one reach to the infinite, the boundless, the eternal."

The mind is surrounded by form. One's first acquaintance is only with form; the form is the first thing seen. The formless is not seen on the outside; whatsoever is seen on the outside is all form. That is why we become obsessed with form and forget that *that* which is must be formless, otherwise how can it take on so many forms?

What is a seed today will become a tree tomorrow. The seed which can become a tree must contain something formless within, which is able to take the form of a seed as well as the form of a tree. That formlessness must be hiding in the seed because that one seed can produce enough trees to cover the whole earth. One seed produces one tree, and one tree bears millions of seeds. If we sow these millions of seeds, each and every seed in turn will bear millions of seeds again; one seed can cover the whole earth with trees. Only the earth may run out of space, deny it and say, "Enough! No more."

There is so much hidden within a seed which cannot be contained in its physical form. The form of the seed is insignificant, almost nothing. That which is formless must be hidden in the seed, because one seed can bear an infinite number of seeds. The form cannot produce the infinite; whatever is born out of form will be finite. The seed should have a finite capacity, only then its form would have some meaning. But I have told you that one seed can fill the whole earth – even this is just a way of expression. Otherwise, if we were to expand the mathematics of it correctly, one seed could fill the whole cosmos, and even the cosmos would become insufficient and the seed require more space because there would be no end to it. One seed producing millions of seeds, and out of millions, again millions and millions of seeds...there is no end to it.

So can what was hidden in that first seed be contained in the form itself? Infinity cannot be contained in the form. The form can only contain the finite. Form itself is a limitation, so how can it contain the formless, the limitless? So when we only see the form in the seed, that is the fault of our vision because we are not able to see the whole seed with all its potential. That which it can be, in a way, is inherent in it right now, otherwise how could it manifest in the future? If this one seed did not contain all the seeds of the world, how could they ever manifest in the future? They are hidden in it today, here and now, only our eyes are not able to see them. So the form of the seed is our illusion – the real nature of the seed is formless. Wherever form is seen, it is because of our faulty vision.

It is like looking at the sky through a window. If you have never seen the sky outside, the sky will look as if it is framed. The form of the window will appear to be the form of the sky. The window is giving a form to the sky – but the sky is formless. Even when we are standing outside the house looking up at the sky and there is no window, then too the earth works like a window and the sky appears arched. The only reason for the arched appearance of the sky is the roundness of the earth. The sky is not round – the earth becomes the window and gives it a form. Our eyes are not more than the window; our eyes will fix a form on whatsoever we see.

So, in fact, looking outside we will always meet the form and not the formless. In order to search for the formless we have to look inside where we can be rid of all windows. With closed eyes we don't need to remember the window – we don't need any eyes, any window, or even an earth. Entering within, we enter into the formless.

Truth exists within and without, but first the seeker has to know the truth within. The day he knows the formless within, the formless becomes apparent outside too. Then form remains only on the surface as an appearance, created by oneself.

This formlessness is free of all descriptions such as truth, wisdom, the infinite, abode of bliss, it is pure gold-like consciousness and knowing. When such a consciousness is experienced – this sutra is very precious – when such a consciousness is experienced then it is called *twam*; it is called thou, not I.

When this formless truth is experienced there is no way to say I, because I is a limitation. And what you have been calling I up to now does not exist any longer. Now what to call it? It surrounds you from all directions, it is present within and without. And we have only two words we can use: either *I* or *thou*. We cannot say I, because only with the disappearance of the I is the formless experienced. So with the inadequacy of language there remains only one way to describe it, and that is to call it thou. So devotees have called the ultimate reality, thou.

The first reason to call it thou is because there is no way to call it I. Actually, to call it thou is also not right, because thou is always in relation to I; it is a relationship. As long as the I is there, someone exists as thou. And when thou is there, I too exists. In such moments one experiences the futility of language. I cannot be said because it is no more; to say thou is also difficult, because then who will be saying it? Who will be saying thou? But if something has to be said, then it is more correct to say thou than to say I. Even though it is not right, it is not correct to say thou, still it is better compared to saying I – at least it conveys the absence of an I. This is the first reason.

Secondly, we could have called it *that* – neither I nor thou, but *that*. Wise men have also called it *that*. But when existence is called *that*, there doesn't seem to be any loving relationship in it; it sounds as if it is an object. We use *that* for objects, and *thou* for individuals. And when the experience of godliness happens it is not like experiencing an object, it is like experiencing an ultimate entity – the ultimate aliveness full of a showering infinite love. The experience is like the embrace of a lover, so to call it *that* would be disrespectful, and to call it *I* is out of the question. The sage calls this pure consciousness, devoid of all attributes and free of all form, *twam*, or thou.

Martin Buber, a great Jewish thinker of the twentieth century, has written a book, *I and Thou*. He is one of the few people in the history of mankind who has expounded upon the deepest relationship between I and thou.

Man can live in three ways: keeping I at the center and making thou the periphery – the way people usually live – I always at the center, thou on the periphery. We use thou, we exploit thou, and we establish a relationship with thou, but always for the sake of I. Even if we sometimes surrender to thou, it is in the hope of making thou surrender for the sake of I; but the concern is always the I. This is the state of ego – wanting to bring the whole world to your feet and to decorate your I. I stands at the center and the whole world becomes the periphery: this is the state of mind of an irreligious person.

Another state of mind is to keep thou at the center and I at the periphery. This state is where only one thirst remains and that is to surrender oneself, to eliminate oneself, where only one longing remains and that is how to dissolve the I for the sake of thou. This is the state of a devotee, of a religious person: thou remains and the I goes on receding, shrinking. I becomes a thin periphery, thou becomes the strong center. This is the egoless state.

There is a third state which has always been difficult to express, where neither thou nor I exists – neither the periphery nor the center exists. People like Buddha tried to express this state but they failed. There is no way to express it, because all language revolves around I and thou. The very birth of language is in the conversation between I and thou. Hence language is unable to convey that which is beyond I and thou.

That is why the sage has to call it *twam*, thou.

Here the sage is trying to commit the least, the smallest possible error. The whole truth cannot be said, hence an untruth which is closest to it, the least untruth, is being said. This state cannot be expressed exactly because neither I nor thou exist there, but some expression of it is a must, the message has to be conveyed. Returning from that unknown realm the sage desires to convey to his loved ones what he has known, what he has seen.

So the sage calls it thou. This he is saying to the disciple who is sitting with him to learn, who is there with a longing to know. He is told that when the experience of pure consciousness happens, we call it thou.

Thou is a lovely word, and closer to the truth. And if someone starts living his life centered on this understanding of thou, it is also very revolutionary.

The whole spiritual practice of Ramakrishna revolved around thou. A mystic called Totapuri, practicing *vedanta*, visited Dakshineshwar where Ramakrishna lived.

Totapuri asked him, "Why do you keep on repeating thou – thou? Drop it, and attain to where neither I nor thou exist."

Ramakrishna was as humble as a devotee should be. Sometimes humbleness becomes a great phenomenon. Ramakrishna said, "Show me the way. I accept your invitation."

Ramakrishna was a respected man. His devotees called him *paramahansa,* the great swan; millions bowed at his feet. Totapuri never expected that he would agree to learn so easily. Even Totapuri, if asked, would not have said yes so easily. "I am *brahman* – I am God," was all he said. When someone proclaims, "I am *brahman*, I am the divine," there is nothing left to learn. If this proclamation is truthful, then no learning is needed. But this proclamation can also be a deception. If it is said after experiencing godliness, great, but if it is said while still under the lure of I, then it is dangerous. Anyone may rejoice in saying this statement, but if the experience has actually happened, then to say "I am *brahman*" is used only as a means of expression. Actually, then it would be better to say, "The I no longer exists and only *brahman* is."

Totapuri was surprised, but he was not aware that one who keeps thou as the center can easily agree to anything – provided thou is really at their center. It is not possible if I is the center.

Ramakrishna agreed and said, "Take me to where neither I nor thou exists." This is the way of someone who keeps thou at the center.

It happened in an amazing way: when Totapuri asked, "Are you wholeheartedly ready?" Ramakrishna replied, "Let me go to the temple and ask the Mother, the goddess Kali, whether I can renounce her. Let me have her permission to renounce her."

Totapuri said, "Then all talk is meaningless. If you want to renounce her, why do you feel the necessity of asking permission? What then is the need to ask her permission to leave?

Ramakrishna replied, "I no longer exist, so how can I renounce anything? Only she remains – to renounce something or not, that is all up to the Mother. I am not, so I cannot make this decision. The day I left everything up to her even this decision was included. If she doesn't give me her permission I will die ignorant, but there is no other way."

This is the feeling of someone who keeps thou at the center – he even agrees to die ignorant. Not even this much space is available to the I that it can choose to decide even in favor of an opportunity for ultimate knowing.

In their songs devotees say that they do not long for liberation, for freedom, for nirvana, just to be on the streets where Krishna walked is enough, because liberation is for the I, and dancing on the streets of Vrindavan is something to do with the thou. That is why the devotees have said, "We don't want liberation, because liberation means *my* liberation – after all, it is not the divine who needs any liberation. Remember it: liberation is for *me*, nirvana is for *me*, the wisdom of knowing is for *me*. So they sing, "I do not want liberation, nirvana or the wisdom of knowing, just let me wander on the pathways where the divine once walked, that is enough." This is the feeling of the one who accepts thou at the center.

There are many reasons for calling the pure consciousness thou. One of them is that to accept the nature of pure consciousness as thou is helpful for the seeker – it is a very helpful hypothesis. If consciousness is perceived to have the nature of I, it could at times be dangerous. If pure consciousness is accepted as having the nature of I, there is a ninety-nine percent chance that instead of eliminating the ego, the ego will become stronger.

The Upanishads are right when they proclaim "*Aham brahmasmi*, I am divine." But this proclamation has happened only once in a while, to one out of a hundred realized beings. This declaration is the exception. It is the statement of those who dissolved everything into their I, whose I became so vast that even all distinctions of the other, the thou, became contained within it. This is extremely difficult because the I is very satisfying, and the whole pleasure for the I lies in the contrast with thou – otherwise it loses its charm. What is the purpose in proclaiming I, if I am alone and no thou, no other exists in the world?

The fulfillment of the ego depends on others. That is why it is very interesting that the ego may declare itself to be free, unaware that it is basically dependent, that it cannot exist without others. When a person says, "I am an emperor," he is not aware that his existence is dependent on his subjects, that he depends on the very people he rules over. When someone declares, "I am the master," he does not know that he cannot be a master without slaves – and he depends so much on his slaves, how can he be the master? A master is dependent, he is bound to his slaves. All proclamations of I, the ego, only exist to make thou smaller. The ego can also be fulfilled in this way.

When the Upanishads declared "*Aham brahmasmi*, I am divine," the world was inhabited by innocent and simple people. But slowly it became apparent that it is dangerous to keep the I at the center. In keeping the I at the center, ninety-nine percent of people go astray, only one percent attain to truth. This Sarvasar Upanishad is meant to help the majority of seekers by expressing the essence of a large number of truths, hence the word *thou* has been used, not "*Aham brahmasmi*, I am divine."

So be ready to eliminate the I in order to attain to the truth. This journey is the journey of dissolving the I. If you can remember with every breath that the I does not exist, that only thou, the divine, the ultimate reality exists, you will find that within a short time all tensions have dropped, all the anguish of the mind has vanished and worries have disappeared, because worries, anguish and tensions all require the hook of the I to hang onto, otherwise they cannot hang on. If this feeling deepens, that "I am not, only thou art," suddenly one day you will find that your worries have disappeared, and even if you want to be worried you cannot, because worries are the shadow of the I. With the disappearance of the I, worries also disappear. Tranquility is the shadow of thou – with the deepening of thou, tranquility flowers by itself.

Nietzsche tried his whole life to live as if there is no God. He proclaimed that if God ever existed, now he is dead. Nietzsche was a great genius, on a par with any Buddha or Krishna. He had a penetrating intellect, but the denial of God turned his intellect into anguish, his brilliance into worry. It is worth noting that when mediocre people get worried, their worries are also petty; when a man of great genius worries, his worry too is of tremendous proportions. There was no alternative for Nietzsche except to go mad, insanity was the result of his denial. Great geniuses do not have petty worries, they have great worries.

Nietzsche could have attained to the peace of a buddha, he was not lacking anything, but he only attained to the same madness as thousands of mad people. And the reason for it was that he tried to build his whole personality on I.

Nietzsche has written in his diary: "If God exists, I want to become God number one, and he can be placed next to me. If someone can become God, then why not I – what do I lack? Or if God exists, I can announce my denial – I am free to deny him. At least I am total in denying his existence, I cannot be forced to accept his existence. Not even God can force me to accept him. In this regard, I am superior to God – he requires my acknowledgement in order to exist. But if I deny him, he has no way to make me accept his existence." This is the result of living with the I at the center.

It is very difficult to understand the anguish of Nietzsche, but we can understand petty worries because we also live with an ego.

Sometime, do a small experiment; remove the I from the center for twenty-four hours, and place thou at the center. Just for twenty-four hours remember thou continuously. Even if a stone hits your foot, even if you are abused, even if someone throws burning coals at you, even if you are praised, even if someone bows down at your feet – for just twenty-four hours, remember that thou is at the center, not I. It will be a new beginning in your life. If this remembering could be possible for twenty-four hours – or even if you couldn't do that, if it is for a full twenty-four minutes, you will not remain the same. Once you know the moments of tranquility of thou, you will never want to live with the I.

When the emphasis shifts from I to thou, it becomes much easier to realize pure consciousness. Or, if pure consciousness is attained, then the feeling immediately shifts from I to thou; that is why pure consciousness is called *twam*, thou.

Brahman, the ultimate reality, is truth.
It is infinite and the abode of knowing.
Truth is indestructible.

Many have tried to give a definition for truth. What is

truth? Man has pondered over it from many aspects. What is truth? What do we mean by "truth"?

Science regards facts as truth, and this definition is widely accepted today. Science says: a fact is truth. A fact is that which can be tested and checked experimentally, for which there is proof in the material world.

Suppose I raise my hand and only one person out of so many sitting here says that he sees my raised hand and the rest of you do not see it. Science will say that person is dreaming, because he has no other evidence. It is not a fact, otherwise the other people who are present would have seen the raised hand. It must be a dream. Dreams are personal, facts are collective.

A table in your room can be seen by everyone, agreed to by everyone, but if you say that God is present in your room they will say, "You may be seeing him, but we do not. You must be imagining things, you must be dreaming."

It is very interesting that it is not possible to share dreams. Two persons cannot see the same dream, or can they? It has not happened yet! No partnership, no friendship is possible in dreams, dreams are always personal. For science, that which is personal is a dream not a fact, and that which is collective is a fact. For science, truth is defined as that which is a fact.

The Upanishads have no objection to this definition; Eastern wisdom has no objection to this definition. But Eastern wisdom raises a deeper question, one which is unanswerable by science. Eastern wisdom says: "We accept that the objectively present phenomenon is truth. But what is present today may be absent tomorrow and what was absent yesterday may be present today. In the East we call only that phenomenon which is never absent a truth. When it is eternal, we call it truth – the rest we call simply a fact."

Eastern wisdom makes three divisions: a dream is that which belongs to the imagination of one individual; a fact is that which is a collective experience; truth is that which is eternal – because a fact does not always remain a fact. Yesterday you were young and everybody witnessed it; today you are not young. What happened to truth? And if truth can change like that over a period of ten years, then the difference between this truth and a dream which continues the whole night and changes over a span of ten hours is only one of time.

A man dreams for eight hours that he is an emperor and in the morning he again becomes a pauper – but he was an emperor for eight hours. You may say that you were not a witness to it, but all the people present in the dream were witnesses – the dreamer was not alone in the dream; he had servants and attendants, ministers, armies, a big capital – all of them were his witnesses, and they accepted him as the emperor.

So the difference is that a dream lasts only eight hours, whereas youth lasts for ten or twenty years – a difference only of time. Suppose someone remains in a coma for twenty years and continues dreaming that he is an emperor… It happens sometimes.

I went to a village where a woman had been in a coma for nine months, and the physicians were of the opinion that she could remain that way for another three years, alive but in a coma. If this woman had been dreaming for nine months – and she must have been dreaming, firstly because she was unconscious, and secondly because she was a woman, she must have been dreaming! And there is no way for her to know that what she has been seeing for nine months is only a dream – and everyone present in the dream would agree. Will the dream become truth just because it has been going on for nine months? It can also happen that today's dream may become truth for the masses tomorrow.

Abraham Lincoln had a dream three days before his death. He got up at midnight, woke his wife and told her, "I had a bewildering dream in which I was murdered, and my dead body was lying in a certain room of the White House. You were standing near my head, two men were standing near my feet, one wearing black clothes, but he did not look familiar to me."

The wife replied, "Go back to sleep, it was only a dream."

Lincoln said, "I just wanted to tell you, that's all," and went back to sleep.

Three days later, Lincoln was murdered. He lay dead in that very room. His wife stood near his head and two men stood near his feet, one wearing black clothes, and the wife knew that he was not familiar with Lincoln. The whole scene was the same.

So something that was a dream three days earlier became a collective fact after three days. So how much difference is there between a dream and a fact? It was a difference of only three days. The difference was only of a certain amount of time.

Dreams come true, and truths become a dream. What we know as facts may one day disappear and fall into oblivion. Today you love someone and you say, "I am ready to die for you – this love is true." And tomorrow? – tomorrow even the ashes of love are gone. This love was so much afire that it should have left some smoke behind, but afterward there was not even a trace of smoke. It left no trace! This love was so true, so real that you would have given your life for it – now who would have conceived that that love would become so untrue?

The materialist makes only two divisions: one is the dream, nonfactual, fiction; and the other is the fact, a substantial fact. A fact is that which is agreed to by the masses, which has a materialistic existence, which we can test and check objectively. But the Upanishadic sage says that truth is that which is imperishable, indestructible.

We make three divisions. We call that which is a personal experience a dream; it may not necessarily be fiction, it may take the form of a fact. Then that which is a collective experience is called a fact, but it may not always remain a fact, it may become a dream. These two cannot be called truth: truth is that which always remains the same – neither is it dream, nor is it fact. It never changes, it never transforms itself – it simply is.

Nothing less than that is acceptable as truth. The Eastern definition of truth lays its foundation in eternity and indestructibility. That is why we call the world *maya*, illusion; there is no other reason behind it.

When we say the world is illusory, or as Shankara says, "The world is an illusion," it does not mean that this world does not exist, it means that the nature of this world is such that it will not remain the same eternally. When Shankara called this world *maya*, people misunderstood it to mean illusion, as if the world is nonexistent – the tree before you is nonexistent, you are sitting here but you are not... No! Shankara does not mean this. Shankara is saying that you do exist, but your nature is such that you exist now and will cease to be tomorrow. So we do not say that you are real, we say that you are illusory. We call truth that element within you which exists now, will exist tomorrow when you disappear, which existed even before your birth and will exist when you die; will exist in your youth, in your old age; which exists when you are at the climax of your fame and when you fall into the abyss of indignity, which exists in every situation – in *every* situation, no situation making any difference to its existence. Only that we call truth, all the rest is illusory.

So what is the difference between an illusion and a dream? For Eastern wisdom, the collective dream is called the world and the personal world is called a dream. The collective dream is the world and the personal world is a dream – and truth is absent from both of them.

But let us look into it further. Nothing seems to be indestructible – have you ever seen an indestructible thing? Nothing appears to be indestructible; everything appears to be destructible, everything is transitory. Nothing crosses the limits of time into the timeless, nothing transcends time; everything withers away in time. Sooner or later everything withers away, the duration does not matter – in time everything is annihilated.

Have you ever seen an indestructible object, one which will never wither away? We cannot see such a thing in the outer world because the medium itself is not indestructible, the eyes through which we see will perish. The indestructible cannot be seen through the destructible. This is a simple fact, that the indestructible cannot be seen through a destructible medium. The eyes cannot see things higher than themselves. The eyes can see within their limit – the eyes perish, hence one can only see the perishable. Ears perish, hence one can only hear the perishable. Hands perish, hence one can only touch the perishable. How can a hand touch the imperishable? *How* can it touch the imperishable?

An imperishable medium is needed in order to search for the imperishable; a perishable medium will not do for the imperishable, and all the sense organs of our body are perishable. So the sage says that the journey toward the imperishable is the journey within, where sense organs have no use. The capacity to see without eyes, without light, to hear without ears, to touch without hands, exists within.

These visions, sounds and feelings can be experienced within, without the help of our perishable organs. But is that which is not known through the sense organs necessarily imperishable? – because the visions seen within may be visible today, but they can still disappear tomorrow.

A friend came yesterday and said that on the first day of meditation a great light appeared within, but on the second day it did not appear. Certainly this light which appeared and disappeared cannot be imperishable – that which once existed and then was lost was only a form.

I told him that whether the light is seen or not, the one thing that is eternal in both of these situations is the seer, the watcher. The watcher watches both the presence of light and the absence of light: it exists in both situations.

Inner experiences are not necessarily imperishable, because they may exist today and disappear tomorrow. But one quality is always there: the knower, the watcher, that which is eternal. That is the imperishable within us. If we recognize that, we can recognize the imperishable element in the world. Other than that, all is perishable.

Once you were a child, now your childhood has gone, but the one who was experiencing this childhood still exists within. You were young, now your youth has gone, but the one who was experiencing this youth is still within. Now you are old, the old age will go, but the one who is experiencing this old age will still be within. The one who is experiencing all three of these – childhood, youth and old age – seems to have permanence; everything else comes and goes. The witnessing self watches joy and sorrow, dignity and indignity; this watcher remains – all the rest withers away.

If you have even a small glimpse of this witnessing self you can know that this witness has witnessed birth and will also witness death; this way you will have found the eternal thread. With the attainment of this thread, this understanding, the existence at once becomes eternal; with this recognition of the eternal thread we attain the vision that can recognize all that is eternal and all that is transitory. Then all forms become transitory and the formless hidden behind them is seen as eternal.

A fact is a form, truth is formless. That is why religion gives a more penetrating definition of truth, one which is more pervasive than the scientific definition of a fact.

Brahman, the ultimate reality, is truth. It is infinite and the abode of knowing. "It is truth" means it is imperishable, "it is infinite," means it is limitless, because whatsoever has a limit will perish. Actually, disintegration begins with the very existence of any limits. The boundary itself starts disintegrating. Because when you relate with others there are boundaries, and this is where the friction lies. If your body were limitless, then no death would be possible because a limitless body would mean that nothing is left outside of it, outside of your body. So how would it die? Where would death come from? There would be no diseases, no forerunners of death, because nothing other than you would exist.

The body decays because there are so many things outside of the body and therefore there is friction every moment. Scientists say that the body of human beings could live for hundreds of years but it decays just because of this friction, this struggle. Just as iron decays because it rusts and the wind that blows weakens the trees, or the sunshine...all around there is a struggle and the hits on your body wear it out. It becomes exhausted after seventy years. Death simply means that your body has succumbed to the impacts on its boundaries.

The finite naturally becomes exhausted; it cannot be indestructible, because this struggling and warfare from outside its boundaries are a regular feature. The friction is continuous. If we were to freeze a particular body, freeing it of all its struggles and frictions, we could preserve this body for thousands and thousands of years. There is no problem in it, because death only occurs because of this outer friction. But even then, after thousands of years, it would become exhausted. After all, it has a limit. Its duration may be lengthy, but it cannot be eternal.

This is why we say that *brahman*, the ultimate reality, is infinite – without limit, without boundaries. Only that which has no boundary can be the whole, and that which has an end, a boundary, does so because of the other, not because of itself.

Your house ends where the other's house begins. If there were no other houses on the earth you wouldn't need to build a fence around your house, the whole earth would be your house. A fence is needed because of your neighbors; limitations and boundaries come into being because of the existence of others.

If the divine is the whole, it can only be without limits. All that which is not whole cannot be indestructible, because any limitation carries disintegration, destruction within itself, any limitation carries death. This is why the *brahman* is called the truth, the infinite and the abode of knowing.

The greatest experience for humans is that of knowing. This will be difficult to understand. One person might say the greatest experience is that of love, another might say that the greatest experience is that of bliss, or something else, but in fact the greatest is knowing – without which love cannot be felt, without which bliss cannot be felt. Knowing transcends both; without it neither love nor bliss can be known. Knowing can exist without love and bliss, but love and bliss have no existence without knowing. So the sages have called the divine "the abode of knowing."

Jesus has said, "God is love." This is very significant: "God is love." This definition is because of a specific situation; its purpose is quite different. It is just to reassure you that the divine is love so that you may hope for benevolence, help; that you are not alone and helpless. Ask for love and it will be bestowed upon you. Jesus defines God as love so that a person can be reassured.

I too say that God is love, or love is God, just because to say "God is knowing" serves no purpose. We cannot relate with "knowing"; with "knowing" a distance, a gap between ourselves and the knowing always remains. It is difficult to touch it, there is no bridge between this knowing and ourselves. That is the reason why we say God is love.

Certainly God is love, but that is not the ultimate definition. The ultimate definition is as the sage says: "God is the abode of knowing." "God is love" is a situational definition keeping man in mind, for the use of man, because knowing has no use, no charm, even though it is the truest definition, the most right definition.

Some have said God is bliss, the abode of bliss – this is also a situational definition. Man is in so much suffering that unless God is bliss no journey is possible; if it were not so why would you ever seek the divine?

Buddha's philosophy was uprooted from India within five hundred years; the reason was that Buddha did not give any situational definitions. Buddha said that it is all *shunya*, emptiness and void. No one wants to go toward emptiness. In fact one would avoid going there, avoid the danger. Emptiness…what will you do there?

Whenever Buddha was asked, "Is God bliss?" – he would say, "No, there is only an absence of suffering, an absence of sorrow, that is all."

This does not inspire you to go in search for godliness. It is good that there is no sorrow, but this is not enough reason to start the journey. Man is in distress, deep distress, hence the situational definition that God is bliss.

But this is not the absolute definition. If we are not taking human beings into consideration then the exact definition is: God is the abode of knowing, pure knowing.

The Upanishads were never popular with the masses because of these absolute definitions, because people cannot relate to absolute definitions. The Bible penetrates deeper into man than the Upanishads. Although the Bible stands nowhere in comparison with the Upanishads, but because its situational definition is very close to man, it has its utility. A sun may be burning far, far away, billions of miles away, but it is of no use to us. Just a small lamp becomes useful because you have to walk here on the earth. You have to walk here, taking steps in the darkness, so why bother about a sun which is far away? It may be there, but it doesn't help you to walk even an inch on a dark night. Your lamp may not be the sun, yes, your lamp is very small, but it helps you to take some steps and to walk on the path, and these small steps may lead you to the sun where all lamps can be discarded.

But the Upanishads give the ultimate definition, because at the time when the Upanishads were born people were neither in so much distress as to be consoled by bliss, nor so helpless as to be consoled by love. Man was quite innocent and content in himself. The ultimate and absolute definition was possible in those days: that God is the abode of knowing.

And this pure knowing is truth, it is indestructible.

What is not destroyed, even as the mediums
of space,

time and objects are destroyed,
is avinashi, the indestructible.

That which will always remain, even if time and space were to disappear, even if all matter and the universe were to disappear, that which is the essential core of all isness is called *avinashi*, the indestructible.

12

Love Is Freedom

The eternal consciousness,
which is beyond creation and destruction,
is called knowing.
The consciousness which fills and pervades
the whole universe –
like clay in things made of clay,
like gold in things made of gold,
and like yarn in things made of yarn
– is called the infinite.
The joyful consciousness,
the oceanic bliss without limit,
that which is the essential nature of all joy,
is bliss.

The sage has called the ultimate existence, the *brahman*, the absolute, the imperishable one – knowledge, knowing. But it has nothing to do with what we call knowledge. If we can rightly understand what *we* call knowledge, then it will be easy to understand what the sage calls knowledge.

The first thing is: that our knowledge is always about some object of knowing; just knowing, pure knowing never happens to us. We always attain to knowledge *about* some object; just the knowing, the pure phenomenon of knowing never happens to us. We know a tree, a man, a stone in the street, the sun in the sky; whenever we know, we know something as an object. Pure knowing is never experienced.

The sages call the knowing of objects impure knowledge, because in it the emphasis is on the object, not on the knowing itself. When we look at the sun in the sky, the sun becomes our focus, not the phenomenon of perception, of knowing.

If we were deprived of all objects our knowledge would disappear at once because it has no existence without these objects. It means that this knowledge does not depend on us, it depends on the objects. If all the objects were removed and there was only a void around us our knowledge would disappear. We have not known knowledge rooted in itself; our knowledge is rooted in objects. This is a very simple conclusion: with the removal of all objects, our knowledge will also vanish. This is amazing – it means that this knowledge does not depend on us, it depends on the objects we experience. This is the state of our knowledge.

The sage does not mean this kind of knowing when he says, "*Brahman* is knowing," because knowledge which depends on others the sages call ignorance. If you haven't the freedom to be the master of your own knowledge, then where else can you have freedom and mastery?

This knowledge of ours is related to all our other experiences. All our experiences are like this knowledge. Can you remain in the state of love when there is no one to be loved? Can you still love in the absence of your beloved? You may think you can, but it is possible only when you at least bring your beloved into your imagination, otherwise not. This imagination of the object will help, but you cannot be loving on your own, so how can this love be your intrinsic nature? This love is dependent on others.

That is why lovers become the worst slaves on earth – although love should bring the mastery of one's self, love should be your ultimate freedom because it is the greatest treasure. But we do not know this treasure. What we call love is always dependent on others. It becomes such a dependence that it becomes slavery.

Love is freedom, so our love, and the love talked about by Jesus or Buddha as freedom, are quite different things.

We become aware of beauty when we see a flower, we become aware of beauty when we see the setting sun – but are we aware of the beauty which is not dependent on objects, which is direct and pure beauty? No, we have not known such beauty. All our experiences are other-oriented, and we are the sum total of these experiences.

So do we have our own existence, our own individuality, or are we only a collection, the sum total of a few experiences which depend on others? If flowers don't bloom, beauty vanishes for us. If there are no objects, our knowledge vanishes. If there is no beloved, love vanishes for us.

Whatsoever we have, we have received it from others. Our existence is borrowed. That is why we stand begging before others our whole life – because we are afraid all the time that if others refuse to sustain us, we will slip away and disappear.

When your beloved dies you are not pained because of his or her death, you are pained because it is the death of your own love; you have never known a love which is there even without the beloved. When you lose wealth the pain is not due to this loss, it is due to the fact that along with the wealth your reality as a rich man is going. If you take away the scriptures of a learned man, you are not only taking away the scriptures, along with it his very knowledge is going. That's why a pundit, a scholar, values his books more than his head, he values the book above his own existence – he bows down to his scriptures. If his foot happens to touch the book, he is scared. If his knowledge is so dependent on this book, this is not knowledge.

So the first thing is: all our experiences are borrowed – we ourselves are borrowed. If our every experience is taken away from us we would vanish like a machine whose every part is separated and removed. A machine is nothing but the sum total of its parts. And he who is only such a collection will not be able to know the soul which is the ultimate freedom.

Try to understand this knowing which the sage calls *brahmagyan*.

The first thing is that it is not dependent on the other, on the object, on some thing. When knowledge depends on an object it is a relationship, when it does not depend on the object it is a state of being. Try to understand the difference between a state of being and a relationship.

You say, "I love you." Now, this love will disappear if you are not there because this love is a relationship, it needs two entities; a relationship is between two entities. If one of the two is removed, then the relationship also disappears. You cannot build a bridge using just one bank of a river, the other bank is also needed. The bridge is a relationship between the two banks.

But Buddha is as full of love even when he is in solitude sitting under a tree with nobody around him, as when thousands of people are visiting him. It makes absolutely no difference to his love. His love is not a relationship, it is his state of being. Buddha is not attached to any person, love is his very nature. His love will shower even in a deserted place, like when a flower blooms on an untrodden path and spreads its fragrance. The flower does not wait for someone to pass by, it just spreads its fragrance. It is like a lamp alight in the darkness: nobody is there to see it but still it goes on giving light because it has no relationship with the other; spreading light is its very nature.

The sun was shining the same way when we did not exist on the earth. It will shine the same way when we are not here. There is no relationship between the shining of the sun and our looking at it. To shine is the very nature of the sun.

A man like Buddha is always full of love – in fact, only a buddha is full of love – because this love cannot be taken away; even alone, he is full of love. This love is not a bridge, not a relationship, this love is a state of being, a state of consciousness.

When the divine, existence, is called knowing, when the universal self is called knowing, it means knowing is its very nature, not a relationship.

So the sage says:

The eternal consciousness,
which is beyond creation and destruction,
is called knowing.

A relationship is born and it dies, but the intrinsic nature is neither born nor does it die. Today I have love for you, yesterday it was not there – but today it is. This love has a birth, but insanity begins when we want to make something that has a birth, eternal. That is insanity! Death is inevitable for anything which has a birth. The day it was born, it should have been realized that one day it would die. Preparations for the funeral procession are hidden in the trumpets of joy on the very day of birth. It is only a matter of time. A flower is blooming, and it is also the beginning of its withering away. Life is bound to death; if life is one end then death is the other. So a love which is born is bound to die; what is created will be destroyed as well.

Knowledge which is born…and it is born: you opened your eyes, there was a flower before your eyes; knowledge happened to you that there is a flower, that it is beautiful, that it is fragrant. This is a birth of knowledge. This knowledge will die. This flower will die and this knowledge about it will also die.

But the *brahman* is a knowing which is never born and never dies. That means it is not related to some object, it is its very intrinsic nature – it is eternal.

Zen masters ask their disciples to search for their original face: When you were not born, then what was your face? When you have passed away what will your face be? They make their disciples meditate over it. It is very difficult. What will you think? What will you meditate upon? They give you this meditation so that thinking takes you to no-thinking, because you cannot go on thinking the unthinkable. A moment will come when all your thinking has to stop.

Zen masters ask their disciples to meditate upon the sound of one hand clapping. The sound of one hand clapping is not possible – but they insist on it. If a meditator says that it is not possible, the master replies that the disciple should not bother about the possibility; he says that it is possible and that the disciple should first meditate for months upon the sound of one hand clapping – the possibility is not the question.

The meditator comes back again and again and reports that it is not possible; it has already been twenty-four hours. But the master replies that he should not worry about the possibility. "My question is: How does it sound?" He says, "Go and meditate."

Months pass – one's head starts feeling giddy, one's mind starts feeling dizzy, everything stops within. After thinking and thinking and thinking it appears to be sheer madness, but then a moment comes when it is clear that no further thinking is possible. Thinking stops for a moment and the meditator rushes to say, "I have heard the sound of one hand clapping."

As soon as thinking stops, the intrinsic nature of the self is revealed.

Search for the face which was there before your birth. It is not possible, because there was no face before birth – it is birth which gives birth to one's face also – and there will be no face after death, because death takes away the face.

Think! A moment comes after thinking and thinking and thinking when thinking stops, the chain is broken, and then what is seen is the original face – that which is your very nature, that which existed before your birth and that which will be even after your death.

The eternal consciousness, which is beyond creation and destruction, is called knowing. Here knowing is equated to consciousness, not to the act of knowledge, because knowledge is always of some object. Here knowing means consciousness, enlightenment. The word *knowledge* has been contaminated, because we always tie it to the phenomenon of knowing some object.

If you are introduced as a man of great knowledge, immediately there will be a query about what is the subject of your knowledge.

If you say, "Nothing in particular, I am just a man of knowledge, that is all," it will not be convincing to anybody. What does it mean? What do you know? They will want to know whether you know medical science or economics or philosophy or theology – in what subject are you a man of knowledge? But if you say, "No, I am just a man of knowledge," this will appear to be a meaningless statement because for us knowledge always pertains to something, it is in relation to some object.

This sort of knowledge has no relation with the knowing spoken of in the sutra as a definition of *brahman*, the ultimate reality. That knowing is the eternal consciousness, beyond birth and destruction. "Awareness" is the right word for it – or better than that is "alertness," just the pure perceptivity – because awareness too appears to be related to something. No, there is just a lighted lamp with no object to be illuminated, only the lamp burning clearly – nothing around to be illuminated. Nothing is being illuminated, there is only the light. I am saying this as an example so that you may conceive what is meant by knowing.

The consciousness which fills and pervades
the whole universe –
like clay in things made of clay,
like gold in things made of gold,
and like yarn in things made of yarn
– is called the infinite.

This consciousness is not confined by the boundaries of a person. We are all sitting here – our differences are due to our bodies, not due to the consciousness.

If we light thousands of earthen lamps in this room the differences will be of the clay pots, or of the oil, or in the wick, but the light will be one and the same. We can light thousands of lamps here and every lamp can be different in structure, in form, in shape, the oil or the wick; all these may be different, but can you differentiate the light, which light belongs to which lamp? The light will be one, all-pervading – but the lamps can differ. Our differences are the same as these lamps. The matter of the body, the shape, the fuel in the body, the wick, all these may differ but the consciousness – the light within us – is one.

The inner journey, by and by, leads us to oneness, and the outer journey leads us to diversity. So the sage says: "That which permeates like gold in golden things and like clay in clay things, is one."

Now even scientists agree to it. They did not agree fifty years ago because then science believed that one thing cannot be converted into another, and those who believed that such a conversion was possible were thought to be ignorant. In the West these people were called alchemists, and in the East they were called the seekers of the *paras* stone, the "philosopher's stone" which turns base metal into gold. They were engaged in seeking a stone which can turn base metal into gold by touch. Alchemists were also engaged in seeking for the secret of turning base metals into precious metals.

But for the last two hundred years science has believed that this is all madness, that it is just not possible. How can iron be changed into gold? – there seems to be no way. Those people who made these claims were thought to be either fools or cheats who were trying to deceive people. If they could turn iron into gold there must be some trickery involved. Iron cannot be turned into gold, so there must be some deception and cheating. Things came to a point where, even when authentic evidence became available, still those people were not trusted.

A great German thinker and scientist was engaged for years in trying to prove that alchemy was a farce. Hasenhoff was his name. He was sitting at his door one morning when a man came to him and said, "I have heard that you have no faith in alchemy, but I can turn iron into gold right now."

Hasenhoff said, "You seem to be an interesting man, but iron cannot be turned into gold. You have gone mad, I have been studying this for years and it is impossible."

The man said, "Will you trust me if I myself show you?" He opened a small box and said, "This is the thing, its slightest touch will turn iron into gold."

Hasenhoff could not believe it at all; he thought: "This man must be mad. How can iron be turned into gold?" He had been studying alchemy for years. Even then, he felt the thing with his hand and scratched it with his nails. Hasenhoff then asked the man to come back the next day so that he could ascertain that there was no trickery involved. He would then arrange to get some iron and call for an expert to test it.

The man never returned, and Hasenhoff repented and grieved his whole life because he had later touched some iron with his nails, and the iron had turned into gold. That man never turned up, but the stuff that had collected under his nails with that small scratch turned iron into gold.

Hasenhoff has written in his autobiography: "I can wait for that man for lives and lives. Now I am in a difficulty. Even if it is a trick, it is wonderful. Anyway, now there was no way for any trickery, because only a small amount of scratched-out particles was with me and even that turned my iron into gold – pure gold."

All kinds of tests were carried out to their satisfaction, but then they began to doubt Hasenhoff. Was he tricking them? Nobody was ready to accept his version, and how could he prove it? He said: "I myself cannot believe it, but it happened. And now nobody is ready to believe me."

People wrote: "It seems that Hasenhoff has gone mad due to his excessive investigations about alchemy. He has been deceived. Although the man is honest and sincere, above suspicion, still it seems he has in some way fallen into some self-deception; his mind has become confused. Such pure gold – it is impossible."

Now, during these last twenty years, science has come to the conclusion that there is no basic difficulty in doing this. The alchemists were on the right track, the seekers of the philosopher's stone were right because science has discovered that everything is made of the same basic stuff; only the quantity of electrons, protons and neutrons differs. For example, a certain element may contain one hundred electrons and another may contain one hundred and one, but the basic nature of the electrons which constitute the two elements is the same. So if we can separate one electron from the element made of the one hundred and one electrons, it will change into a one-hundred-electron element.

Gold and iron do not differ in their basic nature, they differ only in the quantity of their electrons. If the number of the electrons of an atom of iron were changed, you could have an atom of gold. Or if we change the number of electrons in the gold atom, it can turn into an iron atom.

Science has reached to such depths that it has found that the nature of matter is one, although forms differ. This nature is energy, it is the same in all matter. However science has not yet found any technique to turn iron into gold cheaply because the research for changing atoms is too costly as yet; it is more costly than the original gold. In the future we may find a cheaper process, but that is another matter; we are not concerned with that. Even if a cheaper process is never found, one thing is certain: iron can be turned into gold.

Any object can change into another object; not only into an object but into energy too. That is the secret of atomic energy – to transform matter into energy; hence the atomic explosion. With the splitting of one small atom, tremendous energy is released.

The sages of the Upanishads have always said that the atoms of consciousness are also not different, they are the same; our forms on the surface are different, but consciousness within is one.

So as we go deeper and deeper within, we move away from our external personalities; we are eliminated more and more and the universal is more and more. One dies exactly at one's own center. To go within is to dissolve into one's own death, because when we vanish as a personality, we disappear as the lamp and remain as the light. That light is limitless.

The consciousness which fills and pervades the whole universe –like clay in things made of clay, like gold in things made of gold, and like yarn in things made of yarn – is called the infinite. Infinite, because although it resides within limits, forms, it is not limited. It is in gold but does not end in gold, it is within you but does not end in you – it goes on expanding, and expanding – its very quality is unending expansion, it is all-pervading, universal.

Understand it like a vast ocean, and we are the fish in this ocean. A fish is born in the ocean and dies in the ocean; the fish is created out of ocean water and it merges back into the ocean water. But the fish, when it exists, exists just as a person does: it then disappears into the ocean and again takes form out of the ocean – it *is* ocean.

Or if it is a little difficult to understand about a fish, take the example of an iceberg floating in the sea. It appears to be quite separate. It raises its head, and it appears to be quite different from the water, totally solid – but even then it is the sea, and as soon as it melts it will disappear.

This melting process has been called the dropping of the ego; as we melt, the ego dissolves and we become one with the vast ocean. The iceberg may think itself different but it is not. Any difference we feel is due to our ignorance; our wisdom becomes the declaration of our oneness.

This all-pervading infinite has been called *brahman*, godliness. This word *brahman* is very precious; it means something which is expanding endlessly. *Brahman* means the infinite expansion. *Expansion* and *brahman* have the same root. *Brahman* means that which goes on expanding, goes on expanding; there is no limit to its expansion.

No word like *brahman* exists in any other language in the world. It cannot be translated. *Brahman* is not connected with "lord" or "god"; there is no connection. That is why Shankara has dared to say that even God is a part of the illusion – even God – because your God too has shape and form. Brahma the creator, Vishnu the sustainer and Mahesh the destroyer – all have forms; they are also parts of the illusion. Figure and form belong to the illusion. The formless beyond all these is *brahman* – it is a name for expansion, for infinite expansion pervading the whole of creation; never ceasing, it goes on expanding. Hence, it is infinite.

The joyful consciousness,
the oceanic bliss without limit,
that which is the essential nature of all joy,
is bliss.

Try to understand it: *The joyful consciousness...*

Whenever you experience happiness, you do not experience that *you* are happiness; you feel that you are someone to whom this happiness has happened. Happiness is a happening to you – it is not your nature, because one cannot lose that which is one's nature – but as it is you go on losing your happiness. Your happiness in the morning changes into sorrow by the evening.

So happiness comes, sorrow comes, but they come to *you*. They happen to you and then leave; these are just happenings. So when *brahman* is called the embodiment of bliss, it means that happiness is not happening to it but is its intrinsic nature; *brahman* is always happy, it is happiness itself.

When happiness is our intrinsic nature then it is called bliss.

When bliss is only a happening, it is called happiness.

A happening means it is something foreign or alien. It happens to us, it comes from the outside, it happens outside our house. However much we may think that we are one with it, we can never really be.

Diogenes, a Greek mystic, wandered around naked. Once someone asked him, "Why did you drop wearing clothes?"

Diogenes replied, "I tried my best to hold onto them but I could not, so I dropped them. I tried hard to cling to wearing clothes, to make them become a part of me, but I could not. Then I thought: What I cannot become must be only an outside phenomenon, so it should be dropped. Nakedness is my nature and clothes are only a covering on the surface; they may have been there but I have always been naked within."

Everybody is naked inside their clothes; there is no other way to be. Clothes may deceive others into thinking that you are not naked, but they cannot deceive you. And yet they *do* deceive you. This is amazing: people wearing clothes think that they are not naked – but clothes only belong to the outside.

So Diogenes says, "I did my best to hold onto wearing clothes, but ultimately I found that I could not; they remained on the outside, they remained separate. There was no way to make them a part of me, and that which is not part of me, what need is there to try to believe that it is mine? Hence I dropped them."

When Alexander marched to India, Diogenes was lying by the side of the road. He saw Diogenes and asked him, "You seem to be so happy, so full of joy, and yet you possess nothing?" Alexander could not understand that you can be joyous without any reason. How can you be happy for no reason?

The sages say that the day you are happy for no reason is the day of bliss. But our logic says: "You have nothing – no wife, no son, no wealth, no palace, no comforts; you are lying naked on the road, on the earth, and yet you seem to be so happy! What is the reason?"

Diogenes replied, "I could not be happy as long as there was a reason for my happiness. Then I thought to leave this seeking for the reasons for happiness and to seek that happiness which exists without reasons, that which cannot be taken away from me."

Whatsoever has a reason for its existence can be taken away, because the reason itself can be taken away.

For example, there is a woman and you are happy because of her – but she may die tomorrow or any day, and thus she can be snatched away. And even if she doesn't die she may leave you and the relationship ends; then your happiness will be gone. Or, for instance, you are wealthy today, but tomorrow all your wealth may disappear; then your happiness will be lost. Even if your wealth continues to be with you, your happiness will leave you anyway because whatsoever is continuously available no longer creates happiness.

Happiness will not last long whenever there is a reason for it. Happiness which is dependent on some outside reason is momentary. But is there such a thing as happiness without a reason? Happiness for no reason is what we call bliss. If there is bliss and no reason for it, this means that it is not coming from the outside, it is coming from within. If there is bliss but there is a reason for it, this means that it is coming from without. That is why we depend on the outside – we depend on others. Anybody can take our happiness away, anybody can take it away at any moment. And how can you be the master of that which comes from the outside?

But there is another dimension also – where the bliss comes from within, where the flow is completely reversed.

Radha is the name of Krishna's beloved. The name is a reversal of the syllables of *dhara*, a current, a flow. This name is very interesting, because there is no mention of Radha at all in the story of the life of Krishna, not even a word. No ancient scripture mentions Radha, no episode relates to Radha. It was much later – one could say, in more recent years – that Radha was first mentioned, that Radha's name was added to the story. Certainly there is a mention of a friend in the story of the life of Krishna, but she has no name, she has been left unnamed. It was knowingly done that she was not given a name, because she was that friend who is beyond name and form. Even her figure has not been talked of, how she looked, her face – nothing.

In the middle ages the saints called her Radha. They called her so knowingly, because this was a reversal of the syllables of *dhara*, a current, a flow.

There is a flow of bliss which comes from without – that is *dhara* – and when the bliss comes from within it is *radha*. Krishna can love only this type of Radha, the one who is flowing from within; Krishna has no relationship with a Radha who comes from the outside.

When bliss starts flowing from within, when it becomes this Radha, then you have found that friend who is never lost, who cannot be lost.

The joyful consciousness, the oceanic bliss without limit, that which is the essential nature of all joy... When every cause for happiness has been left behind and when everything has gone but still a happiness remains, that happiness is the nature of *brahman*. This has been called bliss.

We do not know bliss, we are not aware of bliss, because bliss can be known only when *dhara*, the flow from the outside, becomes *radha*, the flow from within. Then a new dimension has opened within.

So Diogenes says, "I am happy because I am happiness, I am not happy for some reason."

Alexander felt jealous: it is an ultimate event in this world when an emperor is jealous of a beggar. And Alexander even said, "If I am born again I would not like to be Alexander, I would like to be Diogenes; I too am seeking for this bliss."

And Diogenes said to Alexander, "Seeking! You will never get anything by seeking. Stop here. There is enough space, relax beside me. I have achieved it without going anywhere – right here! Where are you rushing to? There is enough space – come and lie down here beside me."

Alexander replied, "It is difficult right now. I have set out to conquer the world."

Diogenes said, "It is not only difficult right now, it will always be difficult for one who has set out to conquer the world because the journey of conquest is the journey to sorrow. If you want to conquer something, conquer yourself; in conquering the other is hidden your own defeat. As you go on conquering others, you lose yourself within. Leave others alone, because while you are struggling with others you are defeating yourself within. Conquer yourself, know yourself."

Alexander replied, "I will stay with you for a while when I return."

Diogenes said, "You may not return, and you are losing this moment – this moment, which is certainly here now – and yet you are thinking of a moment which has not yet come."

And as destiny would have it, Alexander could not return. He died in the middle of his journey when returning from India.

No journey of conquest is ever completed; death comes in between. We have undertaken many journeys of conquest, in many lives, and each time they remain incomplete. Death creates a discontinuity. Again we start on a journey of conquest and again it remains incomplete. Death interrupts again and again.

Only one conquest can be completed.

Only one bliss can be achieved, and that bliss does not come from outside, it is present within, at this moment.

Enough for today.

Now get ready for the meditation.

13

You Are More than You Think

That which is truth, knowing, infinity and bliss,
and which is unchanging through the mediums
of time,
space and matter is tat, that,
or paramatma, the universal self.
That which is separate from thou and that,
is subtle like the sky, its sole nature is just being;
this we call the param brahman, the ultimate
reality.

Those who are bound to the I, the ego, find it very difficult to reach up to thou, godliness. How can anyone who is surrounded by the I go to the feet of thou? Surrendering will be very difficult.

That is why the sage says to make thou the center and I the periphery. He also says that pure, conscious existence has the nature of thou. It is a great leap from I to thou; perhaps no other leap is greater than this. To leave your I is so difficult – it is not like taking off your clothes, it is more like peeling off your skin. To drop the I or to discard it is very difficult because in this very attempt the I raises its head again and again.

And who is it who will drop this I? Whosoever drops the I, is the I. So how to drop the I? Whatever device is used, it is still in the hands of the I. But that which appears to be nearly impossible becomes possible if you have courage. Try to understand this courage, then you will be able to understand this jump.

Whosoever endeavors to eliminate the I will be in trouble, because to eliminate it is also a doing, and every doing strengthens the doer. Whosoever desires to drop the I will be in trouble, because in that very effort to drop it you are acknowledging its existence. Whatever you desire to drop, you are also accepting that it is more powerful than you are. You only avoid that of which you are afraid.

So neither can you eliminate the I because elimination is a doing, nor can you avoid the I because where can you escape to in order to avoid it? Whatever you avoid always chases you. Whatever you are afraid of you run away from and it becomes a continuous shadow.

Then what to do with the I so that the jump toward thou becomes possible? The only way is neither to run away, nor to try to eliminate, nor to try to avoid it but to watch it, to recognize it, to know it and to get acquainted with it.

There is only one way to destroy a shadow; a sword cannot cut a shadow – or can it? A sword will break, but still the shadow cannot be destroyed. If it had really existed it could have been removed but it is nonexistent, it only appears to exist. Can you escape from your shadow by running away from it? The faster you run the faster the shadow follows you because it is *your* shadow – where will you escape to, where will you run to?

There is only one way to get rid of the shadow and that is to know the shadow for what it is, then you can be free. Neither removing it nor escaping from it is needed, because as soon as you know the shadow to be a shadow no fear remains, no concern to eliminate it remains. In knowing the shadow you know that it does not exist, it only appears to exist.

There is only one way to be free from the I and that is to come to know the I so deeply that it appears to be a shadow, and at that very moment you are freed of it. That is why people practicing humbleness can never reach to thou.

Humility is a refined form of the ego. The more refined it is, the more dangerous it is, and subtle too. That is why the ego of a person we call humble, virtuous, increases in him and peeps out every moment. Humility is an ornament of the ego, the most beautiful ornament ego can wear. Humility is a beautiful mask which the ego can display.

Humility is never straightforward. In fact, when the ego has no mask it is more simple and straightforward than humility. Bad men are more genuine and clear than good men because bad men are straightforward egoists, while good men are indirect egoists. Their ego is behind many layers – very refined, polished. An ordinary man's ego is unpolished and uncut like a raw diamond, whereas the so-called good man's ego is like a cut diamond – cut and polished, shining. It has a good shine, a brightness, but the sparkle in the ego is a poison. Whether you polish your ego or hide it or avoid it or try to escape from it, you are not freed from it. Come to know your ego, go within and recognize what this ego is. So don't be in a rush, don't make any judgments.

We make the mistake in our lives of making judgments before we have the experience, and we begin from those judgments. We are like children solving sums, who first look at the answers in the back of the book and then start from there. Then they never learn the method – why should they? They already have the answers. Then what need is there to learn methods?

But this answer in the last pages of the book is not your answer, it is borrowed, it will not transform your life. Someone who does not learn the method and does not draw his own conclusions lives a borrowed life, and all of your conclusions are borrowed.

You read in the scriptures that the ego is bad. This conclusion is not yours – it is in the scriptures. You don't even know what this ego is; whether it is good or bad can be decided on later. You are unacquainted with what it is, you have not had even a glimpse of what it is but you will still have a conclusion about it.

'Anger is bad' is a conclusion taken from the scriptures.

From the scriptures you come to know everything that is good and bad, but still you remain the same as you are, even though you appear to know everything.

People come to me and say that they know all this, there is nothing which they do not know – but now transformation has become more difficult because they think they know everything. They have borrowed this knowledge, now there is no room to learn and therefore there is no possibility of transformation.

So keep this sutra in mind: knowledge which does not transform you is borrowed. Your conclusions are not yours because your knowledge is not your own, it is not *your* experience. It is all stale, dead and rotten.

Try to know your ego and don't make any judgments, that this is good or this is bad; look at it directly. And if you cannot even see your own ego you will never be able to see the thou or *that*, because the ego is your outer layer and thou is your center. How can one who has not yet come to know his ego know thou or *that*?

So first know this I and as you come to know this I it will disperse. The fire of this knowing reduces the I into ashes. The I vanishes like smoke, as if it never was, it vanishes like a shadow. As soon as it vanishes the seeker stands facing the thou. But the sage says this thou is also not yet the ultimate because it exists in relation to the I, which existed before; this thou has been founded on the memory of the I.

Even if the situation changes our memory does not, it needs time to change. The memory of the I has come from many, many past lives. So even if the ego becomes a shadow today our language will not change, because language is created only around the I. We will still speak the same language. Although the ego has been proved to be nonexistent and has withered away and is now known to be only a shadow, still our language was born around that shadow; a new language is not going to be created in a day. Our way of seeing was always from that position.

If a blind man regains his sight he will not be able to drop his cane all at once. Even if he has regained his sight he will still walk with the cane for a little while because he has been associating with it for such a long time, and now it is difficult to lose his dependency on it. Although the cane has now become useless, it will take time for him to find full confidence in his eyes and to leave the cane behind.

Even if the I disappears, our language and memory will still move around it. This is why the first glimpse of reality will be in the language of thou. In the first experience of reality there will also be a glimpse of deep love. The reason behind it is that we have always been seeking for love which we never found; we have been searching for the beloved whom we have never met. We have searched for many lives and failed. So when for the first time godliness manifests itself within and the ultimate consciousness permeates, it appears like a meeting with the beloved; that the temple we were looking for is here, that the door we were searching for is just in front of us.

So the first language will be of I and of love. The devotee has always spoken this language. But the sage says that it is not the ultimate language. When the blind man throws his cane away, when the memory of the I vanishes, then how will you be able to call it thou? Who is there to now call it thou? What meaning will there be left in thou? When the I is gone, thou will become useless, it will become meaningless.

That is why the second jump happens from thou to *that*; in this jump thou disappears, in this jump godliness manifests in the form of *that*. Then we can say neither I nor thou – we say *that*. In this *that*, not even a trace of the I remains. Not even that much is left which we once called thou. The I disappears like a line drawn on water. With this, the thou too disappears because it is only the other aspect of the I. Now only *that* remains. *That* is the purest assertion, now no impression of the memory or of the past is casting its shadow. *That* is quite unattached and indifferent.

That has these four attributes:

truth, knowing, infinity and bliss...

...which we talked of in the morning. The sage calls them attributes. "Attributes" are descriptions of how *that* is recognized, or the way in which we recognize *that*. These are two different things.

If the sage says, it is *truth, knowing, infinity and bliss*, that will also create limitations. If he says *that* is infinite, this definition too will make *that* finite.

Try to understand this. It is a very subtle perception – very subtle, minute and delicate. When one says that the divine is indefinable, one has already defined it. This statement looks contradictory but it is not, because you have defined it as being indefinable. You have accepted this much definition – "It is indefinable." That is also a definition, you have said something – and you have said much. If it is right, you have defined it completely. If this is true, that it is indefinable, then this becomes the definition. What else could a definition be?

What does a definition mean? A definition means saying something real about something. Even if we only say this much – that a definition is not possible – we have defined it. If we just say that truth is its definition, we are binding it to a limit; even though we are using a beautiful word, *truth*, it is still a limit. When we say that it is truth, we are drawing a line to exclude the untruth and thereby separating it from the truth. And we are binding truth by this dividing line; untruth falls outside and truth has to remain within that line.

The sage says that this is not correct because if untruth exists, it is also contained within the divine. Nothing can exist outside of *that*. And to say that *that* is the only truth is to give *that* a limit, a boundary. That is why some people have not said anything about *that* – only because to say anything is to commit a mistake. If we say it is knowing, we are drawing a boundary line. If we say it is infinite, which means it has no limit... But if we have come to know that it is infinite, it has then become finite.

Someone says that the ocean is unfathomable. What could that mean? Either this man has already been to the ocean's limits and has explored the whole ocean and found it unfathomable – which is an impossibility, because if there is no limit to its depth, how *could* he come to the conclusion that it is unfathomable? Has he reached its limit, has he explored the whole vastness of the ocean? And if he has, then it has a limit. And if he has not been that far then he should not call it unfathomable; he should only say that as far as he has been, no limit was found.

That is why the sage says "attributes." An attribute means: As far as I could go, I found the ocean to be unfathomable. But this is only my experience, how can I say this is the actual state of the ocean? It might be that the limit was only one foot ahead of where I finished exploring – this is not an impossibility in any way. I could not find a limit, but how can I exclude the possibility of the limit being just ahead of me? All that I know is knowledge, but how can I say that there is nothing more beyond *my* knowledge?

That is why the sage calls them attributes. "Attributes" means that we recognize that it is our perception, that to the extent of our knowing we accept that it is truth, it is knowing, it is infinite and it is bliss. We have found it to be so.

The sages have always taken care that should there be a mistake, it should fall on our part, on the human side. The sages have always consciously accepted that they can make a mistake, but there is no reason that their mistake is to be imposed on the divine.

Our minds work in totally contradictory ways. Whatever conclusions we draw, we immediately impose them on others. We do not understand that we are always using this one approach. A man appears to be handsome and we say, "He is handsome." We should restrict ourselves to saying, "He looks handsome *to me*" – just this much, this is enough. And if a man appears ugly, we should not say, "He is ugly"; it is enough to say, "He looks ugly *to me*, this is my feeling." To someone else he may be handsome. And if a man appears to me to be a saint, I should restrict myself to saying that "He appears to be a saint *to me*." He may not be a saint at all to others – and where is the way for anybody to know what he really is?

What you know from external appearances are your perceptions – your likings, your dislikings. You are present in them. But you immediately exclude yourself and impose your conclusions on others. Then the difficulty arises.

The sage says, these are attributes. Bliss too, he says, is an attribute, because you have been in so much distress for so many lives that the experience may have felt like bliss to you. It is like a man who is hungry for days and then gets a piece of dry bread. He says, "Ah! Today's food is so delicious and satisfying, just the ultimate in taste; there is nothing better." He is saying it for himself. He is simply saying that he had been hungry for a long time and in fact the taste of the food is due more to his hunger and less to the food. That is why someone who knows will say, "I am very hungry and that is why the food tastes so delicious." An attribute means that it is a perception.

There comes a moment when we are completely emptied: the I is completely eliminated, the thou is eliminated and our every experience is eliminated. Then what will we say? Will we call it the infinite? We call it infinite because whatever we had known previously was finite; compared to our previous experience *that* was infinite. What we knew before was sorrow, so in comparison this is bliss. What we knew before was only ignorance and in comparison to this it is knowing. What we knew before was untruth, in comparison this is truth. But when we completely disappear, how then will we define *that*?

Whenever Buddha was asked about the definition of *that* he remained silent, or he would say, "Inquire about something else." When Buddha would enter a town he would inform the people that he should not be asked eleven questions, and one of them included the definition of *brahman*. Many would ask

Buddha, "Are you unable to tell us because you don't know?"

Of course, you would start thinking from your own angle; if Buddha doesn't tell you he himself must not know. So many people would go away concluding that Buddha did not know and had not yet experienced it, hence his silence.

What they should have said is: "As we understand it, those who speak are the ones who know and those who do not speak don't know it. That's why we think that since Buddha is silent he may not know it himself." But no, instead they gave conclusions: "Buddha doesn't know it; that is why he is silent. How can he tell us when he himself does not know?" Many others drew the conclusion: "The experience is so profound that we would not understand, hence he does not speak. He will speak when we are worthy." Many thought, "These experiences don't exist and Buddha doesn't want to hurt us, hence he doesn't deny them but keeps silent."

But rarely would someone conclude that Buddha remains silent because he has transcended both the I and the thou and has reached the point from where the one who sees the attributes has disappeared; from that point onward nothing can be said about *brahman*.

So the sage says *that*, these attributes.

An attribute means something we perceive.

...which is unchanging through the mediums
of time,
space and matter...

There are two ways for change to happen in the world: one change happens in space, the other happens in time. Every change happens in time and space. You came here from your town – so two kinds of change happened: you left your town, you changed the space; and then it took time to reach here, thus you changed the time. You started in the morning, you reached here in the evening, you started from place *A* and arrived at place *B*. Two kinds of change happened, a change in time and a change in space.

Time and space are the bases for change, but time and space cannot make any change to the ultimate reality. What might be the reason for this? The only reason is that we live in time and space, while time and space themselves live in the ultimate reality; *that* has no possibility of leaving one place and reaching another because all space is within *that*, and *that* has no possibility of entering into the next year from this year because all of time is contained within *that*.

This is why we say the divine is beyond time and space, because even for time and space to exist, some "where" is needed – which also exists within the divine. We have defined God as isness, existence, or that which is, so if time also exists it can only be within God. Whatsoever exists can exist only within the divine. This is why time and space do not create any change in the divine.

For us there are three divisions of time: the present, the past and the future. For the divine, time is always the present. For us, here and there exist, but for the divine everything is here. For us, yesterday and tomorrow have a time gap, but for the divine everything is here and now; for the divine it is eternally so. So in the language of existence there are no other words except *here* and *now* as far as time and space are concerned.

What we mean by "God" is existence. Existence is called *that*. It contains both the I and the thou. The I and the thou are born in it and disappear in it also. That which is unchanging is called *that*. These two, thou and *that*, are also attributes.

The sage here is coming down step by step. First he says I is an attribute and thou represents the divine, and now he says thou is also an attribute, and finally so is *that*.

That which is separate from thou and that,
is subtle like the sky, its sole nature is just
being…

Just to exist is its nature – this is the *param brahman*, beyond the ultimate reality. This is actually the ultimate reality – this alone is! A jump has been taken from the I to the thou, then from the thou to *that*; now it has to be taken from *that* to the ultimate existence – where there remains no space even for *that*. Because when we say *that*, the gap still exists – the speaker is present, the finger which is pointing toward *that* is still present. We are still separate somewhere – maybe not in the form of the I, but we are still present. We may have known that the I does not exist and that thou does not exist, but the one who says this is still present.

Even this gap, even this small gap, is not acceptable to the mystics, even this much distance cannot be tolerated. This distance is unacceptable. One more jump – and this jump is to where there is not even *that*.

Buddha calls it the void, because nothing is left – neither I, nor thou, nor *that*. The Upanishads call it existence. Buddha calls it the void, because nothing is left of whatever we knew; the Upanishads call it existence, because whatever we knew was not there in the first place. Only that which truly is has remained. What was not has disappeared. All dreams have vanished and only that which is has remained. Now nothing remains that can be excluded from it. This is why it has been called param *brahman*, that which is even beyond *brahman*.

Up to now all of our definitions have pertained to *brahman*, they were definitions of *brahman*. Now the sage calls it that which is even beyond *brahman*, beyond the ultimate reality. He says, now drop this *brahman* also, and go beyond even this *brahman* which we have just discussed. Now leave even that which we have investigated so deeply; now we will talk about that which is beyond even all of this. It only means that now all words and principles have disappeared, now even the seeker and the sought have dissolved – now what is left?

The sage says: "Only that which now remains, exists." Call it *shunya*, the void, or call it *poorna*, fullness, or remain silent about it, or go on speaking about it for lifetimes. It is what we are searching for. There cannot be any rest without discovering it because unless we attain to it we will continue to die; death will happen again and again, suffering will continue. Unless we realize the space where whatever can perish has perished, death will be inevitable. After attaining to the beyond, to beyond the ultimate reality, then, the experience of deathlessness.

Life and death do not happen to that which is, they happen to that which we have created. The ego is our creation, of our own making; it takes birth and it dies. Consciousness is not our creation; it existed before we were born and will exist after we die. It never dies, it never takes birth.

Bokuju was a monk. As the priest in the temple, he offered flowers to Buddha's statue in the mornings. A few people had come to listen to him. In the lecture hall he said, "Today I want to tell you that this man called Buddha never existed. He never existed, it is all a great lie."

People were taken aback. They thought that Bokuju had gone mad, he was talking like a madman. He was a monk of Buddha's, and earlier they had seen him in the temple offering flowers to Buddha, worshipping Buddha's statue. They asked Bokuju, "Have you gone mad or are you joking? You have just now been worshipping him."

He replied, "I have been worshipping him, and in the evening too I will worship him, but I tell you this man never existed. I did not understand this man until now, that is why I thought that he had been born and that he had died; but now I know. You still think I am mad, but you have not heard one more thing. I can tell you now that I too was never born and I shall never die."

They were certain that he had gone mad. Buddha aside – *he* may or may not have been; that matter was twenty-five hundred years old and may be doubtful, he may not have existed – but Bokuju had just said, "I can tell you one more thing, that I was never born and I shall never die."

A few people stood up to leave and asked for his permission to go. Now his discourse was going beyond the limit.

Bokuju said, "Before you go, listen to the third thing also: I tell you that you were never born and you shall also never die."

If all others are right Bokuju is mad, and if Bokuju is right all others are mad. There is no other alternative. But all the wise men on earth say that Bokuju is right.

For that which is pure essence, pure existence, pure isness, life and death are no more than passing breezes. But life and death become so important to you because you don't know them. That which you know, the ego, is your creation and it trembles even in the slightest breeze; just a small breeze and the flame of the ego starts wavering: "Now I'm gone, now I'm gone!"

The laws of life are very strange. If there is the flame of a tiny lamp, then even a small breeze puts it out. But if it is a huge, burning fire, then a big storm will only strengthen it.

So if it is the ego which is facing the breeze, death appears to happen; if it is pure isness facing it, then a glimpse of life is revealed. A little breeze hits the ego – and death, only death appears. But if storms hit the soul, the being, then you are bathed in the juice of life.

A small breeze blows out a lamp but makes a blazing fire bigger and bigger. The ego is very small, it is our creation – but we are vast because we are not our own creation, we are created by the infinite.

So understand that you are always larger than you see yourself – you are vaster than yourself; you are always beyond yourself. All your pettiness is the result of your own efforts, your own doing; all your wretchedness is the result of your own heroic efforts. It is your own courageous deed that you have remained a small flame of a lamp, fearing death every moment, worrying about the sufferings, the troubles, the pains and the anxieties.

Take a jump out of your madness. That jump starts from the ego.

Enough for today.

Now let us make some effort for this jump.

14

The End of Illusion

That which has no beginning but which ends,
which is present equally in what is seen and not seen,
which is neither real, nor unreal,
nor real-unreal,
and which itself appears most pure, most flawless –
that energy is called maya, illusion.
It cannot be described in any other way.
Illusion is ignorance,
it is of no significance and is false.
But to the deluded ones,
illusion is real in the three states of time:
past, present and future.
Hence its true nature cannot be conveyed
just by saying, "It is this…"

It would have been very simple to understand the reality of life if there had been only two categories within existence – the real and the unreal. Then we could easily have said that something exists or does not exist. There would have been no difficulty had there been a clear-cut division in life, in existence. But there is one more category of existence which we can neither say that it exists nor does not exist. That creates the whole complexity.

It is like when a rope is lying on the road, which to you looks like a snake because of the darkness. Does this snake exist or not? It would have been simple to say that yes it exists, or no it does not exist. Then there would have been no problem. But the snake seen in the rope is in one way nonexistent – because upon investigation you find that it is actually a rope and not a snake – but in another sense the snake is, because it has appeared to you. And it has not only appeared, it has caused you to run away. You could have fallen down in your hurry and even hurt yourself. It could have increased your heartbeat, made you perspire, and if you never returned to investigate it you would have always lived with the idea that it was a snake.

Can one run away from something which doesn't exist? Perspire because of something which doesn't exist? Can the heart tremble because of something which doesn't exist? Can all this happen because of a nonexistent phenomenon? If all this can happen, then we have to accept its existence in some sense, because it is impossible to deny outright a nonexistent phenomenon which can cause these happenings.

You have a horrible dream during the night; your sleep is disturbed and yet you know it was only a dream – but your fast heartbeat is not reduced and your limbs continue to tremble. Accepted, it was just a dream, and now you also know that it was just a dream, but still the real heart trembles and the bewilderment continues. It will take some time for sleep to come again.

The sages say that it is not right to call something nonexistent which influences the actual reality. And it is interesting that this third category is so dominating that our whole life is under its influence; therefore it cannot be denied. This third category is so significant that our whole life is influenced by it and moves around it.

That is why India has invented a new word, *maya*, illusion. *Maya* is neither the real nor the unreal, it is in between. In a way it is and in another way it is not. It has been called *maya* because it only appears to be.

A magician can create a tree. In front of thousands of eyes this tree will start growing and in a moment it starts bearing fruit, and the fruit grows bigger. All of those who are seeing this know that it is not possible, that this is not so, but yet it appears to be so.

The basic meaning of *maya* is the art of illusion. The basic meaning of *maya* is magic. It means that there is a possibility for that which does not exist to be seen. And on the other hand, it is also possible that that which is may not be seen. That which is may hide, and that which is not may manifest.

These are the three states: the purely nonexistent, for which illusion is not possible; the purely existent, for which illusion is not possible either; plus that which exists in one way and does not exist in another way – only here is illusion possible. This third is also a form of existence; it is called *maya*, illusion. This is the linguistic meaning of *maya*. If we can also come to understand the vastness of *maya* then we will know its other dimensions in life.

That which is, is eternally so. It has no beginning and it has no end, it will remain eternally. That which is purely nonexistent, it too has no beginning. How can it have a beginning when it does not exist? It has no end because it never existed! *Maya* has no beginning, but it has an end; it is a category in between. It has no beginning, it is beginning-less – but it has an end.

Take it like this: darkness is, it is eternal, but it can be finished; if a light is lit, then the darkness disappears. The third category, that of *maya*, exists eternally, like darkness. Yet when one is awakened in consciousness *maya* ends; when the consciousness is full of light, the darkness of *maya* vanishes. That which is called *maya* is a vast dream.

A dream has a special characteristic which is that when it is there, it feels real while it lasts. We all have dreams and then realize in the morning that the dream was not real, but when we have another dream the next night, it again feels to be real. While dreaming we never remember that it is false. If we could remember, the dream would vanish.

A dream has an intrinsic specialty; when it is happening it

is completely real – not even a bit of doubt arises, there is not a single doubt. Great doubters, who can doubt whether this world exists or not, still cannot doubt about a dream while it is happening.

Berkeley, a great Western thinker, says: "I doubt whether the world exists or not, because there is the possibility that it may be just a long dream. How can I believe that you are really sitting here? I may be simply dreaming. How can I be certain that the people I am seeing are really there? I may be talking to them in my dream. Any dream is just as real as you are real sitting here." So Berkeley asks: "How to trust? How to be certain that you are?"

We call a dream a dream because it vanishes in the morning. But what we call waking also vanishes in the evening. When we wake up in the morning from a dream we find it was false, it has vanished. Someone who was an emperor in the night while he was dreaming finds himself a beggar in the morning. And then, having been a beggar the whole day long, when he sleeps at night he totally forgets about begging. During the night who remembers about being a beggar? Is there any difference between an emperor and a beggar during sleep? During a dream even an emperor cannot remember that he is an emperor. Thus the dream of the day vanishes in the night.

Then what is the difference? One dream vanishes in the morning and the other vanishes in the evening. We forget the day during the night's dream and we forget the night during the day's dream – what is the difference?

So Berkeley says: "How can I believe that there is some existence outside of me?"

It is a very interesting idea, but even Berkeley is not able to remember while dreaming that what he is seeing can be doubted. During the waking state doubt is possible, but during sleep doubt is not possible. Even the greatest of skeptics is not able to doubt during a dream.

The illusory world of dreams is very strange. Even the waking state does not have that much power; it is less powerful because we can doubt it. We can say that one never knows if what is seen really exists or not. But the illusion within a dream is incredible. In dreams we are totally lost and drowned, we accept situations which are quite illogical. A dream does not allow for any logic; if logic remains, doubt also remains.

In a dream you see a friend standing before you suddenly turning into a horse – and you never doubt: How could it be possible? In your dream you never doubt. When you dream you are full of trust, your trust is absolute. In the waking state even the most trusting person has doubts, but in the dream state even the most doubting person trusts. You never doubt for a moment your friend becoming a horse – but how could it happen?

In a dream everything is accepted – a dream has no logic. A dream has this quality – one cannot doubt while dreaming. Whatever is seen in a dream feels real as long as the dream continues. Anything may happen in a dream, it will not be inconsistent. It is just the same harmonious inner realm.

A dream and what is called *maya* have a common characteristic. Understand it like this – *maya* is the dreaming in the waking state. That is why the more surrounded with illusion a mind is, the more difficult it is to doubt it, to raise doubt about this *maya*. This state of *maya* feels perfectly real to it. You see a face and it looks beautiful to you, it seems to you that your life can be sacrificed for this face.

In the love story of Laila and Majnu, Laila never appeared to anybody else the way she looked to Majnu. The whole village felt Majnu's pain, so the chief of the village called Majnu and said, "You are totally mad. Why do you think only of her? She is just a very ordinary, very common girl. Why are you crazy about her? I feel pity for you" – because Majnu was wandering through the village weeping, crying, going from door to door, calling out "Laila...Laila!"

The news reached the emperor. He also saw Majnu's suffering and felt that it was authentic, that his crying was real, and took pity on him. He called a dozen girls of the palace and told Majnu he could choose any one of them and to forget about Laila.

Majnu looked at these twelve girls; they were the most beautiful girls in the kingdom, but he said, "Where is Laila? They are not even the dust of Laila's feet."

The emperor said, "Either you are mad or you have lost all your senses. I have seen Laila and she is a very ordinary looking girl. Why are you saying that these beautiful girls are not even the dust of Laila's feet?"

Majnu said, "To see Laila, the eyes of Majnu are needed."

But these eyes, the eyes of Majnu, what are they doing with Laila? They are imposing something on Laila which she does not have. These eyes are creating some dream about Laila; these eyes are creating some *maya*, some illusion around Laila which she does not have. Laila, as known to Majnu, contains more of Majnu than of Laila herself. Laila is not even ten percent present, she is ninety percent Majnu. And there is a possibility that she is only one percent Laila and ninety-nine percent Majnu. What Majnu is seeing is his own projection, it is his own creation; it is his own mind that is fabricating a dream around Laila's face. It is the mind of Majnu that is weaving a web, surrounding Laila with a fragrance, with beauty, with a melody.

Man's mind weaves illusions and then projects them from within himself, the way a spider takes the fibers from within his own body and weaves a cobweb. Just a support is needed from the outside – that is all. Even the spider needs a support from which to hang its web, the spider needs a wall or a door on which to hang its web. It just needs a support to hang it from, the rest of the creation is its own.

Man too needs something around which to fabricate his illusion. Laila is no more than a support to hang it on. Laila's appearance is nothing more than Majnu's fabrication, his cobweb. *Maya* means the capacity that man's mind has to create a dream around himself. And it is very interesting also that the spider then starts walking on its own cobweb, lives on it, dwells in it. The cobweb comes from within it and it also becomes its way, its path. It is its home, the means of its food, its subsistence. The cobweb will trap food for it, and the cobweb is the spider's own creation.

Sometimes it also happens that the spider itself becomes caught in its own cobweb and has difficulties getting out. Sometimes the cobweb becomes tangled up, some gust of wind may cover the spider with its own cobweb. Sometimes the cobweb breaks and the spider hangs in mid-air. The interesting thing is that the cobweb was a self-creation of the spider – it comes out of its own stomach – and it can also entrap the spider. Sometimes the spider is so trapped in its own cobweb that it is unable to get out of it; the same cobweb which was its life can one day become its death.

Maya means the capacity of man's mind to weave a dream world around himself. This dream has much pleasure in it, otherwise he would not create it; it also has much happiness in it, otherwise why would he create it? This dream also contains a lot of suffering in it, otherwise why would a Buddha or a Mahavira attempt to get out of it? The pleasure of this dream only lasts as long as we are dreaming it.

And it is very interesting that the object around whom this dream is created becomes the reason of the dream shattering – because, in fact, this person is not at all according to our dream; he has his own existence, his own dreams. You meet a person – very loving, very beautiful, charming – and you project your dream onto that person. It is not necessary that that person also projects his or her dream onto you. This is where lovers get into trouble.

Lovers come to me and one of them asks, "I love him so much, so why doesn't he love me?" He doesn't have to; he has the freedom to fabricate his own dream. He may make you the hook to hang his dream on or he may not – he may have chosen some other hook. It cannot be forced upon him. He is weaving his cobweb from his own support, his own hook, and you are weaving yours on him. Trouble is bound to arise someday: at one time your web will feel like a bondage to him and at other times his web, woven around someone else, will be painful for you. Even if we suppose that two persons weave their webs around each other, then too a struggle is inevitable because each is weaving their own cobweb. Pain is inevitable, their paths conflict, expectations shatter and the dreams are broken. Each has his own plans to weave his own inner dreams.

Understand it like this: if two persons are projecting two different movies from two projectors at the same time onto the same screen – two films on one screen – trouble is bound to arise. Everything will overlap and nothing will be clear. But here not only are two films being screened, but perhaps ten, fifteen or twenty persons are projecting their films on one screen. It creates confusion, nothing is achieved, and it is all sorrow and suffering. Every dream is shattered. At the end of his life the only treasure a man is left holding in his hands is disillusionment; only the ashes of shattered dreams and entangled webs.

Mind has a double capacity: one is of projecting, of spreading an idea, a feeling, a fabrication, and the other is of becoming hypnotized by its own projection – a state of autohypnosis, of getting caught in its own fabrication. First we put beauty in a face, first we say, "You are beautiful" – but we ourselves are creating the beauty and then we are charmed by it! This is the other part, the autohypnosis.

To this day, no definition of beauty has ever been found and there never will be because it is an individual projection, it is not a real fact. That is why as times change, fashion also changes and the criteria of beauty changes. Sometimes a flat nose is beautiful, sometimes a long nose is beautiful; sometimes a fair face is beautiful, sometimes a dark face is beautiful.

We conceive of Rama and Krishna as being dark-skinned; a dark color was most beautiful in those days. It is not known whether they were dark or fair, but a dark color was admired in those days; in those times, darkness was considered to be beautiful. That is why we do not conceive of Krishna as being fair-skinned – even the names Krishna or Shyam are both synonyms for the color black.

Nowadays we do not conceive of black as being beautiful, because during the past hundred, one hundred and fifty years, the color white has become dominant. So when we say that black is beautiful, it raises a doubt – although this will not last long, because American beauties are making a great effort to get a dark color, lying on the sea-beaches in the hope that the sunshine can make them dark. White – too much white – creates boredom, and white appears to be shallow. When a river is deep it becomes dark; a shallow river looks white, has white froth on the surface. A dark color seems to have a little more depth. Even the surface of a river shows its reality – if it is dark it is deep, if it is light it is shallow. But this idea changes with the changing times; sometimes white seems really lovely, then we get bored with it and dark becomes beautiful.

There are tribes who like their women to have shaved heads. We shave the heads of sannyasins so that they look unattractive, there is no other reason. A sannyasin should not look beautiful because he is leaving the world of desires and beauty. But there are tribes, African primitives, who shave the women's heads – but not the men's, because men can do without beauty. They shave the women's heads because a shaved head looks beautiful to them. Perhaps their idea is significant because they say, "Unless the head is shaved, the minute curves on the skull are not visible because the head is covered with hair. An ugly skull may be hidden. But when the head is totally clean then one can know the real shape and proportions; otherwise one may be deceived."

What is beauty? – it is we who project it. We project our conceptions; it then looks beautiful to us and we are charmed by the beauty. First we project an idea, throw it on the screen, then impose our own feelings on the image – and then we become charmed by it. Have you ever been enchanted by yourself standing before the mirror? Then you would understand what I am saying.

There is a Greek story about Narcissus, who looked at himself in the waters of a lake and became enchanted – he fell in love with himself. Then he was in great trouble because it is very difficult to search for oneself. How to do it? He looked everywhere, but he could not find the face he had fallen in love with.

Freud has called people who fall in love with themselves narcissists. Most of us are very close to being narcissists – we are also like Narcissus. We are in love with ourselves, although we may not be saying it. A man like Byron fell in love with hundreds of women. He may not have admitted it, but psychologists say that the reason he fell in love with so many women was that every time the woman would tell him that he was very handsome…so it was only for this reassurance, for this self-admiration. This search is nothing but a search to love one's own self; thousands of women should say that you are very lovable… He is only loving himself; but when thousands of women say it, one's belief in it deepens.

When we love someone, we are loving our own conceptions, our own fantasies about beauty, our own feelings, our own ideals – we are surrounded by ourselves, every one of us is a Narcissus. But all these projections appear so real that it all seems to be true.

If a cobweb breaks on one side, the spider again begins to weave from another support. We also do the same thing. If our dreams are shattered by one person, we catch hold of another as a support and again begin to weave our cobweb. One dream is shattered and immediately we begin another dream, but we never become aware of the fact that what we are doing has nothing to do with reality.

Certainly it is not totally false, otherwise we could not have managed it; it is not totally real either, otherwise we would not have suffered. It is in the middle – it is false, but it looks like it is real. This is what is meant by *maya*:

That which has no beginning but which ends...

...That which never began, yet comes to an end. Memory fails as to when *maya* began. Memory fails as to when we fell into this cobweb. There is no way to know when we fell into this darkness; it is beginningless. But an ending is possible.

When someone asked Buddha how sorrow came into existence he replied, "Don't worry about that. Ask how it can be finished with. Don't ask about the beginning, you should ask how to end it – and I know how to end it."

Buddha further said, "A man hit by an arrow falls to the ground, the arrow is stuck in his chest. I go to him to take the arrow out, but the man says, 'First, tell me who shot the arrow. Why did he do it? When did he shoot it? Where did he shoot from? Is it poisoned or not? Is this the result of my past karmas?'

"I will say to him, 'Don't ask all these questions. I can tell you the technique to take out the arrow and how to end your pain.'"

Maya is beginningless. It is very valuable that the Indian seers have been so courageous in accepting facts. Very few streams of thought are able to accept that something exists which is beginningless. The mind says that there must be a beginning, that somewhere, sometime, there must have been a beginning.

That is why Christians have said that the world came into existence four thousand and four years before Jesus. They even fixed the date. Then they found they were in trouble because science has found that the earth is very old – four billion years old. But man lives in his own dreams and logic.

Christians were in difficulty when fossils were found dating back millions of years, and when scientists found metals and rocks billions of years old. But Christians are saying it began four thousand and four years before Jesus, which means only six thousand years ago. It became a problem, because civilizations were discovered which were at their peak seven thousand years ago. There are references which are tens of thousands of years old. The Rigveda mentions configurations of stars and planets which date back ninety-five thousand years. What to do with all of this?

So now man has created a pseudo-logic: Christians have begun to say that although God created this world four thousand years ago, it was only to test the faith of human beings that he left things lying around which look millions of years old. He created those bones – because nothing is impossible for him. If he could create the whole earth, could he not create a bone which is a million years old, which can appear to be millions of years old? He put those bones there so that human faith and trust could be tested.

It can only be a test of faith when all the reasons for distrust are present and, in spite of these reasons, they can go on accepting the idea of a creation of only four thousand and four years before Jesus. This is a rationalization; we try to rationalize our illusions with logic.

These Indian seers are in a way courageous, they accept the facts. Wise men say that the world had no beginning. Basically, India has the only people on earth who accept a beginningless phenomenon. No one else could accept it: somehow or other there had to be a beginning, even though it may be unknown to us – because how is it possible to have no beginning at all and yet exist? But this is a very superficial type of logic. The truth is that if anything is begun there must have been something before that, otherwise how could it have begun? Even the beginning needs something existent to begin with.

So Indian seers say that even for the beginning, something must have already been present. This is why any concept about a beginning is meaningless. We may conceive of a beginning at any time, on any date – millions or billions of years ago – but whenever it began, that cannot have been the beginning because it is essential for something to have already existed in order for it to begin. That is why we accept that this existence is beginningless. The concept of a beginning causes an infinite regression; it has no meaning and becomes like a game children play. For instance, we say *A* is born out of *B*, and *B* is born of *C*, and *C* is born of *D* – but if something needs to exist in order to give birth to the next thing, there comes a point where we have to accept that this whole chain is beginningless. Otherwise we just go on moving back inventing new words, and all those words will not solve the question – although they appear to answer it. But the question will remain there as before; it only appears to be logical.

For instance, one may ask, "What is the earth standing on?" And we can reply that it is supported on an elephant's back and that the elephant is standing on a tortoise. But this only looks like logic, because if you have to stop somewhere why not stop with the earth itself? The earth is not standing on anything. If we have to say that it is beginningless, that it never started, why go so far on this stupid journey? Just accept the simple truth that something is beginningless, that it never began.

But one very special thing about it is that something which is beginningless may have an end. Now it becomes even more difficult for logic, because that which is beginningless must have no end – this is a simple syllogism. How can a stick without a beginning have another end? Either both the ends exist or neither of them exist. It is a simple syllogism – very clear. Even mathematics will say it is wrong. If it has a beginning then it must have an end – thus, two ends. But you say that there is only one end – the last – and that there is no starting point. This cannot happen.

We also think in the same way. I will give you an example in order to understand this. During the past one hundred years what we call Aristotelian logic, linear logic has failed. A two-thousand-year-long tradition of this type of logic is no longer valid, it has failed because of science. The greatest hit was given by the discovery of the atom, because as soon as physics looked into the atom a unique phenomenon came to be understood which logic cannot grasp. And this phenomenon was that when an atom explodes, its basic particles – electrons – appear to be both particles and waves, simultaneously. According to logic this is not possible, it cannot be possible. Aristotle would have said that this is nonsense: it is either a particle or a wave. How can a thing be a particle *and* a wave simultaneously? A wave means that which is not a particle, and a particle means that which is unmoving, still and not waving. A wave can contain a particle in it, but a particle cannot contain a wave in it – a very simple fact.

But a great difficulty arose. Even physicists were in trouble, because the whole of Western thinking had accepted Aristotle as its basis. For two thousand years it had never failed, Aristotle had always been right; that is why he was called "the father of logic." But this phenomenon of waves and particles, these electrons put Aristotle in difficulty.

Now there were only two possibilities: either to follow Aristotle and to say that it could not happen, even though it was happening – that the particle could be at the same time a wave – to deny it and close our eyes… But how could the scientists close their eyes? It was happening! Or else the only way left was to forget about Aristotle. It had been right to follow him so far, because no contrary concept had come to notice which refuted him. Now this fact denied his logic. Which were we to believe – logic or facts? If we had believed only in logic, the whole progress of science would have been stopped.

Scientists gathered courage and agreed to improve upon Aristotle's logic because there was no way to change the truth. Now what to do? Because a particle is simultaneously a wave, a new term – quantum, a particle-wave – which had never existed before, had to be coined. The Hindi language still has no term like that, this is why we have to say "particle-wave." English has created a new term – quantum: it means that the same thing is both, simultaneously. So Aristotelian logic fell into disrepute.

The sages of India, in their spiritual seeking, also reached those spaces where facts defeat logic. This fact is one of such examples. The Indian seers accept that the logic is correct, that something which has no beginning cannot have an end, but we have seen it ending and we are helpless! We have experienced within us that *maya* comes to an end and it has no beginning. Now what to do? Our difficulty in the realm of the inner experience is like that of the West in respect to quantum mechanics. We too knew logic which we had developed long before Aristotle. Aristotelian logic developed across twenty-five hundred years, whereas the Eastern school of logic has existed for at least seven thousand years. We too knew that this is the rule of logic; we knew quite well, but what to do? What to do if the fact does not agree with logic? We are bound to accept an illogical fact. This fact is beyond logic.

Maya has no beginning; searching and searching we found that no matter what we may call a beginning it cannot really be a beginning, for in order for something to begin, something has to exist before it – and again the search for another beginning starts. But when we go deep within, a moment comes when the whole entanglement of our projections is shattered and we are out of *maya*. *Maya* has no beginning, but it ends; this we know as a fact through our experience. That is why the Upanishads are not logical proclamations; they are the conclusions of our inner observation. Whenever a fact is profound, logic has to be dropped, there is no other way.

Western psychology has now discovered a fact where ordinary logic has to change. I was just speaking about physics... Now with Jung, Western psychology has also arrived at a new concept. We always thought that the male is male and the female is female, but Jung discovered that every man has a woman within and every woman has a man within, only the proportions differ. We call those people men who are sixty percent man and forty percent woman, and those people women who are sixty percent woman and forty percent man. The difference is only of quantity – there is no other clear-cut difference – so in every man there is a woman, and in every woman, a man.

So Jung said: "We should say that the old concept – that a man is a man, and a woman is a woman – has been proven wrong. To call a woman manly, or to call a man womanly, is nonsense. Human beings are bisexual. The old division of sex is out of date."

And Jung has put us in more difficulty. He said: "As I went deep into my experience, I found that the proportion is not certain, it changes many times in a day. A man may perhaps be more of a woman in the morning and more manly in the evening. It is also possible that you behave like a man today and tomorrow you behave like a woman."

Have you ever noticed this? I know a man, a very courageous, bold man: yet when his house caught fire he began to cry, beating his chest and pulling his hair, more than a woman would have done. When I saw him weeping I could not believe that he was the same man. He was behaving altogether like a woman. If we follow the old logic we would say that this shows his weakness, his unconsciousness. But modern psychology would say that it is not weakness, it is just that the ratio has changed and his inner woman has become predominant.

Sometimes we have seen women fighting and struggling like men. Sometimes a Queen of Jhansi, India's Joan-of-Arc, behaves like a man, then we call her manly, believing that she is a special woman. It is not so, it can manifest in any woman.

And many times it happens that when a woman's male side manifests she is more manlier than a man, because her manliness is fresh and virgin. It was dormant and had remained unused, like soil which remains uncultivated for hundreds of years and is then very fertile; if seeds are sown in it the yield is immense, the surrounding fields yielding for so many years look arid. Thus, when a woman is manly, her hidden man, her dormant male, is very fresh and intense because it has remained unmanifested – hence the explosion. And when a man is womanly, his tenderness surpasses even a woman's; he is more womanly than any woman.

With the new psychology, linear thinking and logic failed. Logic says that a woman is a woman and a man is a man; a man is not a woman and a woman is not a man, but the facts are that both are both. It is time to abandon the old concepts.

Jung says that attraction is due to this, otherwise there would be no attraction. A unique phenomenon has been noted, that a man searches for a woman who resembles his inner woman. Love happens only then, otherwise it does not happen.

And that is why it can happen that you can love a woman or a man, and then tomorrow that love is gone. Then you get angry, saying that perhaps this man or this woman was not right. But the reason is only that the rapport with the inner woman or inner man has been lost. You have a male or female image within which you search for, and when you are in rapport with that image, you call it love.

Love is nothing but to be in rapport with someone who is harmonious with your inner image. But everyone keeps changing, that is why today's rapport may not work tomorrow. It is there in the morning and may be gone by the evening.

Wise men of India have experienced that which has no beginning but has an end, and that which has no end but has a beginning.

Now I will tell you the second part: *maya* has no beginning but has an end, enlightenment has a beginning but has no end.

Enlightenment, *moksha*, means to be free from *maya*. It has a beginning – because one day you rise above *maya* – but it never ends. Mahavira became enlightened, and now this enlightenment has no end.

Indian seers could comprehend that *maya* is the state which has no beginning yet ends: enlightenment is the other state which has a beginning but has no end. If we put both of them together the circle is complete. What is beginningless in *maya*, is endless in enlightenment. What is in the beginning of enlightenment is at the end of *maya*. The end of *maya*, is the beginning of enlightenment. The circle is complete.

This circle is a spiritual experience, it is not logic. If one wants to have this experience through logic, it is like trying to walk with one's feet and hands tied together. If you are then unable to walk, it does not mean the phenomenon of walking is false, it only means you are tied down with your own logic.

That which has no beginning but which ends,
which is present equally in what is seen and not seen,
which is neither real, nor unreal, nor real-unreal,
and which itself appears most pure, most flawless –
that energy is called maya, illusion.

It appears as flawless because while it is seen it appears, like a dream, very real and factual. When it disappears, it is not that it is seen with flaws, it just disappears. When it is seen it appears as a solid reality, when it is not seen, it is a complete unreality. This existence of *maya* between these two states has been called *sansara*, the world.

It cannot be described in any other way.

Nothing more can be said about it. To know more one has to experience it. Enough has been said and nothing more is needed. More than this is not possible. The sutra is complete. If one wants to know more, one has to know through experiencing.

Illusion is ignorance,
it is of no significance and is false.
But to the deluded ones,
illusion is real in the three states of time:

past, present and future.
Hence its true nature cannot be conveyed
just by saying, "It is this..."

There are three things here: ignorance – we do not know and that's why illusion appears; our ignorance is the basis for it.

When a rope appears to be a snake, what is the basis for it? Proper recognition of the rope was lacking, therefore it appeared to be a snake. Had we gone closer to it, lit a lamp and looked at it, the snake would have disappeared; the snake exists because of our not-knowing, not because of the rope.

Try to understand it correctly. The snake exists because of our ignorance, not because of the rope; the rope is still a rope even after recognizing it. It was a rope even before we recognized it. But then a moment came when we saw an illusion in the dark, we saw it from a distance and ran away. It was dark and there was no snake; where did this snake which we saw come from? It came from our not-knowing and from our memory. In our past we had seen a snake and the rope resembled that snake – the rope looked like a snake because it was dark, and we ran away. The fear worked, the memory worked – the old memory of a snake projected onto the screen, together with the darkness, worked. We did not go close enough; ignorance worked and the rope became a snake.

Sometimes the opposite also happens, sometimes a snake becomes a rope. It happened to Tulsidas. He secretly went to meet his wife, but he could not enter by the front door because not even a day had passed since she had come to her mother's house to stay, and he was so shy that he could not go to the front door so he climbed up the back of the house. It was a rainy night and a snake was hanging down. He took it to be a rope and grabbed it and climbed up. This also happens: if a rope can look like a snake, why couldn't a snake have looked like a rope?

The reason for this also lies in the memory – that it looked like a rope. He was in such a hurry that he had no time to look at what it was. He was afraid someone might see him, might catch hold of him. There was no opportunity to investigate it, to check it out, otherwise he could have gone through the front door. There was no way to take a lamp with him because thieves do not carry lamps. A deep infatuation, a deep desire to be with his wife…so the snake becomes a rope. The snake is still a snake – the basis is again ignorance.

…it is of no significance and is false. Because that which is, is so very insignificant and trivial, you yourself make it big. You give significance to your dream and make it very important. That is why when your dream shatters, the person on whom your dream has been projected loses all their charm and becomes boring. The person is the same, it is only that now you have dropped your dream.

Everything around us is so petty and trivial, everything you project your illusions onto is trivial. It is like a movie screen: there is nothing to it, just a blank white screen, but then you project so many images on it and then take great joy in them – you go almost crazy about the images! These pictures are only the play of light and shadow, only patterns of light and nothing else, but you go crazy about them.

Now there are three-dimensional films. When three-dimensional films were first produced they looked absolutely real. So when a three-dimensional film was first shown in London, and a man on a horse came galloping along and threw a spear, everyone in the hall ducked their heads to escape the spear because it looked so real. The spear had length, breadth and depth, and when it was thrown it seemed to be rushing toward the spectators. There was no time to remember that they were sitting in a cinema. They ducked their heads, because there seemed to be no difference between a real spear and this spear in the film. And what happened? – nothing, only a play of light and shadow. But the illusion is possible: *…and is false.* Here, *false* means that which is not, which does not exist, but really seems to exist. *False* is a synonym for *maya*. We produce pseudo-facts through *maya*. *False* means pseudo-facts, and *maya* is the energy to produce these pseudo-facts.

But to the deluded ones... A deluded one is not a fool. Understand that to be deluded does not mean to be a fool. Even intelligent people may be deluded, great, learned people may be deluded. To be deluded does not mean to be stupid, deluded means to be submerged in *maya*, to be lost and hypnotized by *maya*. So a great pundit may be deluded – Tulsidas was a great scholar, and nothing was lacking in his scholarship, but he was deluded.

In the East there's a saying that a mother takes twenty-five years to grow an intelligent son, and it only takes two seconds for a young lady to make a fool of him. The mother wastes twenty-five years to make him intelligent – in study, in learning – and the mother is not aware that an ordinary young woman will fool him in minutes, and then all intelligence is lost.

To be deluded does not mean to be a fool, to be deluded means to be in the state of delusion. Anyone may be deluded, and when one is deluded intelligence does not count. Someone may be intelligent one moment and the next moment all his intelligence may be gone, as if he has become intoxicated, or like a man walking on the street, conscious, and suddenly he is given a tablet to make him unconscious and he begins to stumble and falter.

We all have within us this potential of *maya* energy. When we give it the opportunity, it spreads its umbrella and we are covered by it. To be under the umbrella of *maya* is called delusion.

So we have three words: one is *maya* – *maya* is an energy; another is *mithya* – *mithya* means the false or pseudo-facts born out of this *maya*; the third is *moodhata* – idiocy, delusion, a consciousness covered by *maya*.

So when we call someone a *moodh*, an idiot, it does not mean he is a fool, it simply means he has made a fool of himself. He may also become intelligent. Great intelligence is not needed in order to get rid of this delusion. Understand this second part: it is not necessary for the person to be very intelligent to do it, it is possible even for idiots to get rid of their illusions – because intelligent people can also be idiots.

Sometimes it happens that an unsophisticated village person attains to ultimate wisdom. It means he is out of the illusion, that is all. Kabir or Nanak, Taran, Dadu or Farid, all were illiterate people. Mohammed and Jesus were not knowledgeable in any sense; they had no sophisticated, educated mind. They were very ordinary men, but suddenly they jumped out of their illusions and attained to ultimate wisdom, to become supremely enlightened ones.

This ultimate wisdom dawns after the elimination of illusion, and ordinary knowledge, scholarship, comes after the elimination of ignorance, stupidity. It is easy to eliminate ignorance, it is eliminated with the accumulation of knowledge. Not to know about many things is called ignorance. A person who knows about many things is called a scholar, but the scholar and the ignorant one are in the same category, they differ only in quantity. The person who is ignorant knows less, the scholar knows more. The difference is of quantity, not of quality, because both of them can be deluded; at any time either of them can become deluded.

The opposite of illusion is called wisdom and the opposite of ignorance is so-called knowledge. That is why knowledge can be learned but wisdom cannot. Knowledge may be borrowed, but there is no way to borrow wisdom. Knowledge is only an accumulation, but wisdom is an inner revolution. Delusion can vanish. Delusion means to be hypnotized and overpowered by *maya*. The ability to move out of the influence of *maya* is called wisdom.

But to the deluded ones, illusion is real in the three states of time… What are these three states of time when *maya* appears to be real to the deluded person? Everything has three moments of existence: when it is not yet, when it is, and when it again moves into nonexistence. Everything passes through these three dimensions of time.

I saw you just now and I am not in love with you; this is one state. Seeing you, I fall in love; this is the second situation. Tomorrow, the love vanishes; this is the third state. These are the three states of love – it was not, then it is, and it is not again.

The sage says that the deluded person sees *maya* as real in all three states. When it is not there, he thinks love does not exist and that this is reality; when it happens, he thinks it exists and that this is reality; when it ceases, he again thinks it does not exist and that this is reality. None of the three are realities, they are just three states of time. Every experience of *maya*, every delusion has three moments: before being, being, and after being. Of all the three states, whichever is happening to the person at that time he believes it to be real.

What does this mean? It means that if a person in love believes that there is love and that it is something real, then as this love disappears he will believe that there is no love – and he will believe this with the same depth and conviction as he had previously believed that there was love.

But he will not be able to see that this thing which has now become nonexistent possibly had no existence in the first place, or that something that now exists and was not there a moment ago. Could it be that its present existence too is nothing but an illusion, that between two moments of nonbeing only the delusion of being is happening? Because that which is, is always, and will always be there; that which comes and goes or appears and disappears can only be an illusion, a trickery, a hypnosis.

To the deluded ones it is real in all the three states of time. Hence it is very difficult to make a deluded person understand what *maya* is. The sage says: *Hence its true nature cannot be conveyed just by saying, "It is this..."* What is it that cannot be conveyed? – because when his love affair is over and he is told that the existence of this love was only an illusion, he believes it. But again, tomorrow, when a new love affair appears

– then try to tell him this again! He will refuse. He will say that the previous love may not have existed, but this one does. Man has this recurring capacity to become deluded.

I have heard about a man who married eight times. In a way it is good that there may be so many opportunities to marry; perhaps he might come to his senses after repeating his delusion so many times. But man has an infinite capacity to be deluded.

He was astonished when he married for the first time and became disillusioned after six months. Everything was lost, his dreams were shattered and he thought that he had chosen the wrong woman. He married a second time and after six months found that he had again chosen the wrong woman. The second woman proved to be the same as the first. He chose eight times and each time the woman proved to be of the same type.

But even then he could not understand that it was he who was making the choices, so how could a new choice differ? How could it happen? It was still the same man who had made the first choice! His way of making a choice – his way of seeing, the projection of his illusions, his concept of beauty, his fantasies about love – all were the same the second time, and the third time and so on, but every time he thought that he had just picked the wrong woman. It never occurred to him that the chooser, the one who was choosing, could not make anything other than a wrong choice. It is only this wrong one who would qualify, who would fit his criteria.

The difficulty with being deluded in the three states of time is that you never perceive that it is your own cobweb that you are weaving, you always blame the other. If I fall in love with you, I do not see that it is I who have fallen in love, I only see that you are so lovable, so perfectly lovable. Then tomorrow, because of these projections I have made, the trouble begins. I should only have said: "Because of being the type of person I am, my falling in love with you is unavoidable. You are not responsible for it – you are only a clothes hanger and I am the coat; I am hanging myself on you, you are in no way responsible for it. You are not involved in this. Had I not met you I would have searched for some other kind of clothes hanger that fits with me. It is just coincidental that we met and I hung my coat on you."

But the person to whom I say, "I love you because you are so lovable," is also not seeing the point that tomorrow there will be trouble. That person should immediately say, "Please, excuse me. I am not lovable. I only appear that way to you. But soon a moment will come when all your love is gone and you will start taking your coat off this hook. And then too you will say it is because I did not prove to be a lovable person, that is why you are taking your coat back."

When someone says to you, "You are such a loving person that I can't help but love you," you don't wish to deny it; you feel that you are that loving person, and that is why the other loves you. Nobody likes to be a clothes hanger, so you are always willing to go along with the idea that you are a very lovable person and that is why he is loving you.

But you do not know that you are inviting trouble. Tomorrow, when he gets bored with this hanger and takes his coat down, he will say, "This hook is rotten. I can't hang my coat on it," then there will be pain. But in both situations he is doing the same thing – putting the responsibility onto the other and not on himself.

In illusion, the responsibility is always put onto others, whereas in wisdom one feels responsible oneself. Hence if you abuse someone like Buddha, he knows that you are in search of a hook; if you bow at his feet, he knows that you are in search of a hook. In either situation he never takes himself to be important. When you bow down at his feet he remains like a stone and when you call him names, then too he remains like a stone – because he knows it is your need, it has nothing to do with him. It is just a coincidence that he was there, it is pure coincidence. So when you say, "You are a bad man," he just listens knowing that the way you are you can only see a bad man in him, that is all. There is nothing more to it. And when you say, "You are the wisest man," then too he understands; he knows that the way you are, he appears to be the wisest man to you. It is your eyes, he neither takes any pride in it nor any condemnation.

But we feel difficulty with such a man. We feel uneasy, such a man throws us back on ourselves again and again. We desire to ride on others, to make others vehicles for us, to use the shoulders of others, and this man throws us back on ourselves again and again.

Hence even a man like Buddha becomes only a cause for our distress as long as our illusions are there. Even a man like Buddha is only a cause for our suffering as long as we are deluded. No matter what he says or does, whatever we perceive in it through our delusion is going to be a cause for our suffering. Until we are ready to shatter our illusions we cannot see the real face of Buddha – because what we see is our own projection.

So, to a deluded man nothing more than this can be said: that this is the situation – awaken out of it. Recognize it, explore it, and become conscious of it.

15

The Servant Has Become the Master

I am never born.
I am not the body. I am not the ten senses.
I am not the intellect. I am not the mind.
I am not even an eternal ego.
I am without prana, the vital breath of life.
I am without mind.
I am ever the pure self-nature.
I am ever the witness beyond intellect.
I am eternally consciousness itself.
About this there is no doubt.

The real "I am" can only be talked about when the I is eliminated. We are acquainted with one I, and this I that we know is nothing but the sum total of all our illusions. We create this I, we nourish, feed, enrich and strengthen it and make it powerful. But because it is false and our own creation we are troubled by it, we become worried, anguished, because that which is not our nature always becomes a burden.

Scientists say that tens of millions of years ago, animals with huge bodies existed all over the earth. An elephant is nothing compared to them, they were ten times larger than an elephant. Researchers investigating the evolution of life are having great difficulty in finding out why those animals became extinct. There are no apparent clues to some great calamity on the earth that would show the cause of their extinction. Their complete disappearance would have been impossible, even if there had been an earthquake or a volcanic eruption affecting the whole earth. So what happened?

Recently, during the last fifty years, a new clue came to their minds. It is possible that these animals enlarged their bodies so much that they died under the weight of their own bodies. There is no other apparent reason that might have been the cause of their death. The bodies of these animals became so huge – bodies which were their means of life – these bodies grew beyond the limit and became the cause of their death. It became difficult even to move with such a weight and to feed this body became even more difficult as the demand for food increased. This demand for food went on increasing with the growth of their bodies. So the body is, in a way, a means for the continuance of life, a vehicle for life, but only to a limit; it can become fatal beyond that extent.

I have told you this to help you to understand that the ego, our I, is also an essential part and parcel of the system of our life. But it goes on growing and we forget that what we chose to use as a means is now using us as a means. What we wanted to use is using us, and what we created for our protection, we are now protecting at the cost of our lives. But it is very difficult to know when the boundary has been crossed, when the master becomes the servant to his servant, when the leader becomes the follower of his own followers. But it happens – it happens because the seed of this is intrinsic to its system.

As I have told you, it is difficult to know when a leader becomes the follower of his own followers. To become a leader he has to satisfy his followers, and in trying to satisfy them he has to follow his followers; to remain ahead, first he has to follow. If you don't follow the followers whom you are to lead, they will not be ready to accept you as their leader. This is a very interesting happening: the leader has to follow because he has to lead. The leader gets lost in the very process of becoming a leader, because he has to appease those whom he rules and without noticing it, slowly,

slowly during this appeasement, he becomes enslaved.

The same happens with the I. It is needed. As I told you it is necessary for our life-system, it is functional. But the I has no existence, it is just functional – functional in the sense that it is representative of and indicating toward something. It is like our names – one person is called Rama and another is called Krishna; nobody is born with a name, the name is altogether a lie. But it is very difficult to function without names. There are six billion people on this enormous earth, and if we tried to live without names it would be very difficult, it would be impossible to know who is who. So we have to be labeled. The labels are false, but they are functional.

When I say they are functional I mean that it is convenient. We know that this man is called Krishna and that man is called Rama – although no one is Rama and no one is Krishna; all names are absolutely false. We are born without names and we die without names. We adopt the name on earth and we abandon it when we depart, but it has a utility in between. There is no harm in it, as long as there is an understanding of its utility. But you know how easily you can forget that the name has only a utilitarian purpose.

When a man is ready to die for his name trouble arises. He says, "It is a question of my name. I will not let my name be sullied even at the cost of my life." This shows that the name has not remained a mere utility. You are being used by the name; save the name and you are saved, lose the name and you are lost.

One evening, when Swami Ramateertha was in America, he returned home laughing and his friends asked, "What happened? What are you laughing at?"

He replied, "Some people met me on the way and they began to abuse Rama. I laughed loudly because they were insulting Rama – as if I were Rama."

His friends were new people, unacquainted with his way of

speaking, so they asked, "What are you saying? Aren't you Rama? You are Rama. If they were insulting someone, they were insulting you."

Ramateertha replied, "If the name is not just utilitarian and I identify myself with this name then the insults are meant for me, then I have to react. But I am well aware that a name is only functional. If tomorrow I become Krishna instead of Rama, it will not make any difference to me; only the name will change and I will remain the same. I can have a thousand names and they will all be superficial. To insult the name does not mean to insult me. I am more than a name, and separate from the name."

If we can remember this also in relation to the I, then the I is also only utilitarian. But we are not aware of an interesting phenomenon: we call others by name, but if we call ourselves by name it would be inconvenient. If I were to call myself by my name it would seem as if I were calling someone else, hence the common way we describe ourselves is as I. We use a name to describe others and we use I to describe ourselves. Hence I works for each one to refer to himself. When we use I, we know that we are pointing toward ourselves, when we use a name it is pointing toward someone else.

That is why the people around Ramateertha found it difficult to understand him, because when he spoke he did not use the I. He used to say, "Rama was walking down the lane and a few people began to insult him." He would say, "Rama is going to a town to deliver a speech." He did not say, "I am going to deliver a speech." Listening to him, it seemed as if he was talking about someone else.

There is nothing wrong in using the word *I*; there is no sin or no crime in using I, it is practical and convenient. Only this much should be remembered: the I is for convenience and it is not real. Then what is the problem in getting rid of the I? The problem arises when the label becomes our soul; as long as it is only superficial no problem arises.

But we become so attached to labels that we paste these labels all over ourselves. All over we are only labels and labels, it becomes difficult to find the person. These merely utilitarian labels stick so fast to us that sometimes, instead of being useful, the labels become harmful.

I have heard:

Nasruddin was working in a big office. Some glassware needed to be dispatched and the boss asked him to stick a label on the box showing which way is up, so it would not be put upside down. So he stuck the labels on and the box was sent.

When his boss asked him, "You did not forget to put on the label, did you?" Nasruddin replied, "Forget? I put them all over – they are visible from every side."

Such is our situation. The label would have been useful had it been put only on one side, on the upper side, so that care could be taken. But Nasruddin put them on every side, visible on every side. Now this box cannot be taken care of because each of its sides is the "up" side.

With us the utilitarian aspect also becomes suicidal. It could have worked, but the entity whose name it is, is forgotten and only the name remains. It would have been alright if only others were to fall in this illusion, but it happens that the person himself falls prey to this illusion and it goes deeply inside him.

If all of us sitting here were to sleep here tonight and if someone were to call out, "Rama," no one would hear this voice except for the man whose name is Rama. It clearly shows that even in sleep he is aware that he is Rama. The rest of the people would remain sleeping. They would not even be aware that somebody is calling Rama. But this man, even in deep sleep or sunk in dreams, knows that he is Rama.

The name goes so deep, it goes on penetrating like an arrow in the chest – the name enters like that, power enters like that, money enters like that. The ego is the accumulation of all of that which is our personality: name, fame, money and power – all this together creates the ego.

The sage first talked about dissolving the ego, discarding this *maya*, and now he gives this very interesting sutra. He talks about the jump from I to thou, from thou to *that*, then from *that* to existence itself. Then he talks about *brahman*, the ultimate reality, and *maya*, illusion – and suddenly comes this sutra:

I am never born.
I am not the body. I am not the ten senses.
I am not the intellect. I am not the mind.
I am not even an eternal ego.

A journey was begun which started with the I, progressed to thou, arrived at *that,* and then came to empty existence. Again the I is being used, but now it is not the same I that was mentioned in the beginning; that I has been abandoned. Now we have arrived at another I. This I appears only when the previously known I is dissolved. This I is the real self. This I does not mean ego, it means the soul. We have not created this I; it does not mean our name, fame, prestige, power, culture or education. This I means our existence, our being.

Remember one thing: the I which is renounced, which we discussed renouncing, which is discarded, was our "doing"; this second I is our "being." That I was our doing, this I is our being. So try to understand the difference between doing and being. This will give you a clear glimpse of the second I.

There are things we do, which if we didn't do them they would not happen. For example, if you don't get an education you will remain uneducated; if you don't learn a language it will be unknown to you. If you want to be a scientist you can become one, or if you try to become a blacksmith you can become one – if you do something you will become someone. But there is something existing within you which is not your doing – it is your being. Your being is not your doing. You exist before your every action; otherwise who would be doing it?

A child is growing in the mother's womb. The child doesn't even have to breathe in the womb, it doesn't even need to do this much. But try to understand this very interesting phenomenon: the child is existing, he is not breathing yet he exists. His being is, his isness is, his soul is; the soul is totally present.

Physiologists have always raised this question: When does life start? From when? If we think that life stops with the stopping of breathing, then life must begin with the beginning of breathing. So when a child cries for the first time after his birth and takes the first breath his cry works as a shock, a push to start his breathing, the heartbeat, now the mechanism starts functioning. When the child makes his first scream this is his first doing; his first cry is his first doing.

But the question is, whether the child existed before the cry or not. If he was not, then who cried? If he was not, then who took the first breath? He was, otherwise this could not have happened. So this thing that is existing before the first breath is our being; that is our isness, that is our soul.

Stretch it to the other side also. In the first case physiologists may agree with me about this phenomenon – that if nobody is already present before the first breath, then who is it who breathes for the first time? But on the other side, physiologists will feel more of a problem when I then say that when the breathing stops, that which was present before the first breath will still be present afterward. It is not concerned with the stopping of the breathing, it existed perfectly well before the breathing, so it can exist perfectly well after the breathing has stopped.

You will easily understand the first argument: Who will breathe if someone is not already present? The second argument is that much more important: Who is it who lets go of the breathing if there is no being inside, other than the breathing? But the second argument cannot be understood as easily. If the first is understood, there is no difficulty in understanding the second.

So let us get one categorization clear: there are things which we do. This is the reason why the more a person does, the bigger an egoist he becomes. Then one might say that blessed are those who are lazy, because there is not much "doing" around them on which they can build their egos. Still the human mind is very tricky: they can consider their laziness to be a kind of doing. They may say, "We are in the act of relaxing or non-doing."

Whatsoever we do, we use it only to enhance our egos. Whatever we do, we strengthen our I. Our I is the sum total of our doing – the grand total. That is why the ego goes on increasing every day. Because of this children are simple and old people are complex. It has no other relationship to age except this factor, that the ego has had time to become stronger in old people. That is why old people can easily become quarrelsome, angry and irritable. This happens naturally; the children of today will also prove to be the same tomorrow, they will also become like this.

There is a reason for it, but it has nothing to do with age, it has to do with the doing which goes on increasing every day. The old man has done too much. That is why old men always talk about their doings – I did this, I did that. What can children talk about? They haven't done anything yet. Right now they are only existing; they are breathing, moving their limbs – this cannot create much ego. So children look simple and the reason for their simplicity is that they have not yet had an opportunity to develop their ego.

That is why the sages say that when an old man again becomes childlike it is the ultimate flowering. Yet normally the situation is quite the opposite: children become like old men and old men do not become like children. If an old man is childlike it is the ultimate flowering; if children become like old men it is the ultimate loss, the ultimate fall. But that is what is happening.

We all try to help the child to develop his ego; the child is also trying to do the same. Sometimes the child makes such an effort that it is incomprehensible, but if you go deeply into it you will understand.

One day I was passing by the post office and I saw a small boy smoking a cigarette, a very small boy. He was wearing a false mustache worth one or two annas. The sun had not risen yet – it was just about to rise, and we were alone on the road. When he saw me he hid behind a tree. I followed him, and when I spoke to him he quickly put out his cigarette and took off the mustache. I went to see his father and saw that the boy was only trying to imitate him – he wore a mustache and was smoking a cigarette. So this poor child was trying to enjoy adulthood. And the imitation of his father's walk was worth seeing – smoking and walking, and wearing a mustache!

Fathers preach to their sons not to smoke, but they do not know that a cigarette doesn't only create smoke, it creates ego as well. The cigarette has become a symbol of adulthood – only adults smoke! It is symbolic that only adults can smoke. If some minor smokes, people say, "Not at your age – first become an adult, then you can smoke." So the child thinks, "If cigarette smoking symbolizes adulthood, what is the harm in smoking? It will only cause a little bit of coughing, a little bit of trouble, a few tears in the eyes. I will get used to that, and with a little practice it will be alright."

So children are trying to imitate adults; the ego is trying to express itself. It will grow and it will expand. Our doing is our ego, our being is our soul.

'Being' means that which we already are, which one doesn't have to create. We did nothing to achieve it or to create it. How can we do anything for it? Being precedes all our doing.

Now we will begin to talk about the I which means the being, which means *to be*. We will have to express it in a negative way, otherwise we will not be able to understand it. We understand only the I which says, "This is *my* house. This is *my* shop. This is *my* position."

Try to understand it. The vaster the "mine" the bigger is the

I. That is why the I in someone who says this is *my* nation, this is *my* religion, becomes even bigger. You have a small piece of land – then certainly you cannot have a huge I. How can you? Another man has a larger piece of land, and still another claims the whole country, the whole nation; certainly his I is the biggest.

The expansion of "mine" is the expansion of doing, of ownership; the I also grows with it. So when your wealth is stolen from you, it is not only that your wealth is taken, something of you is taken away as well. You have been robbed and it feels as if your soul has gone. This feeling of having been robbed is not just related to your wealth, it is related to you because now your "mine" has diminished with it. Your "mine" has been trimmed along with your wealth; some of your I also dies with it.

Our false I is related to "mine." "Mine" is the empire, the kingdom in which the I lives. Using the metaphor of a lamp, it is the oil, the fuel of "mine" which keeps the wick of the I burning. If the energy given to "mine" runs out, the flame of the I is extinguished.

Certainly, the discussion of the other I will have to begin with a denial: *I am not the ten senses.* Forget wealth – it is outside; forget fame – it is outside.

The senses are very deep and inner, and yet: *I am not the ten senses.* The senses are still somewhat outside.

I am not the intellect. The intellect is even deeper. *I am not the mind.* I am something which is simply never created: I am not born: *I am not the body.* And the final thing: *I am not even an eternal ego.*

We have discussed one type of I, the ego. This ego is not eternal, it just comes and goes, it forms and it vanishes. This last sentence in this sutra is marvelous. The first ego is transitory, it disappears, so we often wish to destroy this transitory ego just so that we can attain to some eternal ego.

The religious leaders preach to people to drop this transitory ego because it is momentary. It is very interesting that they say,

"Drop this ego, it is momentary, attain to the soul which can never be destroyed."

Greed arises in our minds and we think, "This is great! Then we will attain an eternal ego. Let us drop this momentary ego, it will be left behind anyway, it is petty; if I drop this one then I will attain the other one."

The person in whose mind this greed appears will never be able to rise above the ego. Hence the sage gives a very revolutionary sutra. He says: *I am not even an eternal ego.*

Don't think that there is an I which will remain forever, the I is always momentary; there is nothing like an eternal I. The I dissolves, becomes a nothingness, and no ego of any kind is left.

But our greedy minds are ego-obsessed minds. They perceive even the soul as nothing but some kind of a pure state of the ego. When we say "soul" we see it as meaning an eternal ego – that the petty ego will be dropped but the real inner me will never be lost. The sage says there is no such I within, and only when you come to realize this will you know the inner one.

I am not even an eternal ego. This sutra is similar to Buddha's word *anatta*, "no-self." Buddha used to say there is no self, there is only "no-self." That is why it became very difficult for Buddha to grow roots in India. Buddha's concept could not have a deep appeal to people because he did not provoke any greed.

Listening to Mahavira you can become greedy, even though he did not intend it. Mahavira says, "You will be in *moksha*, you will be in a state of pure, awakened consciousness." And the listener thinks, "So, I will still be there." Something has already gone amiss here between Mahavira and the listener. Mahavira says, "You will remain pure, awakened and eternal," and the listener has no idea of which "you" Mahavira is talking about. He thinks, "That's great! So I will be there, I will survive."

But the one who is speaking is none other than the I which he has accumulated. He says, "No harm, then there is nothing to worry about. Even if this house is left behind it is no problem, even if this money is left behind it is no problem, even if this body dies there is no problem, I will still be there." And this I is nothing other than the sum total of these very things.

Buddha said, "You will not remain at all. Everything else may remain, but not you."

A greedy person could not accept this statement. He would say, "Then what's the use? Why should I lose everything and gain nothing? What's wrong in a momentary ego?"

And you say, "Because this pleasure is momentary."

Then he says, "Okay, if there is some eternal pleasure, I can take the risk."

But then you say, "There is no eternal pleasure either."

"Then I may as well enjoy these momentary pleasures."

The greedy person says, "I accept that the ego is misery, it is painful, I suffer – but what will I gain if I abandon it?"

If something bigger can be achieved, our business mind agrees. We are happy with the deal. The investment is not a bad one – leave a little and gain more; leave the momentary and gain the eternal; the drop disappears and the ocean is achieved. What is the harm? What is wrong in it? Our greed says, "The mathematics are clear, a risk can be taken."

But Buddha says, "No, there is no self, the self does not exist. There is no soul within you, you are only ego. And ego is only suffering, therefore abandon the ego. Don't ask me what will be achieved. Nothing will be achieved."

So the seeker thinks, "Then I will hang on tight to what I have."

Consequently, Buddha could not be understood, because he did not use the language of greed. Buddha may be the only man on earth who did not use the language of greed. This sage is also saying the same thing. He is saying: *I am not even an eternal ego* – I do not exist even to say I. This is absolute denial.

I am not the ten senses. But do you understand the meaning of this? You might not comprehend what it means: *I am not the ten senses.* Have you ever had an experience without the senses? Whatever you have known, you have known through these ten senses. Just imagine: *I am not the ten senses.*

It means your every experience is lost, you are left empty-handed, nothing is left. The love you have known, the respect you have known, the insults you have received, the flowers you have seen, the beauty you have experienced through the eyes, the music you have heard through the ears, fragrances, everything will be lost; this touch – everything will vanish. Will you have anything left?

When the sage says: *I am not the ten senses,* he means that whatever experiences of the ten senses you have accumulated you are not those. Then you are totally empty, only a begging bowl remains with nothing in the bowl, because everything had been put into it by the ten senses.

It is like the River Ganges saying, "I am not those rivers which have merged with me." The trouble that the Ganges will face will be faced by us. What is the Ganges without them? – it is a mixture of all the rivers and tributaries merged together. If the Ganges were to say, "Whatever rivers have merged in me, I am not those. All the waters which have flowed into me are not me" – would the Ganges then remain as a river? Only a dry desert would be left.

We are also the sum total of those rivers which the senses have brought to us. Every sense has contributed a flow of pleasure within us. The eyes have brought seeing, the ears have brought hearing, the tongue has brought taste. We are the total of all of these. Remove the senses one by one – the journeys done by your feet, the achievements of your hands, the statements made by you through your words and heard by your ears. If all were to be removed, what would remain within? And the sage says: *I am not the ten senses.* So you may think: "Nothing may remain – but even then there will be enough intellect left to know that nothing has remained." But then the sage says:

I am not the intellect. Why? This is a very surprising statement: *I am not the intellect.* The denial of every other thing is understandable. There is not much of a problem in denying the senses because they are part of the physical body, but the intellect – thoughts and mind – are deeply rooted.

Actually, the intellect is born out of the struggle between the consciousness within and the world without. The intellect is a product of that struggle. That is why if you have no challenge in your life your intelligence will not flower. Hence, the sons of rich people remain unintelligent, there is no challenge to awaken their intelligence and no opportunity for its creation and expression.

Just imagine that you immediately get whatever you desire. For instance, imagine that one day we could produce a *kalpavriksha*, the mythological wish-fulfilling tree on earth – and man is trying, man is trying hard – would the person sitting under it have any intelligence? Make a wish, and you immediately get what you want without a struggle, without a challenge – what intelligence would you need? So intelligence is like the sharpening of a sword. The sharpness of a sword is due to friction. If there was no friction against the sword it could not have a sharp edge.

So one may have intelligence within, but it only grows and manifests after there is struggle without. That is why intelligent people are born in times of struggle; when the struggle is over they disappear. The more challenge you have in life the more sharpness you will have, and if there is no challenge at all, sharpness is lost.

Today, if young Americans are dropping out of schools, colleges and universities, the sole reason is that they do not need them; all the conveniences and comforts of life are readily available. In order to obtain these comforts students used to have to sharpen their intelligence, to study against all odds and inconveniences, doing their homework by the light of lampposts on the street. Today they all look like fools. Today many American students are saying, "What's the point of going to college? What is the point of studying?"

It will not be a surprise if in the coming fifty years American universities become more and more empty – and they have the best universities. This is a strange specialty of human beings. In fact the struggle is missing, the challenge is missing.

Today, America has the best means for developing the intellect, but America's own level of intellect is not growing. Most of its intellect has been borrowed from other countries. America can purchase it, but for how long? This situation is now creating problems for other nations, and many countries in Europe have begun creating regulations that do not allow their intelligent people to immigrate to America because it is creating a brain drain. Intelligent people born anywhere are sooner or later all ending up in America; it is becoming unavoidable because most countries can neither provide the facilities for academic work nor as much money, prestige, nor the laboratories – none of it – as America can. So the brain drain goes on happening in all countries; intelligence goes on moving away from the other countries in subtle ways.

Just as there was a time in the past when wealth from all over the world was siphoned off toward London, now all the intelligence is drawn toward New York. And the exploitation of wealth was a trivial matter, no big deal, but the intelligence now being siphoned off is an important matter. And how long can America live on borrowed intelligence? America can attract the intelligent people from India or from England and so on, but then their children are bound to refuse to attend universities. When there is no struggle, intelligence does not grow.

So the sage says: *I am not the intellect*, because the intellect too is external, the intellect too grows from an outer struggle. "No," the sage says, "I am also not this sharpness which comes from an outer struggle."

I am not the mind. After all, what do we contemplate? We only contemplate some object in the outer world when it becomes of value to us. We think, we contemplate, we ponder.

Intellect is that system of logic which sharpens the personality of a man and makes him more efficient in his struggles in the world. And mind means the capacity to contemplate, think and ponder, which gives man entry into and the ability to reflect on the abstract, the unmanifest.

Try to understand it like this: if you know or have seen the game of chess, you will know that the person who can imagine at least five moves ahead will become a skilful player. He has to imagine ahead: "I will move this way, the reply will be this, my counter reply will be this, and then this will be the move of the other; then I will move this way and my opponent will move like this."

One is thought to be an expert to the extent that he can contemplate ahead in this manner. Still those moves have not yet been made, and as yet the moves have not been countered, because they are not yet created on the other side. The capacity to plan ahead is called contemplation. But even that is external, the calculation of external moves – it is not concerned with the inner.

When a baby is born it has neither intellect nor mind, there is only the potential. Then the potential becomes an actuality. How it becomes actual depends on the opportunities, circumstances.

We are none of these. Then what are we? Then what is the meaning of our existence? This is only a negation – not this, not this, not this, not this.

I am without prana, the vital breath of life.
I am without mind.
I am ever the pure self-nature.
I am ever the witness beyond intellect.
I am eternally consciousness itself.
About this there is no doubt.

"I am never born, always without vital breath of life, and without the mind..." I just told you, the vital breath of life is that which starts as soon as the child breathes. This is how yoga came to search for techniques which would enable one to live just as a child can exist without breathing. Why should there be a problem in controlling our breathing in such a way that we can also exist without it? Yoga found such techniques, and from its understanding that, as a child can exist without breathing we should also be able to do so, a practical method was created.

Yoga did much work on *pranayoga*, the discipline of the vital breath, and with very, very slow exhalation tried to bring it to that neutral state in which a child is before his first breath, or in which he would be after his last breath.

There was a yogi in South India called Brahmayogi. Suddenly, in 1930, his name spread all over the world, because he could suspend his breathing for ten minutes. When he gave his first performance at Calcutta University ten doctors, the most intelligent medical brains of Calcutta University, were gathered around him. Brahmayogi had told them to write his death certificate in case he were to die during the course of the experiment. All ten doctors signed his death certificate when his breathing stopped because all the symptoms of death were apparent, according to medical science.

But after ten minutes this yogi came back to life. When he folded up the certificate and was putting it in his pocket, the doctors asked him to return the certificate and said, "Are you going to sue us, take us to court or what? If so, we will be in great trouble."

Ten doctors had certified that this man had died. But his breathing revived. Brahmayogi used to say, "I bring the breathing to the point where it is in a child just before birth, until just moments before the birth. Slowing down, more and more and more, the breathing comes to a stop, and with the stopping, the heartbeat and the pulse also stop."

But the soul is still there, otherwise who would come back? This man came back. He performed this experiment in Rangoon and in Oxford also.

The doctors told him, "If you are right and we have not been tricked in some way, we will then have to change our definition of death. Up to now we were certifying a man dead who showed all the clinical symptoms of death. We have certified many people as dead; now one cannot know how many of them were actually dead or not. Now there no longer seems to be a way to double check it!"

The truth is that none of them were dead. If we take the meaning of death as annihilation, none of them were annihilated. The only definition of death that we have is that the mechanism which used to breathe is no longer capable of breathing. Brahmayogi is doing it the other way; the mechanism is capable but he is not breathing anymore. The dying man is in the opposite situation: he wants to breathe but the mechanism is no longer capable. If one of the above two are missing, breathing will stop: either the mechanism becomes incapable, or the person does not want to breathe.

For brief moments, we also stop our breathing – anyone can. But if we can stop even for a moment, for that moment we have managed without the vital breath. And if we can manage without it for even one moment, we can manage just as well for ten moments; it is not a big thing. Then it is only a matter of practice.

...without...vital breath...without mind. We are, even when we do not think. Even in deep sleep, when all thoughts disappear and dreams disappear, we still are.

Now scientists say that even if they take out a man's entire brain his isness is not destroyed, he is still there. Mind is not essential in order to exist. In fact we have to sleep daily because we get so tired of the mind that it is necessary to leave it behind for a while, otherwise we feel old and stale.

I am not the mind... I am ever the witness beyond intellect. One can try to be a witness using the mind. Whenever you are practicing being a witness, you are doing so intellectually. You say, "I will remain a witness, I will try to be a witness."

All effort, all endeavor belongs to the mind. No one can be a witness through the mind; witnessing is only possible when the mind dissolves. The mind can never become a witness. Try to understand it carefully.

The mind cannot remain without judgments, and witnessing means not to judge. Witnessing means that if I see a flower, I remain just seeing it; neither does the thought that it is beautiful arise in my mind nor the thought that it is ugly; neither does the thought arise that it is a roseflower nor the thought that it is jasmine; neither does the thought to pluck it arise nor to leave it – mind does not come in between. The flower is there and I am here; nothing arises in between, no thought waves come in between. It is all an emptiness, a void in between – the flower there and I here. Only then am I the witness.

If you say to yourself in a conceited way, "Alright, this moment I am a witness to the flower," even as you are saying this you are related to this thought and not to the flower. And if in seeing the flower a small flash comes in that "It is beautiful" – not even words, just a flash – then too the mind has entered. The mind cannot exist without making judgments.

In fact, the very function of the mind is to judge. You will have to judge for or against, this side or that. You will have to be somewhere – with the mind you cannot be neutral. And you can only be a witness when the mind ceases to do anything.

I am ever the witness beyond intellect. You see, but you don't think; you are, but you create no opinions. Consciousness is there in its totality, but no shadow of thought falls over it.

I am eternally consciousness itself. It is not that sometimes you are conscious and sometimes you are unconscious; you are always consciousness.

With effort we can sometimes be conscious for a moment. A man puts a dagger at your chest and you are conscious for that moment; lifetimes of sleep are gone in a moment. The sharp edge of the dagger has cut through the darkness deep within, transcending all the five bodies, all the senses and all thoughts, you are just a witness.

There is a sect of Zen monks in Japan who teach meditation through swordsmanship. They say meditation cannot be obtained for less than this, that man is so lazy and sleepy that unless there is a sharp sword in front of him no meditation can happen. The training centers for swordsmanship are called meditation centers. Above the entrance it says "Meditation Center," but going inside you will be surprised to see that they are practicing with swords. You cannot even conceive what a sword might have to do with meditation.

Japan has given birth to a very special kind of warrior called samurai. A samurai is a soldier who combines meditation with the sword. Nowhere else on the earth are there soldiers like the samurais. The Rajput soldiers in India are also nothing compared to these samurais because the essential part of the training of a samurai is that the intellect, the mind, should not be there when he is using the sword. This is the training: when you take the sword in your hand the mind should not be there to interfere. Let the sword do its work without the interference of the mind.

When two samurais are engaged in combat, victory and defeat are very difficult to decide. The swords move without any interference from their minds. The samurai masters say: "You miss a movement only when your mind comes in and that's when you make a mistake, because that's when you become unconscious in the act."

You are in a pitched battle, in a sword fight, and suddenly a thought flashes in your mind that you have left the tap in your house running; you are gone! That is how thoughts come in – not only in a sword fight but also when you are sitting in the temple to worship or to meditate. You miss the moment! You are transported away from there. "It is during this gap," the samurai masters say, "that the sword of the other will have penetrated your body." The sword should move, but there should be no thoughts within.

Then who will be there within? There will be only the witness within – only the witness. It will witness the sword moving, and even if the sword penetrates the body it will witness that too – but only if there is a witness; then it will see the sword penetrating within. The sword will have nothing to do with the witness, the sword can never penetrate the witness.

That is why Krishna said: "*Nainam chhindanti shastrani* – weapons cannot cut it, fire cannot burn it." Burn it in fire and it remains unburned, untouched.

I am eternally consciousness itself. Not just occasionally. We only become conscious occasionally, in an accident or in some intense moment. It is very interesting that whenever we are totally conscious, that is when we get a little glimpse of bliss in life. Rarely, very rarely – maybe once or twice in life – a few such moments occur when we suddenly get a glimpse, which we never get again. The reason we get a glimpse is the same: for some reason we become conscious within. Any reason, the reason can be anything. This consciousness which flowers for a moment, this peak we never achieve again. And we go on searching for another experience like this for the rest of our lives.

It can happen anywhere. It can happen in the deep still moments of a night when there is no thought within, when only the sound of a cricket remains; the bliss experienced in that moment was never known before. In the morning, seeing the sunrise, it can sometimes happen. The sun goes on rising and as you watch it there is no thought within; not even this much thought, that "It is the sun"; not even the word *sun* comes to mind. In that experience the sun becomes divine. That experience can never be forgotten.

Such things happen accidentally, sometimes. But to cause it to happen through using a method is called meditation – that one remains aware. But there is effort in it.

The sage says: "When effort is not there and the awakening is natural – that is my real nature, that is what I am."

About this there is no doubt. There is no doubt about it. Why? – because this is not a theory. The sage says: "There is no doubt about it because I am saying it from my own experience."

Vivekananda went to Ramakrishna and asked, "Does God exist?"

Ramakrishna did not say yes or no. He did not sit down to

discuss or explain, no, all he said was, "Do you want to meet him right now, this very moment?"

Vivekananda has said somewhere, later on, "I hesitated for a split second; did I want to see God right now or not? That man did not hesitate, and the question I had asked was a difficult one: 'Does God exist?' He ought to have hesitated, because the question is very complex. Nor is it all that easy to say yes or no. If you say yes you will have to prove it, and who has been able to prove the existence of God?"

Perhaps many people are not able to accept God just because no one has so far been able to prove his existence – otherwise atheists would have disappeared long ago. But they have not disappeared, so this only goes to show that God is something which cannot be proved – otherwise nonbelievers would have disappeared long ago.

The earth has produced so many great theists, and yet the atheist remains unaffected; the theists do not even create an iota of change in him, he remains as he is. Even if we could bring all the theists together, they could not change a single atheist. What could be the reason for this? There is only one reason: an atheist demands proof and there is no proof – hence the helplessness.

So Vivekananda had thought, "Ramakrishna will be in trouble; he is only a villager, illiterate. He has studied only up to the second grade in Bengali language, so what could he know?"

Vivekananda was an atheist, and he was intelligent, well-educated, one of the greatest geniuses Bengal could produce, an expert in debating, in logic, in Aristotle and Indian philosophy. Vivekananda asked this villager who was just a rustic, and this villager had put Vivekananda into a state of hesitation. He asked Vivekananda if he was ready to meet God – right now!

There is a special quality in this answer, and that is the confidence of Ramakrishna – as if God is there, right in the next room, and it is only for you to ask and you can meet him. This man knows beyond a doubt – no doubt at all. Doubt can only not exist when there is experience.

So the sage says: *About this there is no doubt.*

All that he is trying to say is: "I have known it and I am saying this from my existential experience. This is not a theory or a dogma. This is not my thought, my idea, my concept. I have known it to be so; I have lived it as such."

Prior to this Vivekananda had gone to the father of Rabindranath Tagore, Devendranath. He was a Maharishi, a reputable man. Ramakrishna was nothing at that time; Maharishi Devendranath was a great man. First, he was from the respected family of Tagore – his father was called a king – and then he was wise and respected as a great sage. He had the personality of a sage.

Most of the time he lived on a houseboat on the river. So at midnight Vivekananda swam over to the houseboat. Soaking wet, in the dark of night, he pushed the door open. It was not latched, because there was no question of anyone coming in the middle of the night; and who would come onto a houseboat? That was one of the reasons why he was living on the houseboat. Vivekananda pushed open the door and entered. Devendranath was sitting in meditation with closed eyes. The push on the door, the sound, the shaking of the houseboat, the door opening – and suddenly there was this young man catching hold of Devendranath by his collar, shaking him and asking, "Does God exist?"

Devendranath said, "Just sit down and calm down your breathing. Is this the time to ask such questions? Is this the time to visit? What kind of manners are these?"

Vivekananda said, "When the house is on fire who cares about manners? Answer my question, forget about everything else – no formality is needed: Does God exist?"

There was a flash of hesitation within Devendranath; it was difficult to say yes, and no was out of the question. But how to answer a man like this, who says that the house is on fire, who has come swimming to your house at midnight, soaking wet – even his face could not be seen clearly – asking about God? Is this the way of a seeker?

He said, "Sit down, I will explain."

But Vivekananda jumped back into the river. The sound of the splash… Maharishi Devendranath called out, "Young man, wait!"

Vivekananda replied, "Your hesitation has said everything – there is nothing left to wait for."

That is why the sage says: *About this there is no doubt.*

This hesitation was enough to reveal his doubt. But Vivekananda bowed down his head before Ramakrishna – in front of a villager, a rustic, he bowed down. Devendranath was one of the wisest men, but there had been hesitation.

The mind always hesitates; it is only experience that is without hesitation. No matter how much you can think, hesitation will remain. How can there be no hesitation using the mind? You can go on thinking, believing and convincing yourself endlessly that God exists, but some voice within you will go on saying: "You have not known it yet, you have not attained to it yet, you have not experienced it yet." Even if logic and evidence have all said to you that God exists, yet your inner experience will go on reminding you that you are still empty and unfulfilled.

That is why the sage says: *About this there is no doubt.* I am saying a truth which I have experienced.

16

Beyond All – the Witness

I am neither the doer nor the experiencer.
I am but a witness to all manifestation.
It is because of my closeness to them that the body,
etcetera, appears to be conscious, and begins to
function accordingly.
I am the unchanging, the eternal.
I am ever the home of bliss, of purity and knowing.
I am almighty.
I am the clear soul
which is present in all sentient beings as a witness.
About this there is no doubt.

In order to enter into the depth and profundity of existence, it is essential to understand a few more negations. Yesterday we discussed that you are neither the body, nor the senses, nor the mind, nor the intellect; you are consciousness. But still more subtle layers exist, and those subtle layers are created only because of their proximity to consciousness.

Consciousness illuminates whatsoever is in its proximity. It is like a light which shines on everything that is nearby. We light a lamp, and instantly everything within its field is illuminated. Similarly, everything within us near to consciousness is illuminated. And it is with this illumination that the troubles begin.

Try to understand it like this: when there is no light, it is dark and nothing is visible. Then a lamp is lit. If the light of the lamp had any consciousness it would be under the illusion that all that became illuminated, visible, is part of the lamp itself. The light would be under the illusion that all that became illuminated is not separate from it, because "When I am not, it is not there; neither the walls nor the furniture of the room are visible. When I am not there, there is nothing. Things only exist when I am there. Naturally, it is simply logical that the existence of everything is contained within my existence."

It is the same with consciousness. If there were no consciousness there would be neither the five bodies, nor the mind, nor the intellect, nor the senses – nothing! Everything comes into existence with the emergence of consciousness. If consciousness becomes unconscious, if it disappears in a deep sleep, then even the body is not felt, the mind is not perceived. That is why when you have to have an operation a layer of deep unconsciousness is created around your consciousness so that you will not feel pain even if your hand is amputated. You would not even know if your whole body was cut into pieces, because the light of the lamp which illuminated all this is covered with unconsciousness.

So consciousness, illuminating anything that is close to it, becomes identified with it. Because of the proximity it feels that "I myself am this." This is the whole mistake of identification. And then we start behaving according to whatsoever it is that we have identified ourselves with.

For example, we breathe; if our consciousness leaves the body the breathing will leave too. The process of breathing runs only when the light of consciousness falls on it. Naturally, consciousness identifies: "When I am, breathing is, and when I am not, breathing is not. So I must be the breathing itself, I myself am the breathing."

But this is not true. You have never taken a breath. Breathing happens: you are only a witness. Certainly, awareness of breathing happens only when you are, but the process of breathing as such is totally separate; it can go on even if you are unconscious. And now scientists claim that even if you are dead they can keep the breathing process going with the help of machines.

Breathing is a separate mechanism, a separate system. You are only the awareness of it. Have you ever taken a breath? If it were you who had been breathing you would have died long ago, because if you had forgotten to breathe for a while everything would have fallen apart. And man may go on committing all kinds of other mistakes – and that is okay – but if he forgets to breathe that will not do. That is why it is not you who is breathing, it happens on its own; you are not the doer, you are only a witness to it. The blood circulates in your body, you do not circulate it. You are not the doer. The heart beats – you are not the doer, you are only a witness.

If you understand this phenomenon about the heart, the breathing, the pulse beat and the circulation of the blood, it will not be very difficult to understand how the mind also works. You do not make it work, it too is a mechanism – mind too is a mechanism.

A person is possessed by sexual desire; if he thinks that he is doing it he is mistaken. It is just happening. This too is nothing more than a few glands, some fluids being released in the glands. When the sex glands have matured at the age of fourteen they make sexual desire possible. If you were to remove these glands, the possibility of any sexual desire would be gone. You are not even the creator of your sexual desires, and that is why it is very difficult to get rid of them. How easy it would have been if you were creating them. If you had been the creator of your sexual desires then there would have been no difficulty, you would have just said, "I don't want this," and it would be finished. But you go on saying that you will not have any sexual desire and still it goes on arising, it doesn't leave you. Why? If you are the doer, the creator, then where is the difficulty?

The difficulty is that you are not the doer and, believing yourself to be the doer, you get into double trouble. First you consider yourself to be the doer, and then because of it you think that if you wish you can be the controller also. You think, "I am myself the doer and I can stop sexual desire if I wish to." But it doesn't stop; you can neither arouse it nor can you stop it.

Does that mean you can never get rid of sexual desire? Yes, you can be free of it at this very moment. If the feeling of the doer vanishes, and if you remain only a witness, then you are freed from desire. Desire remains on one side, the mechanism remains separate from it and you stand aloof; a gap happens in between.

One more thing needs to be understood. You are not the doer with regard to this mechanism, but your presence is necessary for it to function – just your presence. You are not the doer.

The sun when it rises in the morning makes no effort to open each bud individually. Perhaps it is not even aware of how many flowers have bloomed because of it, how many birds have started singing their songs. It is not the creator of all this, still it could not have happened without the sun. If the sun doesn't rise tomorrow morning the birds will not be able to sing, the flowers will not bloom and the lotuses will remain closed. Yet the sun is not the doer because there is no question of doing. Its rays don't come and open each bud, one by one. Its rays don't reach out to create songs in the throat of each bird. There is no effort, only its presence works.

Science accepts one fact which is called a "catalytic agent." Science says that there are times when just the presence of a catalytic agent creates an effect. For example, water is comprised of hydrogen and oxygen together, but if you mix hydrogen and oxygen the result will not be water. You can go on mixing them, but they will not make water as the catalytic agent is not present. Everything else is present – because water contains nothing other than hydrogen and oxygen.

This phenomenon of the catalytic agent should be properly understood because it will be very helpful in understanding the witness. When we analyze water we find nothing except hydrogen and oxygen – only these two things. Then why don't we get water when we mix hydrogen and oxygen? These two should become water, but it doesn't happen unless electricity is present. That is why when lightning is flashing in the sky during the rainy season it is a sign of rain, otherwise the clouds would just continue wandering and there would be no rain. Science has remained puzzled as to what part electricity plays, but it has been found not to have any direct contribution in the creation of water. That is why when we analyze water we don't find any electricity. Then what does the electricity do? It does nothing, but its presence is essential; water would not happen without its presence. So electricity has worked as a catalytic agent.

A catalytic agent means that the phenomenon cannot happen without it being present, and yet it is not doing anything. So breathing is not possible without the presence of consciousness, the heart will not beat without the presence of the consciousness, the intellect will not work without the presence of the consciousness. And yet the consciousness is not the doer.

But this creates within us the illusion of being a doer – "If something could not happen without me, then I am the doer" – because we can understand only two concepts in our minds: firstly, "If I am the doer, then things happen," and secondly, "If I am not, then they don't happen." So the natural conclusion is that "I am the doer."

We don't know the third dimension at all, when only the presence of the consciousness works. When we assume the role of the doer because of this presence, then this becomes our bondage. If this presence remains an unidentified presence, then that is the witness. We only need to know that we are the witness, that things certainly happen in our presence, but we are not the doer. When this is understood a distance is then created between ourselves and our mechanisms.

Then many profound things happen because of this unidentified presence. For instance, your sex center may try to assert itself, but if you remain a witness it will not be able to, because as soon as you become the witness you are disconnected from the sex center. As soon as you are a witness you have receded back into yourself and you have distanced yourself from your sex center. The proximity of the consciousness, which your sex center needs in order to function, is disconnected. The sex center can remain throbbing and calling, the sex glands can continue asking for sex, but your presence is not available.

That is why amazing things sometimes happen. You are sitting there, full of sexual desire, your mind totally absorbed in it, and suddenly someone shouts that your house is on fire. Why is it that your sexual desire vanishes from the mind within a split second? – because the consciousness moves from there and becomes connected to the thought of the house being on fire. Otherwise try separating your mind from sexual desire and you will know that it doesn't work! You cannot separate from it. But as soon as you hear the news of the fire – even though it may be a false alarm – the whole mechanism of your sexual desire comes to a standstill; you forget about it and it is finished.

What happened? The presence of your consciousness shifted. An emergency has arisen, and now the mind cannot afford to be anywhere else. It moved away from the desire, and the desire disappeared in this very moving away. The mechanism of sexual desire was there, and you too were present within this mechanism – but then what changed? What has changed is that you are no longer present near the desire; your consciousness has shifted from it, your attention has moved away. Freedom from sexual desire is not attained through effort, it is attained through effortless witnessing, because you are not a doer.

So the sage begins this sutra:

I am neither the doer nor the experiencer.

"I am not the doer" – this is somewhat comprehensible; "I am not even the experiencer" – this is more difficult to comprehend. In doing, we are doing something on the outside, doing is always external, but experiencing is internal. When we are doing something we move without, and when we are experiencing something we move within.

Experiencing is internal, hence it is nearer. That is why, maybe, you can understand that you are not a doer, but it is very difficult to understand that you are not the experiencer either. But one who is not the doer cannot be the experiencer, because deep down experiencing too is an act, a doing. To say "I experienced" is also a subtle doing. "I did" is a gross doing, "I experienced" is a subtle doing.

So when the feeling of doing is outside, simultaneously the feeling of the experiencer happens inside – and the bigger the sense of doing, the bigger the desires of the experiencer. Therefore the bigger the sense of doing the more anguish in life, because the desires of the experiencer increase in the same proportion – the greater the passion, the greater the discontentment. That is why those who strive more are often found to be very miserable because they feel that they have done so much, but what did they achieve? What could they enjoy? In fact you go on doing and doing in the hope that one day you will sit back and enjoy. It goes on this way for the whole of your life, but the moment to enjoy never comes.

There is another example of this proximity. You know when you are eating food that you do not create the hunger – hence you are not the doer. This is not so difficult to understand. You do not create hunger, it simply comes. If it does not come, there is no way to create it. So this much is clear, that hunger happens, we do not create it. We eat food because there is hunger. But we experience the taste – it feels good or bad, bitter or sweet. So let us accept that hunger is not created by us, we do not produce it – it comes. We do not create hunger but we certainly do experience the taste. Taste is more subtle. Do we really experience the taste? Or does that also happen in the mechanism of our bodies and because of our proximity to it we think, "I am tasting it."

Taste also happens in our mechanism. That is why when

you have a fever you cannot taste anything. You are the same, but your mechanism is dull and incapable of experiencing it. Taste happens in the mechanism.

Pavlov has done many experiments in Russia. There is something to be understood in this context from those experiments. Pavlov asks: "Is taste a pleasing experience or an unpleasant one? If a foul smell is released around you each time you are eating food, by and by eating will become a suffering. Or if you are given an electric shock through the chair whenever you are eating, after ten or fifteen days each mealtime you will be expecting the pain, 'Now it's going to come!' Once this pattern is established, then even if you are not given the shock anymore you will not be able to relish the food."

Many mothers have a problem with their children, that they do not enjoy eating. They make a thousand and one efforts, but their children do not want to eat. And it never occurs to them that the child is not at fault. In fact the way the mother may have behaved whenever the child asked for milk is what has spoiled its interest in food. An association has formed. Whenever the child has asked for milk, the way the mother responded has created a bad association, a bad taste. So the mother's behavior has become associated with the food.

In fact men's attraction for women's breasts is the result of their mothers' efforts to discontinue breast-feeding. Every mother is trying to take her child off the breast as soon as possible, and the result is that he will not be able to forget breasts his whole life. He is looking at breasts even in his old age. The attraction that men have to breasts is not without a reason. In his childhood when his mother's breasts were everything to the child – they were his very life – they were taken away so forcefully that they will haunt his memory for the rest of his life. They are stuck in his mind and an idiotic obsession is born around breasts. People are totally obsessed. Only these parts of a woman's body appear to have any significance. Painters waste their entire lives painting them. People call these painters geniuses, but all they are doing is painting women's breasts; sculptors sculpt them, and poets write poetry about them. And these are the so-called intelligent people!

That there is so much poetry, sculpture and paintings of breasts are only indicators of man's insanity. Man is insane, but the incident that triggered all this was very trivial. That is why in those tribes where mothers enjoy breast-feeding the people are not interested in breasts. In primitive tribes, in the so-called undeveloped tribes, mothers enjoy breast-feeding.

And it is also interesting that the fact that children enjoy sucking milk is only half the truth; the mother also enjoys breast-feeding, even more than the child. If civilization and conditioning and all these things did not interfere, the child would be freeing her of a thousand and one tensions.

That is why there is no such interest in breasts in primitive tribes. We feel surprised that these tribal women go around with their breasts uncovered. In reality we should be surprised that our women cover them. It is insane to cover that which is. And the amazing thing is that the attempt to hide them is nothing more than an effort to expose them, because if the breasts were completely naked no one would look at them. There is nothing in them to look at. Nobody looks at any of those parts of the body which are naked. Whatever is to be shown needs to be covered and decorated, then it attracts. It is a double game: cover that which you want to show, hide that which you want to expose. This game creates the complexities which have their aftereffects.

You are eating: whatever pleasant or unpleasant feeling you have while eating is created by your environment. Your mechanism receives impressions and upon these it decides whether what you are eating is good or bad. That is why people who do not eat fish are surprised to see how others can enjoy eating it. It has such a foul smell, but it is very tasty for those who eat it.

So what is taste? It is a conditioning, a habit. That habit happens in your mechanism and you are present just behind it. You are so close to it that whatever is highlighted because of you, you take that to be yourself. Taste cannot be experienced without you, so you become the taste, you become the experiencer.

In fact deep down you are just a witness to the taste. You recognize the taste as sweet or bitter – the one who recognizes it is you. You are not the sweet taste, you are the one who recognizes the sweetness. There are three happenings: you are eating a sweet thing, you are experiencing the sweetness, and you are aware of this experience. The one who is aware of this experience is you.

That is why the sage says:

I am neither the doer nor the experiencer.
I am but a witness to all manifestation.

"I am only witnessing, and everything is happening outside of me." Consciousness only witnesses, everything else is happening in the manifested world. Everything is happening around you – you are only witnessing it. But we lose this witnessing when we either become a doer or an experiencer. And suffering begins as soon as we become a doer or an experiencer.

I have heard about a house which caught on fire. The owner of the house is crying and beating his chest. Then one of his neighbors comes and tells him, "Why are you crying? I happen to know that your son sold this house yesterday and has also received the money."

The tears disappear, the crying stops, and the man becomes totally normal. What has happened? The house is still on fire, the man is the same; no change has happened. If we look, nothing has changed on the outside. By now the flames are rising even higher, he should be crying louder, but he is not – the identification has been broken, his consciousness is not involved in it. The house no longer belongs to him. The matter is over.

But suddenly the son comes running, shouting, "Why are you just standing there?" The father is standing there as an onlooker and the son demands, "Why are you standing idle? The deal was only in process. The house has not been sold yet."

Again the father starts crying and beating his chest, although the outside phenomenon is still the same. What has happened in between? What has changed during those few moments? The flames are still there, but why have the tears disappeared? His identification has been broken.

When we take something to be "mine," we feel a closeness with it. When we know it is "not mine," this proximity disappears. This proximity, this identification, is the clue to all our joys, all our sorrows, to our becoming a doer and to our becoming an experiencer.

I have heard that a man was staying as a guest for a night at an inn and left at four o'clock in the morning. After one year he returned, and again stayed at the same place. The innkeeper stood up in astonishment and said, "You are still alive!"

The traveler replied, "What do you mean? Did you hear a rumor that I had died?"

The owner said, "It is not a question of a rumor. The last time you stayed here all the people who had eaten here that night were found dead in the morning except for you, and because you had left before dawn we could not be sure about you; the food had been poisonous."

Hearing this, the traveler fell down unconscious.

This was a real fact. But what really happened? – the same kind of phenomenon that occurred at the time when the house was on fire. But in that case the identification was broken, while in this case the identification was created. The traveler identified with the idea of being poisoned, became unconscious and died. Fewer people die of poisoning than die of their identification with the idea of being poisoned. Poison in itself is not that effective, it too needs some identification.

I was talking before about Brahmayogi, who used to stop his breathing for ten minutes. He could also contain any kind of poison in his body for thirty minutes. He would swallow it, store it in his stomach, and then release it through his urine. He was able to keep it inside for up to thirty minutes, but no longer. But he died in Rangoon, because he could not contain it inside for more than this. Thirty minutes is also not a short time! Chemists were all amazed and astonished, because this poison would even cause a person's death the moment it would touch his tongue. One would not be able to remain alive long enough even to say something, not even to say, "I am dying" – and this man was able to contain even this type of poison in his system for thirty minutes!

But he died while doing this experiment in Rangoon. It was a surprise. What happened? What was the secret? He took the poison at Rangoon University and left to go to the place where he was staying, but the car he was in broke down on the way so he did not reach there until thirty-five minutes later, he was unconscious. He was not able to contain the poison for this long, and the five-minute delay because of the car breaking down caused his death. That had been his secret, to reach where he was staying within thirty minutes and release the poison through his urine.

Whenever he was asked how he could keep the poison in his system for this time he would reply, "I don't become identified with it; I don't allow any feeling that I have taken poison. But I am unable to prolong it for more than thirty minutes. After that length of time I will begin to be overpowered by it, and then it will occur to me that I have taken poison and that I could die. As soon as this thought comes, the trouble starts. The identification! Instantly this thought will bring my consciousness into identification with it and I will become the doer or the experiencer."

If the consciousness can remain unidentified, anything is

possible. If you have ever seen a hypnosis experiment you would have been amazed. If your body were laid across two chairs, stretched out, your feet on one chair and your head on the other, could you lie like that? With your feet on one chair and your head on another chair, could the middle of you remain straight? How could it stay straight? You would fall immediately. But if you are hypnotized and told that you are a board which cannot bend, then someone can even walk on you and you will not bend. What has happened? The body is the same, it has not changed. The bones still bend at the joints where they used to, yet someone is sitting on top of you and your body does not bend. What is happening? The identification has been removed. The idea of falling, the idea of collapsing which you have always carried, that you would fall if such a thing were done to you, has been removed and a new idea has been given to you.

Ramamurti used to support an elephant standing on his chest. What was his secret? The chest is not so strong as to allow an elephant to stand on it – no one's chest is, not even Ramamurti's. It cannot happen, the very question does not ever arise. A man's chest is a man's chest, and no matter how strong it is, an elephant's foot will smash it into pieces. Ramamurti's experiments contained nothing more than the art of removing the identification. If you can remove this identification you can even have an elephant standing on your chest without your bones breaking. Bones break because the idea that they will break has become so concentrated in you. The weight of the elephant itself does not break them – that is the most interesting thing.

Lao Tzu has told a story about four persons who are sitting in a bullock cart. One of them is a drunkard and the other three are sober. The cart has an accident and turns upside down, but the drunkard remains unhurt and the other three all have multiple fractures. What is the drunkard's secret? He should have the most injuries! Totally drunk with wine, you would think he was preparing to travel to hell, but his bones did not break.

He is lying relaxed by the roadside, and the other three are screaming and crying with broken bones.

The drunkard is not even aware that the cart has turned upside down, and that he could have broken his bones. This much awareness is needed to create the identification. He is unaware. He had not even been aware that the cart was moving or that it had turned over or whether he is now inside or outside of the cart, so an identification with his bones was not created and he remained unhurt. That is why children go on stumbling and falling. You see drunkards fallen over, lying on the road, but they are never seriously hurt. In the morning they again get up fresh and go on their way. You try falling and see what happens – without drinking! One time will be enough to make it difficult for you to get out of bed.

It is the identification. Consciousness immediately identifies with the body when it sees an accident about to happen. So whatever you are thinking within that short space of time, it outwardly materializes. If the distance is maintained, it makes a difference, it makes a difference.

I am neither the doer nor the experiencer.
I am but a witness to all manifestation.
It is because of my closeness to them that the
body, etcetera,
appears to be conscious, and begins to function
accordingly.

The body assumes that this is so. But this is only our belief. Our world is our belief, and unless this belief is broken we have no way of attaining to liberation.

I am the unchanging, the eternal.
I am ever the home of bliss, of purity and knowing.
I am almighty.
I am the clear soul

which is present in all sentient beings as a witness.
About this there is no doubt.

As soon as the ideas of being the doer and the experiencer disappear, the phenomenon of witnessing begins. Or, to put it another way, as soon as witnessing begins the ideas of being the doer and the experiencer disappear. It depends on you where you want to start from. Start from anywhere, and the phenomenon starts happening. Cease to be the doer while doing, cease to be the experiencer while experiencing, and the witness starts emerging. Keep on trying to give birth to the witness, try to remain constantly alert and the doer and the experiencer will start disappearing. These are the two ends of one phenomenon.

There are two ways: one is meditation, and the other is asceticism. Asceticism is a method which removes the experiencer and the doer. Meditation is a method used to become a witness, a watcher. Start from anywhere, the outcome will be the same.

It needs to be understood why the ascetic moves into suffering. Why after all, does the ascetic choose to suffer? Why did Mahavira need to stand naked in the scorching sun? What need was there for his naked body to shiver in the cold? Why walk on rough roads with bare feet and deny yourself any food for months on end? Either he was mad, which was not the case… In fact it would have been difficult to find anyone as peaceful, as centered, as wise as he, so there is no way to call him insane.

Sometimes Western psychologists suspect that Jesus was a madman, but even they cannot have had doubts about Mahavira. Some of Jesus' statements are such that he appears to have been mad. For instance: "I am the only begotten son of God, I am the king of the whole of creation. In heaven I will be sitting next to God. Those who follow me will be saved, and those who leave me will fall into eternal hell." And then suddenly he is crucified, and dies like any ordinary man. What happened to his kingdom? He had promised to save the whole world and could not save himself! And if he was the only begotten son of God, how could God permit his son to be crucified?

Western psychologists suspect that he must have been deluded. But there is no truth in that suspicion; they are making a mistake. They do not understand the language of Jesus. Jesus was speaking to people who were just villagers, rustics, uneducated, who would not have understood the language of sophisticated philosophy. His language had to be of this mundane world.

Such doubts cannot be raised about Mahavira because he was using a very cultured language. There are no loopholes in it to prove him insane. Then why did Mahavira invite self-imposed suffering? The reason is that it was an experiment in breaking away from the doer and the experiencer.

It is a fact that you can easily become the experiencer in pleasure, but it is not as easy with suffering. The very suffering, the very pain does not allow you to be just the experiencer. A thorn pricks your foot and at that time you easily become a witness of this pain – you have to, because how can you enjoy it? There is no joy in it, you have no taste for it, you want distance from it. A distance is automatically created from the pain, the suffering; the identification is broken because nobody wants to live in suffering. We have no desire to be close to it. It comes – that is another matter – but we want to keep it at a distance.

But when pleasures come we get very close to them, then we don't want to keep any distance. When people welcome you with garlands as a celebrity then there is no desire to be a witness. In such a moment you don't feel any interest in being a witness. In such a moment your only longing is to reap as much praise as possible. It never occurs to you that this person may be doing something wrong, or that he may be mistaking you for someone else – that it may be a joke, an illusion. No, in such a moment your mind says, "This is not an illusion. It ought to have happened long ago – it has taken this long because of your stupidity. At last you have finally recognized me; what should have happened a long time ago is finally happening now."

But if someone were to put a garland of shoes around your neck – an Indian insult, a sign of rejection – a distance would be immediately created. You would think that it cannot have been meant for you, that there must be some misunderstanding, that it must have been meant for someone else. Or else this person must be mad, a scoundrel, or a crook. You don't think it is right, you throw it back on the other. But if a garland of flowers is brought for you then you claim it, you think you deserve it – you don't consider it as simply a gracious act on the part of the other. You get identified with the garland of flowers. You want to be identified with pleasure because you want pleasure. You become identified with what you desire. You have never wanted to suffer, in fact you always wish suffering to go away, so even if it comes you try to distance yourself from it.

So this becomes the principle of asceticism – to stand in the middle of suffering so that slowly, slowly, by and by, it becomes clear that you are not the doer, that you are not the experiencer.

Mahavira would live without food for thirty days, so that when he was hungry, then he knew that it was not he that was hungry – it was the body, and he was only a witness to it. On the thirty-first day he would visit a village, eat some food, and know that he was neither the earlier hunger nor the satisfaction now. Both the phenomena were outside of him. In his suffering he saw its separateness from his self, and then he would try to maintain the same separateness with regard to the pleasure as well.

So asceticism is a technique. It is a way, a means to break our identification with the doer and the experiencer; then the birth of the witness begins. On one hand the doer and the experiencer disappear, and on the other hand the witness begins to take birth.

Try this experiment sometime. There is no need for you to go looking for suffering because so much suffering already comes to you on its own. So when sorrow comes, experiment with this technique of asceticism. You don't need to take up a life of asceticism like Mahavira. He belonged to a family where he had already enjoyed plenty of pleasures, so perhaps he had had no experience of suffering at all, and that is why he had to make this choice.

Your life is already layers of suffering upon suffering – you need not go in search of it. Just try to disidentify with the doer and the experiencer in that very suffering. When you are ill, keep a distance from the illness and remain a witness. Don't experience yourself as being ill, only experience yourself as a witness to that illness. You will be amazed: as you experience it in this way the illness starts to disappear, and an enormous distance is created between you and the illness. As you experience yourself in this way you suddenly find that everything is healthy within. It is as if someone suddenly lights a lamp in the darkness and everything becomes clear. That moment of clarity is the moment of witnessing.

The other technique is meditation. Mahavira's emphasis is on asceticism, Buddha's emphasis is on meditation. That is why the followers of both could not understand each other. They were contemporaries, but their followers could not understand each other at all because their emphasis is different and they look opposite to each other.

Mahavira says: "How can there be meditation without asceticism?" And Buddha says: "Asceticism preceding meditation is nonsense." And both the statements are right.

And the interesting thing is that in this world two things do not become wrong just because they are opposites. Two opposite things can be simultaneously right. The world is so complex, so full of mystery, that two things in opposition are not essentially wrong.

Ordinary logic holds that if two things are opposite, either both of them are wrong, or one may be wrong and the other right, but both can never be right. This only proves ignorance of the mystery of life. The mystery of life says both can be simultaneously right. So Mahavira and Buddha are both right at the same time, equally right; only the directions of their paths are different.

Mahavira begins with the experiencer, the doer, and what remains after disidentifying with it is the witness. Buddha begins with the awakening of the witness. When the witness awakens, the feeling of being the doer and the experiencer starts withering away. When the witness awakens totally, both the doer and the one who enjoys disappear. That is why Buddha could influence the whole world more than Mahavira. The basic reason is that nobody has so much happiness that he will go looking for suffering. Everybody already has enough suffering, so that the very idea of choosing anymore suffering seems ridiculous; suffering is already available in abundance.

Buddha's teachings could be understood more easily because they do not increase one's suffering. They are an experiment to awaken the witness directly, which reduces the suffering.

Someday Mahavira's teachings may become influential and someday maybe, when the world becomes too affluent, Buddha's teachings will disappear. It is also possible that in the coming century, in America, the teachings of Mahavira may be revived – prosperity may have increased to such an extent that even suffering may start having an appeal; so much prosperity and pleasure may be available that even suffering may look like a welcome change.

Here, two Western women sannyasins have been sleeping out under the trees. They told me in the morning that every Indian seems to be worried about this. They said, "Whoever meets us says, 'What are you doing? Don't do that! It is dangerous to sleep outdoors on the ground, during the night.' And we are enjoying it."

I told them, "You may not realize why the Indians can't enjoy sleeping beneath the trees – they are so poor they are already living under the trees! You can enjoy it because so much distance has happened between you and the trees that to be there is an adventure for you."

So both techniques can help this phenomenon to happen, that only the witness remains. Then, even though this witness may be within us, it is not ours; it is all-pervading. With the experiencing of the witness the ego disappears, because the ego is nothing but the sum total of the doer and the experiencer. "I did," "I experienced," "I achieved" – all these create your I, the ego. If I did not do and I did not experience and I did not achieve, then where can your I stand? The whole accumulation falls apart.

So the witness is not "mine." Understand it rightly: the witness is not "mine" – you become a witness to all that you have been calling "mine." As soon as the witness awakens the I dissolves. The witness is like an infinite ocean within us. It is within me, within you, within everyone; somewhere it is asleep, somewhere it is awake, somewhere it is tossing and turning, somewhere it is dreaming, somewhere it is totally awake and somewhere it is dormant, in sleep, but the witness is the same. It is the same in a tree, it is the same in a rock – in deep, deep sleep. It is the same in animals – it is just beginning to stir. It is the same in us – once in a while awake for a moment. It is the same in Buddha and in Christ – totally awake. These differences are only quantitative. But someone who knows it in its fully awakened state finds instantly that it is a vast ocean.

The witness is oceanic, permeating us all. We are all in it, and it is in all of us. But it is one, and it is omnipresent. The sage says: *About this there is no doubt.* "I say it after knowing it, I say it after realizing it, I have found it to be so."

It often looks as though the statements of the sages are very egoistic assertions. Those who don't know are bound to feel like that. Those who don't understand any language other than that of the ego are bound to feel that way. To say that there is no doubt about it, is it not authoritarian? If we were to ask Krishnamurti, would he not find it authoritarian and an effort to create an ultimate dogma? Krishnamurti would not like to say, "What I say is beyond any doubt." He would say, "This would mean that I am putting pressure on you to believe me." And perhaps he is also right.

There are people who declare things authoritatively only so that it is accepted. But it is also wrong to believe that all people are like that. People like these sages also exist, people who are not imposing any authority on anyone, who are just stating a fact – some humble information about which they have no doubt. And if they *have* no doubt – is it then wrong to say so? Or should they say that they have doubts just because of this fear that their statement might look authoritarian? Or do you think it will be right for them to say that they do not know whether they have doubts or not? Or should they not say anything at all, out of the fear that it may look like an authoritarian statement to someone? Anyway, does this fear make any difference?

Krishnamurti has been saying his whole life that he is not anybody's spiritual master, that his statements should not be taken as ultimate dogmas, that there is no need to accept what he says; that he is not an authority. But the most interesting thing is that hundreds of people accept him as an authority. And it becomes even more interesting, and in fact a joke, that people accept him as an authority because he denies it to be so; people regard him worthy to be a master just because he denies that he is a master!

It is a very interesting game of the human mind that when someone says to you that he is not a master your ego feels satisfied – "This is great, this man can be a friend; bowing down to this man's feet is not necessary, we can hug him, we can be friends with him, he is not above us."

It is true that when someone tries to be superior that is the ego. But when someone declares that he is not above anyone just so that others may feel good, this too is the ego – of course, from the other side, from your side. If someone tells you to touch his feet he will seem egoistic to you. But when someone asks you not to touch his feet because there is nothing special about him, then you are not aware that the satisfaction you are getting from this is your ego. And if, on the contrary, this man touches your feet, then what to say of your ego!

A friend came to me and told me, "I only like Krishnamurti – he seems to be the only wise man."

I asked him why, and he replied, "When I went to meet him, he moved near me and started patting my foot."

Krishnamurti may have done this in a moment of love, but he was not aware that while he may have been patting this man's feet, what was really being patted was this man's ego. And Krishnamurti appeals to him because of that!

Man is a very complex riddle.

So when the sage says that there is no doubt whatsoever, he does not mean that you should believe what he says. No, he only means that his statements are not mere statements, they are coming out of his realization. And there is nothing wrong in saying it. He declares that within him there is no doubt. This declaration that *About this there is no doubt* – if this is how it is, what is wrong in it? If he knows it, he should express it. To say the truth is humbleness.

It is very interesting that we go on repeating – especially during the past one hundred years this idiotic idea has gone deeper and has become very influential – that we are all equal, that no one is lower and no one is higher. This has not changed anything. It doesn't mean that we have stopped thinking of ourselves as higher. No, all it means is that we have stopped thinking of others as higher than us. When we say no one is lower and no one is higher, it doesn't mean that we have stopped treating someone else as lower, it only means that we have stopped treating anyone else as higher.

When we say that all are equal, in the deepest sense this is right, but we have no understanding of that depth. We have not yet come to that point where this statement is true; where we are, this statement is totally false. There, where we are, we are not at all equal, in fact we are altogether unequal. But we have accepted this idea that equality exists. But where we are, we are all completely different and unequal.

Another problem arises when a person believes that everyone is equal: then he will never discover the point where equality is truly possible. Someone who begins from the premise that everyone is unequal will one day reach the point where equality will become possible, because he will do something about it: he will go on a journey, make some endeavor toward improving himself, refining himself, changing the situation. But someone who believes himself to be equal with Buddha… This does not harm Buddha in any way. If it were to harm Buddha in any way there would still be no problem, but it harms the person who believes in this idea.

Yet if Buddha were to say, "You are wrong" – then to you Buddha would appear to be egoistic by proclaiming that you are unequal! Then what should Buddha do? He can either say, "Yes, you are equal to me, not only equal but superior to me" – this satisfies your egos, but your journey for transformation and improvement will not begin. Or, if Buddha says in a natural and spontaneous way, "No, we are not equals" – then it hurts your egos.

Buddha, Mahavira, Krishna or Christ have not declared that where we are now we are equal. Certainly they know that at some point, at the center, we are all equal, but that is at our final destination; we are not equal where we are now. There are big gaps, big distances between us on the path, on the journey, but there are no gaps between us at the destination.

That is why Krishnamurti's statement appeals to people, but it is dangerous because he says we are all equal even on the path; that no one is a master and no one is a disciple, that no one is ahead, no one is behind. This is true at the destination, but not at all on the path. And he who believes that we are equal while on the path will never reach the destination.

When the sage says: *About this there is no doubt,* it is only a humble statement about himself. What he means is that he is not saying so through a process of thinking about it but through knowing. And it is meaningful in one more way: because we are living in skepticism, in doubt.

As I have told you: a bird just hatched from its egg tries its wings sitting outside the nest, but cannot gather courage to fly because he has never flown. He has no idea that these wings are for flying. He is also not confident because his wings are tiny, and the sky is so vast. How could they be helpful in this vast sky? And how is trust to arise in the unfamiliar, the unknown, the untrodden path, the vast sky in which one has never flown? Seeing some other bird flying, even then trust does not arise that "I can also fly," because it is not necessarily so that one can do what others are doing.

But if another bird could say to this bird, "I too have passed through this phase. One day, sitting outside my nest, I too was worried. I too was unable to trust in my wings that I could fly in the sky, because I had no previous experience. But now I can tell you from my experience that there is no doubt about it; although you have tiny wings, this sky is made for your wings and you can fly. Your wings are big enough, this whole sky is even too small for them. You can fly – this is beyond doubt. I say it from my own experience."

Experience means that one has known both situations, otherwise it will not be experience. One who has known the first situation in which the small bird is today, fluttering his wings, unable to gather courage, and who also knows the second situation, the experience of flying in the sky, this one can say to this bird, "Don't be afraid, take the jump!"

About this there is no doubt. This declaration is helpful. This proclamation does not mean what Krishnamurti inevitably takes it to mean – that meaning is also true, but not necessarily so. It does not mean that the other bird is trying to create his authority and is compelling others to believe in what he says. It does not mean that the other bird is trying to become a master and make the little bird a disciple. No, it is none of that. Yes, it could be so, but it is not inevitable. The big bird is simply saying to the little one to look at him, that what he is saying is not just baseless, that he is saying it after knowing it. "If you are able to see me and know me, then this trust may become infectious and give birth to a self-confidence within you too."

A master becomes a trouble, a hindrance to you when he asks for your trust in him; a master becomes helpful when he arouses your trust in your own self. In both situations, a proclamation that there is no doubt about it is essential.

17

Such Is This Mystery

I am this brahman known by all vedanta,
the state beyond knowledge.
I am not perceptible even as sky and air, etcetera,
I am neither form nor name nor action.
I am this brahman, the ultimate reality:
the abode of sat, chit, anand – truth,
consciousness, bliss.
I am not the body –
how can there be birth and death for me?
I am not the vital breath –
how can there be hunger or thirst for me?
I am not the mind –
how can there be sorrow or pleasure for me?
I am not a doer –
how can there be bondage or liberation for me?
Such is this mystery…

Here ends the Upanishad.

As far as the expansion of knowledge may reach, it will be called *veda*. *Veda* means the act of knowing, to know. *Veda* and *vidvan* – scholar – come from the same root. *Veda* means knowledge.

But there is also a dimension of life, a hidden state of existence where even knowledge cannot throw any light, where knowledge has no access, where access is possible only if knowledge is left outside. Hence India has coined a unique word – you must have often heard it but perhaps without understanding it: the word is *vedanta.*

Vedanta means that state where even *veda*, knowledge, comes to an end, where even knowledge cannot approach, where you have to go even beyond knowledge, where knowledge becomes meaningless, where knowledge has no access. *Veda* means all knowledge, as far as it can go. But even that does not help. All that has been known does not help; all that has been experienced, all the treasures of knowledge are of no help. This is the point from where *vedanta* begins. Where veda comes to an *anta*, an end, there *vedanta*, the state which is beyond knowledge begins. At the dead end of *veda* is the beginning of *vedanta*. If we translate the word *vedanta* into English, the exact meaning will be "no knowledge."

Let us understand these three steps. One is *agyan*, ignorance, the next step is called *gyan*, knowledge, and above it is a step called *gyanatit*, beyond knowledge. Ignorance is when we do not know, knowledge is when we know; in other words, when we have gone beyond ignorance. *Gyanatit* means that we have gone even beyond knowledge.

Not only does ignorance create bondage, knowledge also binds you. Liberation is the state when knowledge has also been abandoned. Ignorance has to be dispelled, but that is not enough. Many methods to destroy ignorance have been created on earth, and many schools of thought have come into existence throughout the world which have tried to dispel ignorance. But probably it is only the wise men of the East who created a school of thought which said that a state comes when even knowledge has to be dropped, where even knowledge becomes a bondage. Not only is ignorance a bondage, knowledge too can become a bondage because knowledge is finite. Howsoever much one may know, knowledge cannot be infinite. If you want to know the infinite you will have to drop all knowledge.

That is why, in a deeper sense, the man of ultimate wisdom appears as an ignorant man. In a way he becomes an ignorant man because he too is without knowledge. But in another sense he is quite the opposite from an ignorant man; the ignorant man is that way because he has no knowledge, and the man of ultimate wisdom is ignorant because he has let go of this knowledge too.

Try to understand it like this, one man is born a beggar and he grows up begging on the streets. Then there is Gautama the Buddha, who renounces his palace one day and suddenly goes to beg on the streets. The street is the same, the begging bowls may be the same, and the beggar and Buddha may be walking together on the same street to beg. So what is the difference? Both are out to beg, both have a begging bowl in their hands, both will stand begging at many doors; both are beggars – but are they really the same? The difference is not visible on the surface, but a great difference lies within.

The beggar is just a beggar, he has nothing at all. He has never known any riches and so he is suffering from having nothing. He has no money – Buddha too has no money – but the beggar has never known money, that is why the lack of money is like a hollowness to him, a pit; it is a suffering, a wound – it oozes. His very being is empty; his begging bowl is not only in his hands, his begging has gone deep within him. And this Buddha who is standing near him is also a beggar, but he has known riches. His trouble was not lack of money, his trouble was too much money. He had too much of it, more than enough, and therefore it became meaningless. He has left money after knowing it, money has become meaningless to him. But for the beggar it is very meaningful.

Both are beggars, but Buddha's begging has the grace of an emperor. Even in his begging Buddha has a grandeur which emperors would envy. Even in his begging Buddha is a master. For him money has become meaningless, it has dropped. The other man is also a beggar, but he really is a beggar; money is very meaningful to him, and the desire for money continues.

The situation is the same between an ignorant man and the man of ultimate wisdom. The wise man renounces knowledge the same way that Buddha renounced wealth – after knowing it, after enjoying it, after having it. He sees that even knowledge has a boundary, that all knowledgeability stops there and no meeting with the infinite happens, so he renounces knowledge. He puts fire to his knowledge, puts his knowledgeability on the fire and burns it. He becomes like an ignorant man, but he is not ignorant. The ignorant man is still seeking knowledge, whereas this man has completed his journey for knowledge and has gone beyond it.

Hence, the sage says:

I am this brahman, known by all vedanta,
the state beyond knowledge.

He does not say: "I am that *brahman* who is known by all the Vedas, the ancient scriptures," because he is not the *brahman* which the scriptures talk about. That *brahman* is finite, bound by the concepts of knowledge. "I am the *brahman* which is known in that state which is beyond knowledge. Even the scriptures cannot know of it. Only someone who dares to renounce his scriptures, his knowledge, is able to know it; I am that *brahman*." It will become easy if we try to understand it from the inside.

We can know everything through knowledge except ourselves, because everything is in front of knowledge and we are only behind it. We can know everything through the faculty of knowledge, it is only a means for us.

Understand it like this: we can see everything through our eyes except our eyes themselves. And if you are seeing them in a mirror you are not seeing your eyes, you are seeing only the reflection of your eyes. The reflection is something else. The eyes see everything, but why can't they see themselves? What is the problem? In order to see a thing a distance is needed, a gap is needed to see something; it is necessary that they are facing each other in some way. Now how can your eye face itself? It is not possible. That is why the eye can see everything except itself.

Knowledge too can know everything in this world except for the *brahman*, the ultimate reality – that which is hidden within us, that which we are. Knowledge is the eye of that *brahman* within us and all else can be perceived through it. The collection of all that perception is called veda, knowledge. What the *brahman* knows is called veda, knowledge, and that through which the *brahman* can be known is called *vedanta*, the state beyond knowledge.

Now, how to know the *brahman*, the ultimate reality? Who is it who will know it? In fact the very language of knowing has to be abandoned because knowing always implies the other. How is it possible to know oneself? How can you know what you yourself are? – and who will know it? From what dimension, in which way will you come to know it? That is why whatever we come to know about ourselves will become something other than ourselves – just in the very knowing of it. In fact one's own self is beyond the reach of one's knowing.

There is only one way and that is to take all our knowledge off like clothes and to put it aside, to become naked, as it were, without clothes. In the same way, when you can become naked of all knowledge then the revelation that happens is not knowledge, it is an inner revelation. The thrill of ecstasy that spreads within, the recognition that happens without any formal knowing, is called *vedanta*, the state which is beyond knowledge. A mind that discards all knowledge enters that state.

Man is very clever, he has created scriptures even around *vedanta* – that state which is beyond knowledge. He has created knowledge even out of the state which is beyond knowledge. Pundits go on propagating that *vedanta* is not the end of the scriptures called the Vedas, the knowledge, but the very essence of these scriptures. They go on insisting that *vedanta* is a physical part of these scriptures. This is an absolute lie, it is absolutely wrong.

The whole effort of the sages has been to somehow free you from words, dogmas, knowledge so that you can become settled in that ultimate realm which is not available through knowledge but only through being. Knowledge is a barrier to being, because knowledge is nothing but an extension, an expanding outside of oneself. Being is to sink within oneself, to settle within one's own self, to come to the original center.

So *vedanta* means the state when you are ready to renounce all your knowledge, just as Gautam Buddha is ready to renounce all his wealth. Your knowledge too is a kind of wealth, it is an accumulation of an inner wealth.

It is very interesting that even our wealth is not ours, we only possess it as a middle link in a great chain – a son inherits his father's wealth, then his son inherits it from him. No one is born with wealth, this much is certain: it doesn't matter where it comes from, no one is born with it. It may be given by the state, it may be given by the family, by society, or a tradition, it may be earned through hard work, or else it may be stolen, but one thing is certain: no one is born with it and no one dies with it. So wealth is a phenomenon that happens in the middle somewhere and is outside of us.

It is the same with knowledge: it is obtained from others. Knowledge is the accumulated earnings of society. That is why animals cannot be knowledgeable – they have no language through which to accumulate their knowledge. That is why when the father animal dies, he is unable to hand over his experience to his son, there is no way. The son has to start again from where the father had started; hence animals cannot develop.

Illiterate societies cannot make any progress. The oral information from the father is not enough. Many things get lost and the sons have to start afresh – from *ABC*.

As language evolved it created treasure troves of knowledge.

And when we also created a script and discovered how to write, all fear of losing that knowledge disappeared. That is why this phenomenon has become possible only with man. With animals, the son begins exactly at the same point again where the father began – the son dies at the same point where the father had died, his sons have to start all over again from the very beginning – that is why no progress becomes possible.

All human progress happens because each son takes over where his father left off; the volume of knowledge goes on growing and the wealth of knowledge goes on accumulating. Every generation accumulates knowledge and hands it on to the next generation. That is why the more knowledge a society accumulates, the more intelligent it becomes. Knowledge is an accumulation.

Just imagine that for twenty years all universities, colleges, schools were closed, that all libraries were burned, and for twenty years there was no available means for any education; that fathers stop teaching their sons, teachers stop teaching their pupils. Do you know what would happen? In twenty years you would be where you were two million years ago. Everything would be lost.

Knowledge is an accumulation and it has to be handed over constantly, hence the existence of schools. What do the schools, colleges and universities do? They hand over the accumulation of knowledge from the father's generation to his son's generation, nothing else. The teacher's work is this transferring, his whole business is to hand over what the older generation has accumulated to the new generation – that is his only work, that of being an intermediary link.

Knowledge is also wealth obtained from others. All knowledge put together may be called veda. In India we call the Vedas, *samhita*. *Samhita* means that which has been collected, everything known which has been compiled. That is why I do not agree that veda consists of only those four Indian scriptures called the Vedas. Whatever has been accumulated in the world as knowledge is veda; knowledge as such is veda, a *samhita*, a collection, because it has been accumulated.

That is why the sage says it very consciously, knowingly – they are not words said in passing …*known by all vedanta, the state beyond knowledge*. Not known through the Vedas, because that which is known through accumulated knowledge is not knowing. The knowing of the ultimate reality is not an accumulated knowledge, it is already within ourselves; it does not need to be brought in from the outside.

So it is possible that universities may be closed down and the education system discontinued – this movement seems to be happening all over the world. If the movements of young people, hippies and others succeed, then universities will not run and libraries will be burned; soon everything will end. But there will be no harm done to the *brahmangyan*, the knowing of *brahman*, experiencing *brahman*. All the Vedas may be burned, the Bible and the Koran may be destroyed, but the knowing of *brahman* will not be affected because it is never attained through them. They have no relevance to it. Whenever the knowing of *brahman* happens, it comes from within. It may have been expressed on the outside, but its attainment is never from the outside.

The Vedas may have tried to say what the realization of *brahman* is, but it is never received from the Vedas. They may contain the expression – everyone who has known this state has tried to convey it, and the compilation of all this has created the Vedas – but whosoever has known this state has not known it through the Vedas, he has known it by *vedanta*, by going beyond knowledge. And when I say "the state beyond knowledge," I mean the end of knowledge – when knowledge is transcended, when he lets go of knowledge.

Such a man says: "I have known everything, but all that knowledge has come from the outside. Now I renounce it all and want to know that which is within, which never comes from the outside. Now I want to seek and know that purest reality which is never available from the outside and is always present inside."

Hence the sage says: *...known by all vedanta, the state beyond knowledge.* This needs to be understood. If the sage had only said "that has been known by *vedanta*," it would have been slightly wrong. But the sage says "that has been known by *all vedanta*." Because it is not that the understanding of *vedanta* is born only in India, no. Wherever it has happened, wherever this state beyond knowledge has happened, all is included.

What Jesus realized is also *vedanta*, this state beyond knowledge, although he was not aware of the Upanishads – that was not necessary. When Lao Tzu came to realize it, it was through *vedanta*; when Eckhart came to realize it, it was through *vedanta* – whenever anyone in the world has realized it, it has happened through *vedanta*, the state beyond knowledge. Whatever collection of knowledge they had, it was only through dropping it that they came to realize the ultimate reality.

So the sage says: *...by all vedanta.* Wherever, at whatever time, at whatever place, and under whatever circumstances it has been realized, it has always been realized through *vedanta*, that state which is beyond knowledge, which is the cessation of knowledge. This is the comprehensive meaning of *vedanta*, the state which is beyond knowledge.

But as man is, and as the mind of man is, we still come across people who claim to be *vedantins* – adherents of *vedanta*. Nobody can be a vedantin, this is sheer foolishness. Nobody can be a vedantin because *vedanta* is not an "ism," a doctrine, a dogma. Any "ism" is again a scripture, a Veda. So if someone says he follows *vedanta* he is absolutely mistaken, because where there is still a following, how can knowledge have been dropped? To be a follower as such belongs to knowledge, so no one is a *vedantin*, a follower of *vedanta*. And when I say this, what I mean is that no one can make an "ism," a theory out of it. Whosoever tries to do that has not understood it, he has missed the point; he has missed the real thing. The very meaning of *vedanta* is: no "ism," no theory, no scripture, no knowledge. How then can you become its follower?

In fact to enter into this state every theory, every scripture, every principle has to be left behind. Even the most ancient scriptures are to be abandoned. Then we can say that such a man is in the state of *vedanta* – but he is not a vedantin, a follower. He has entered into the state beyond knowledge, this much can be said, but he cannot say that he is its follower. This would be an inconsistency, the very meaning of the word would be lost.

I am this brahman known by all vedanta, the state beyond knowledge. "I am that which the sages realized when they dropped all their knowledge." What the sage is proclaiming is a proclamation from ultimate reality. One may think that this proclamation is very egoistic: "I am *that*, which has been known by all *vedanta*, the state beyond knowledge!" No, not at all, there is no trace of ego anywhere. The sage is only saying: "Now I am talking about that reality, that ultimate reality which cannot be approached through knowledge. I dwell where even knowing has no reach; where only being has access, where only pure 'isness' can enter; where knowledge becomes a barrier, where knowledge is a disaster, where knowledge is an obstruction, where knowledge creates disharmony, where knowledge creates restlessness. I dwell there, where not even a ripple of knowledge exists."

We have all heard that if thoughts cease, meditation happens. But now try to understand something deeper – when knowing ceases, *brahman* happens. With the cessation of thoughts meditation happens, but the notion of knowing remains in this meditation. When the notion of knowing also disappears, when there is no ripple of knowing, when all knowledge disappears, then *brahman*, the ultimate reality happens.

I am neither form nor name nor action.
I am this brahman, the ultimate reality:
the abode of sat, chit, anand – truth,
consciousness, bliss.

I am not the body…

The last part is a very precious statement, extremely precious.

I am not the body –
how can there be birth and death for me?
I am not the vital breath –
how can there be hunger or thirst for me?
I am not the mind –
how can there be sorrow or pleasure for me?

The last statement is the reply to the original inquiry, where this Upanishad began. The reply that has come after such a long journey is astonishing. The reply is:

I am not a doer –
how can there be bondage or liberation for me?

This Upanishad began with: *What is bondage? What is liberation?* These were the first questions. The sage has discussed things in such detail, entering deeply into the reality of life, that you could never have imagined that this would be the final reply which he gives. He should have said so in the very beginning!

What the sage is now saying is that "When there is no bondage in the first place, how can there be any liberation? I am not something which can be bound, I cannot be bound; freedom is my nature, so who can put me in bondage? How can I be bound? How can any bondage stick to me? I do not have even this much existence that I can be bound. Where is the body which can be bound? Where is the form which can be imprisoned? Where are its outlines?" It is only after going beyond all the boundaries, having discussed freedom from all forms at length… Perhaps by now the seeker himself may have forgotten that his original inquiry was: *What is bondage? What is liberation?* That inquiry has receded so far into the distance that perhaps you did not remember it either! The query has been left so far behind, the discussions have gone so deep, to such profundities, that now the sage says:

I am not a doer – how can there be bondage or liberation for me? "If bondage does not exist, then what meaning is there in liberation? If bondage is not possible for me, then where does the question of liberation arise?"

This Upanishad began with a question and it ends with a question. The sage says, "How can there be bondage? – and therefore how can there be liberation? Where I am, bondage and liberation cannot exist." But if this were the answer, he could have said this at the very beginning!

I remember a Sufi story. Hassan, a fakir, left his village and set out in search of a master. An old fakir was sitting beside a rock and Hassan said to him, "I have set out in search of a master. I have no hope of attaining to truth in this village" – in one's own village no one has such hope – "and if the people I know have any truth in them it is beyond my imagination, this much is certain. That's why I'm leaving this place. Would you please guide me as to where I should go, where I should search?"

The old fakir said, "The way is very difficult, it is arduous. But since you have asked, I will tell you. If you find a man with such and such features and who fits such and such a description, don't let go of him, follow him at all costs; a man with such and such a face and eyes, a turban of such and such a type on his head, wearing such and such a kind of robe, sitting in such and such a posture on such and such type of a rock, under such and such a tree – if you find this man, don't leave him."

Hassan continued to search and search for this man. It is said that he went to every town and village but he could find neither the tree, nor the rock, nor the man. He wandered for thirty years. He wandered until he became tired, thoroughly fed up, exhausted, worn out. He did not find even a glimpse of truth and his very thirst for truth almost faded away and it lost all its intensity. Now he even began to doubt that there was such a thing as truth anywhere, so how could he find it?

He became angry with that old man: "What nonsense! He put me to so much trouble, telling me to look for a man of this description, at a particular place. Had he not done so, perhaps I would have succeeded in my search. I have been ruined by seeking for this man, by this search; neither could I find the place he described, nor the man."

Hassan returned to his village. That old man was sitting just at the entrance to the village. Seeing this, Hassan was surprised – the tree looked like the one he had been told about, the rock was also the same. He came close and found that the eyes were also the same. Hassan fell at the old man's feet and cried, "Are you mad? If you are the man I have been searching for, why didn't you tell me in the very beginning? Why did you make me wander about for thirty years?"

The old fakir replied, "I did tell you that very day, but thirty years of wandering were necessary in order for you to recognize me. I had told you everything on that very day but you didn't look at me, nor did you notice the rock or look at the tree. You were in such a hurry, all ready and eager to go on the search. You had already taken it for granted that truth could not be found at this place which you were leaving behind. I described the eyes – you didn't even look at my eyes. I described the features too. It is not only you who has been put to a lot of trouble, what about me? – I couldn't leave this rock for thirty years! I had to wait for you, until you came back.

"This much was certain, that you would return; where else could you go? All the descriptions I had given couldn't have matched anywhere else except this rock, this tree. So you have also created trouble for me. But your thirty years of wandering were necessary; it has been essential for you to pass through this suffering. This anguish was a spiritual discipline for you."

The sage could have also given him the answer in the very

beginning. He could have said, "What bondage? – who is it that can be bound? And when there is no bondage, what meaning does liberation have? Who is to be freed?" But then no journey to the inquiry would have been possible and perhaps the seeker might have returned quietly, but not at peace.

Perhaps he might have kept his mouth shut, perhaps he might not have been able to say a single word in response, but this would not have been a solution; it would have been no help to him. The sage had to wait. It was a long journey. Inch by inch on this long journey he effaced the seeker.

It is remarkable that the sage totally ignored the initial inquiry. He paid no attention to what the seeker had asked and instead just began to eliminate the seeker by saying: "...not the body, not the senses, not the mind, not the intellect, not I, not you, not *that*, neither the scriptures, nor the knowledge – beyond all and everything." The sage went on dismantling him, dissolving him. And now, when the process of dissolution was complete and he saw that the iceberg which had come as a seeker had melted and become one with the ocean, he asked the seeker, "What bondage? Bondage to whom? Who do you think you are that you can be bound? Where are you that you can be bound? And when the reality is that you have never been bound, what is this liberation that you are now seeking? Who is it you want to free? Who will attain this liberation?"

This Upanishad is wondrous in this respect. It begins with a question and it ends with a question, but the form of the question, the context of the question, the quality of the question has changed. In the beginning the disciple had asked the question, and now at the end the master is asking the question. And somewhere in between these two, lies the answer. That is why both had prayed: *...protect us both; may it care for us both. Together may we strive...* "Protect us both, lest we drown in the middle."

To have just given an answer would have been very easy, but to help someone to reach to the solution, to the questionless state, is very difficult. Anyone can give answers, giving answers does not make one a master; one may become a teacher, but he will not be a master.

This is the difference between a master and a teacher. The master gives a solution: the questionless state; the teacher gives answers. You can ask a teacher what is what and he will tell you. But even this answer may not necessarily be his own, he may have received it from someone else. It is also not necessary that the answer he gives will have solved his own problem. This too is not a necessity. It is a fixed answer, it is traditional; the teacher just passes it on to the student. But the master does not give answers, he only gives the solution. And the solution can be given only through your enlightenment – there is no other way. In fact only enlightenment brings the solution, the questionless state.

The whole process described by this Upanishad is the process of enlightenment. If you go on moving step by step through this process you will attain to enlightenment. Enlightenment is the solution.

The day the solution is attained, the master puts the question back to the disciple: "Now I am asking you!" Because all these inquiries were, just as I said earlier, like that illusion when you see a snake in a rope at twilight, and then you come running to me to tell me about the snake and to ask me how to drive it away, how to remove it. Should it be killed with a stick or with a bullet – or whether to just stop going that way?

If I just say to you that there is no such thing as a snake there, that you are under an illusion, that it is your mental projection and that you are mistaken, then it is impossible to expect you to accept my statement. You may keep quiet, but the snake is more real for you than my statement. I am only making a statement! The snake is more real. No, I can give you an answer, but that will not solve the problem. It would be more appropriate to take a lamp and come with you and say, "Let us see how big the snake is so that we can bring a sword or a stick of the appropriate size, or we will make some other suitable arrangements to kill it – but first, let us go and see the size of this snake."

Someone who knows that there is no snake and yet takes a lamp and comes with you, is not a teacher. A teacher would have only given you an answer. It is possible that he might have even explained to you how sometimes people mistake a rope for a snake. He might have explained everything, but if you ask him to come and walk along that path with you he will say, "My answer is only what I have heard. I don't want to get in any trouble – there may be a snake there, I don't want to get involved with it. My answer is taken from the scriptures. I know it. My teacher told it to me, his teacher told it to him; I know it all well. I am ready to tell you everything but I am not going to go there."

The master will go with you – knowing full well that there is no snake. But the reality that there is no snake has to become your own experience. He will come with you, carrying a lamp. This whole Upanishad goes ahead of you, carrying a lamp. Inch by inch the path is being lit, darkness is being dispelled, and soon the master arrives at the rope. You may still be seeing the snake but he says, "Look, where is the snake? This is not a snake's tail, this is a rope; this is not a snake's body, this is a rope; this is not a snake's head, this is a rope."

This is what has been discussed here, that you are neither this nor this nor this – which is nothing but eliminating the snake. When the I has been totally eliminated and only the rope remains, then the master asks the disciple, "Now how to kill this snake? Which snake is to be killed? And if there is no snake, what will the sword kill? And if there is no snake, what advice can I give you about being safe from it? You tell me!" And with this question, the Upanishad ends.

Here ends the Upanishad.

There is not a single answer from the disciple. The disciple should say something now; at least a thank-you – at least show some gratitude, at least show some expression of devotion and delight – something! He should say something! But the disciple is utterly silent. The disciple is silent because in a sense he no longer exists, not even to speak. Not only has the snake been eliminated, the disciple too has been eliminated. The person who had come to inquire is no more, the mind which had come inquiring is no more, the ego that had questions and wanted answers is no more. In fact he who had come is no more and he who now remains never existed before, so who is to give thanks? To whom to give thanks? What response can there be?

Zen Master Lin Chi used to say to his disciples, "If you do not answer my question this staff will hit your head; and if you do answer, then too the staff will hit your head."

Certainly, it was a koan because he didn't leave any way out. And it was Lin Chi's practice to ask his disciples questions. He used to say, "You can ask me questions only if you first answer mine, this is the condition."

The master used to tell the disciples to answer his questions first, and only then would he answer theirs. And Lin Chi kept his staff in his hand. Then he would say, "I will hit you if you answer and if you don't answer, then too I will hit you." Often people would run away, but those who knew of his ways stayed.

When Bokuju went to meet him for the first time, he said to Lin Chi, "Let us do it this way – first complete your hitting, let's get it over with, then the questions and answers can happen later on. Otherwise this will create a distraction and an unnecessary disturbance. This is an easy job, let's get it over with first; questions and answers are difficult matters. First you do your hitting – here is my head."

And Lin Chi said, "So the man has arrived. I will not ask you questions – you can ask me."

If your questioning is just out of curiosity that is another matter, it has no value. But if the questioning is a part of your quest then it is a gamble, it is a big gamble, because to ask such questions as: *What is bondage? What is liberation?* is to put one's life at stake. After eliminating everything, after wiping the whole slate clean so that not even a word is left on it, in the end the master puts the question back to the disciple. So that not even knowing may be left behind, finally he wipes that off too and says, "No scriptures and no sense of knowing has any entry there."

He destroys everything, burns everything to ashes, burns the very seed itself. And then he asks, "What bondage? Who is there to be bound? What liberation? When one has never been bound in the first place, then what liberation is needed?"

Had the disciple spoken, even said "Thanks," this entire Upanishad would have to begin all over again, because it would have meant that while the snake may no longer be there the disciple is still there. He still speaks, he is still there to say, "Your compassion is great. You have explained everything, I have understood it all. I have attained to knowing."

If you return from a master as a knower, it has been a waste of time going to him. A master is one who destroys you, from whom *you* cannot return because you no longer exist; only then has your going to the master been meaningful.

Religion is the art of dying, of annihilation; it is the science of extinguishing your I on your own accord. It is like when someone blows out a lamp and the flame disappears: similarly, our ego, our I, has to disappear in a way that it can never be found again, so that only an emptiness remains behind – the void. It is only in that emptiness that we can realize our real being. Hence the last statement: *Such is this mystery*:

Such is this mystery...

Here ends the Upanishad.

"Upanishad" means mystery, and "mystery" means that which even if we understand, it remains beyond our understanding, or that which we may not understand and yet seems to have been understood. This is what mystery means. Those who don't understand carry the false notion that they have understood, and those who understand know that it is beyond comprehension; this is the meaning of mystery. If something is understood through your understanding then it is not a mystery, if something is not understood just because you did not understand then too it is not mystery. "Mystery" implies that those who do not know, feel that they know; and those who know, feel that they do not really know.

In the last days of his life Socrates said, "It was good while I didn't know; at least the illusion of knowing was there. But now it has become difficult because since I have known, I know that I don't know."

This is what is being called the mystery.

The oracle of Delphi had declared that Socrates was the wisest man in Greece. People ran to Socrates saying, "Do you know that the oracle of Delphi has declared that you are the wisest man?"

Socrates replied, "The oracle is late in her declaration; when I was wise, no one came to tell me this. There was a time when I was wise, but then nobody declared it. At that time, I myself wandered around declaring it! And now, when I have come to know that I know nothing, now this strange idea has entered the oracle's mind. There must be a mistake somewhere. You go and ask her again."

They went back. They went back happily, in a way, because they were hurt to hear that Socrates was a wise man. If Socrates had said, "Yes, I am a wise man," then they would not have believed in him that much. But he said, "I am the most ignorant man." They said, "Socrates must be right, and the oracle must have made some mistake."

They went back and asked again: "It seems there is some mistake..."

But the oracle replied, "I never make a mistake."

So they said, "There must be a mistake because Socrates himself says, 'I am an ignorant man.'"

The oracle replied, "That is why I declared him the wisest man – this is the reason. As long as he was a wise man, I could not declare it."

This is what is being called the mystery. "Upanishad" means mystery. Otherwise the word *Upanishad* literally means that which has been realized by sitting near the master – not by hearing the master but by sitting near him; because in hearing one only receives words, but by sitting near him one receives something more. But sitting near him is an art. Listening is very easy, sitting near him is very difficult.

The word *Upanishad* means that which one attains to by sitting near the master – simply by sitting near him, by coming closer to him, by surrendering to him, being in love with him, being as a nothingness near him, forgetting oneself near him. In fact that is why what the master says is not as important as what he is, because what he says is heard, but what he is, is received by sitting near him.

It often happened that when Gurdjieff had a disciple sitting near him, he would look at the disciple with so much anger that the disciple's heart would be shaken. Many disciples simply escaped from him. Gurdjieff was quite an expert in it; he was so expert that those who were close to him said that people sitting on one side of him would see anger in one eye, while he would be expressing love through the other eye to the people sitting on his other side. And the people sitting on opposite sides would sometimes get into an argument over their observations as to what kind of man Gurdjieff was.

One would say, "What a loving person Gurdjieff is – there was pure love pouring out of his eyes." The other would say, "Are you mad or something? I was also there, and his eyes showed only evil and fierceness and nothing else."

Alan Watts, a great Western thinker, has called him the "rascal saint" – a saint and still a rascal. But Gurdjieff was a wonderful man. It is very easy to be an ordinary saint or to be an ordinary rascal. But the people who knew him, who had sat close to him, always told others not to worry about what he does, what he says, how he moves his eyes, but only to concern themselves about being in his company, near him. "What he speaks through his eyes, through his words or through his facial gestures need not be your concern, because in order to learn something from him it is enough to just be with him, near him." They said, "Don't worry about his expression or whether he is calling you names, showing anger or showing love; don't care about all that, these are all his devices. Through them he finds out whether you have come just to listen to him or to be with him."

If you have come only to hear and understand him he gets rid of you, because he says that a person who has come only to hear him cannot go far. One should come close to him – an intimacy, a closeness, a nearness is needed. In that nearness, consciousnesses start merging into each other – the doors between you open and the consciousnesses begin to move into each other.

The day this inner flow of consciousness happens, the Upanishad happens. On that day – only on that day, and not before that.

About Osho

Osho's unique contribution to the understanding of who we are defies categorization. Mystic and scientist, a rebellious spirit whose sole interest is to alert humanity to the urgent need to discover a new way of living. To continue as before is to invite threats to our very survival on this unique and beautiful planet.

His essential point is that only by changing ourselves, one individual at a time, can the outcome of all our "selves" – our societies, our cultures, our beliefs, our world – also change. The doorway to that change is meditation.

Osho the scientist has experimented and scrutinized all the approaches of the past and examined their effects on the modern human being and responded to their shortcomings by creating a new starting point for the hyperactive 21st Century mind: OSHO Active Meditations.

Once the agitation of a modern lifetime has started to settle, "activity" can melt into "passivity," a key starting point of real meditation. To support this next step, Osho has transformed the ancient "art of listening" into a subtle contemporary methodology: the OSHO Talks. Here words become music, the listener discovers who is listening, and the awareness moves from what is being heard to the individual doing the listening. Magically, as silence arises, what needs to be heard is understood directly, free from the distraction of a mind that can only interrupt and interfere with this delicate process.

These thousands of talks cover everything from the individual quest for meaning to the most urgent social and political issues facing society today. Osho's books are not written but are transcribed from audio and video recordings of these extemporaneous talks to international audiences. As he puts it, "So remember: whatever I am saying is not just for you...I am talking also for the future generations."

Osho has been described by *The Sunday Times* in London as one of the "1000 Makers of the 20th Century" and by American author Tom Robbins as "the most dangerous man since Jesus Christ." *Sunday Mid-Day* (India) has selected Osho as one of ten people – along with Gandhi, Nehru and Buddha – who have changed the destiny of India.

About his own work Osho has said that he is helping to create the conditions for the birth of a new kind of human being. He often characterizes this new human being as "Zorba the Buddha" – capable both of enjoying the earthy pleasures of a Zorba the Greek and the silent serenity of a Gautama the Buddha.

Running like a thread through all aspects of Osho's talks and meditations is a vision that encompasses both the timeless wisdom of all ages past and the highest potential of today's (and tomorrow's) science and technology.

Osho is known for his revolutionary contribution to the science of inner transformation, with an approach to meditation that acknowledges the accelerated pace of contemporary life. His unique OSHO Active Meditations™ are designed to first release the accumulated stresses of body and mind, so that it is then easier to take an experience of stillness and thought-free relaxation into daily life.

Two autobiographical works by the author are available:
Autobiography of a Spiritually Incorrect Mystic,
St Martins Press, New York (book and eBook)
Glimpses of a Golden Childhood, (book and eBook)
OSHO Media International, Pune, India

OSHO International Meditation Resort

Each year the Meditation Resort welcomes thousands of people from more than 100 countries. The unique campus provides an opportunity for a direct personal experience of a new way of living – with more awareness, relaxation, celebration and creativity. A great variety of around-the-clock and around-the-year program options are available. Doing nothing and just relaxing is one of them!

All of the programs are based on Osho's vision of "Zorba the Buddha" – a qualitatively new kind of human being who is able both to participate creatively in everyday life and to relax into silence and meditation.

Location
Located 100 miles southeast of Mumbai in the thriving modern city of Pune, India, the OSHO International Meditation Resort is a holiday destination with a difference. The Meditation Resort is spread over 28 acres of spectacular gardens in a beautiful tree-lined residential area.

OSHO Meditations
A full daily schedule of meditations for every type of person includes both traditional and revolutionary methods, and particularly the OSHO Active Meditations™. The daily meditation program takes place in what must be the world's largest

meditation hall, the OSHO Auditorium.

OSHO Multiversity

Individual sessions, courses and workshops cover everything from creative arts to holistic health, personal transformation, relationship and life transition, transforming meditation into a lifestyle for life and work, esoteric sciences, and the "Zen" approach to sports and recreation. The secret of the OSHO Multiversity's success lies in the fact that all its programs are combined with meditation, supporting the understanding that as human beings we are far more than the sum of our parts.

OSHO Basho Spa

The luxurious Basho Spa provides for leisurely open-air swimming surrounded by trees and tropical green. The uniquely styled, spacious Jacuzzi, the saunas, gym, tennis courts…all these are enhanced by their stunningly beautiful setting.

Cuisine

A variety of different eating areas serve delicious Western, Asian and Indian vegetarian food – most of it organically grown especially for the Meditation Resort. Breads and cakes are baked in the resort's own bakery.

Night life

There are many evening events to choose from – dancing being at the top of the list! Other activities include full-moon meditations beneath the stars, variety shows, music performances and meditations for daily life.

Facilities

You can buy all of your basic necessities and toiletries in the Galleria. The Multimedia Gallery sells a large range of OSHO media products. There is also a bank, a travel agency and a Cyber Café on-campus. For those who enjoy shopping, Pune provides all the options, ranging from traditional and ethnic Indian products to all of the global brand-name stores.

Accommodation

You can choose to stay in the elegant rooms of the OSHO Guesthouse, or for longer stays on campus you can select one of the OSHO Living-In programs. Additionally there is a plentiful variety of nearby hotels and serviced apartments.

www.osho.com/meditationresort
www.osho.com/guesthouse
www.osho.com/livingin

Books by Osho in English Language

Early Discourses and Writings

The Art of Living
Astrology
Breaking All Boundaries
Compassion and Revolution
A Cup of Tea
Dimensions beyond the Known
Earthen Lamps
The Eternal Quest
From Sex to Superconsciousness
The Great Challenge
Hidden Mysteries
I Am the Gate
The Independent Mind
Keys to a New Life
Life Is a Soap Bubble
Love Letters to Life
New Dimensions of Yoga
The Path of Meditation
The Psychology of the Esoteric
The Search for Peace
Seeds of Wisdom
Silence: The Message of Your Being
Work Is Love Made Visible

Meditation
And Now and Here
In Search of the Miraculous
Meditation: The Art of Ecstasy
Meditation: The First and Last Freedom
The Inner Journey
The Perfect Way

Buddha and Buddhist Masters
The Book of Wisdom
The Dhammapada: The Way of the Buddha (Vols 1-12)
The Diamond Sutra
The Discipline of Transcendence (Vols 1-4)
The Heart Sutra

Indian Mystics
Bliss: Living beyond Happiness and Misery (Shiv Sutras)
Die O Yogi Die (Gorakh)
Enlightenment: The Only Revolution (Ashtavakra)
Krishna: The Man and His Philosophy
Showering without Clouds (Sahajo)
The True Name (Vols 1&2) (Nanak)
The Last Morning Star (Daya)
The Song of Ecstasy (Adi Shankara)

Baul Mystics
The Beloved (Vols 1 & 2)

Kabir
The Divine Melody
Ecstasy: The Forgotten Language
The Fabric of Life
The Fish in the Sea Is Not Thirsty
The Great Secret
The Guest

The Path of Love
The Revolution

Jewish Mystics
The Art of Dying
The True Sage

Jesus and Christian Mystics
Come Follow to You (Vols 1-4)
I Say nto You (Vols 1 & 2)
The Mustard Seed
Theologia Mystica

Western Mystics
Guida Spirituale (Desiderata)
The Great Challenge (Treatise of St. Dionysius)
The Hidden Harmony (Heraclitus)
The New Alchemy: To Turn You On
(Mabel Collins' Light on the Path)
Philosophia Perennis (Vols 1 & 2)
(The Golden Verses of Pythagoras)
Reflections on Kahlil Gibran's The Prophet
Theologica Mystica
Zarathustra: A God That Can Dance
(Nietzsche's Thus Spake Zarathustra)
Zarathustra: The Laughing Prophet
(Nietzsche's Thus Spake Zarathustra)
The Voice of Silence (Mabel Collins' Light on the Path)

Sufism
Just Like That
The Perfect Master (Vols 1 & 2)
The Secret
Sufis: The People of the Path (Vols 1 & 2)
Unio Mystica (Vols 1 & 2)

Until You Die
The Wisdom of the Sands (Vols 1 & 2)

Tantra
Tantra: The Supreme Understanding
The Tantra Experience: The Royal Song of Saraha
(same as Tantra Vision, Vol. 1)
Tantric Transformation: The Royal Song of Saraha
(same as Tantra Vision, Vol. 2)
The Book of Secrets: Vigyan Bhairav Tantra

The Upanishads
Behind a Thousand Names (Nirvana Upanishad)
Finger Pointing to the Moon (Adhyatma Upanishad)
Flight of the Alone to the Alone (Kaivalya Upanishad)
The Heartbeat of the Absolute (Ishavasya Upanishad)
I Am That (Isa Upanishad)
The Message beyond Words (Kathopanishad)
Philosophia Ultima (Mandukya Upanishad)
The Supreme Doctrine (Kenopanishad)
That Art Thou (Sarvasar Upanishad, Kaivalya Upanishad,
Adhyatma Upanishad)
The Ultimate Alchemy (Vols 1 & 2) (Atma Pooja Upanishad)
Vedanta: Seven Steps to Samadhi (Akshaya Upanishad)
The Way beyond Any Way (Sarvasar Upanishad)

Yoga
Yoga: The Science of the Soul (Vols 1-10)
-The Path of Yoga (Vol.1)
-The Heart of Yoga (Vol.2)
-Yoga: The Mystery beyond Mind (Vol.3)
-The Alchemy of Yoga (Vol.4)
-Yoga: A New Direction (Vol.5)
-Essence of Yoga (Vol.6)
-Yoga: The Science of Living (Vol.7)

-Secrets of Yoga (Vol.8)
-Yoga: The Path to Liberation (Vol.9)
-Yoga: The Supreme Science (Vol.10)

Tao
The Empty Boat
The Secret of Secrets
Tao: The Golden Gate (Vols 1 & 2)
Tao: The Pathless Path (Vols 1 & 2)
Tao: The Three Treasures (Vols 1-4)
When the Shoe Fits

Zen and Zen Masters
Ah, This!
Ancient Music in the Pines
And the Flowers Showered…
And the Grass Grows By Itself…
A Bird on the Wing
Bodhidharma: The Greatest Zen Master
The Buddha: The Emptiness of the Heart
Christianity, the Deadliest Poison and Zen, the Antidote to All Poisons
Communism and Zen Fire, Zen Wind
Dang Dang Doko Dang
The First Principle
God Is Dead: Now Zen Is the Only Living Truth
The Great Zen Master Ta Hui
Hsin Hsin Ming: The Book of Nothing
I Celebrate Myself: God Is No Where, Life Is Now Here
Kyozan: A True Man of Zen
The Language of Existence
Live Zen
The Miracle
Nirvana: The Last Nightmare
No Mind: The Flowers of Eternity

No Water, No Moon
One Seed Makes the Whole Earth Green
The Original Man
Returning to the Source
The Search: Talks on the 10 Bulls of Zen
A Sudden Clash of Thunder
The Sun Rises in the Evening
Take it Easy
This. This. A Thousand Times This
This Very Body the Buddha
Turning In
Walking in Zen, Sitting in Zen
The White Lotus
Yakusan: Straight to the Point of Enlightenment
The Zen Manifesto: Freedom from Oneself
Zen: The Diamond Thunderbolt
Zen: The Mystery and the Poetry of the Beyond
Zen: The Path of Paradox (Vols 1-3)
Zen: The Quantum Leap from Mind to No-Mind
Zen: The Solitary Bird, Cuckoo of the Forest
Zen: The Special Transmission

Osho: On the Ancient Masters of Zen
Dogen: The Zen Master
Hyakujo: The Everest of Zen – With Basho's haikus
Isan: No Footprints in the Blue Sky
Joshu: The Lion's Roar
Ma Tzu: The Empty Mirror
Nansen: The Point of Departure
Rinzai: Master of the Irrational

Responses to Questions
Be Still and Know
Beyond Enlightenment (Talks in Bombay)
Beyond Psychology (Talks in Uruguay)

Come, Come, Yet Again Come
From Bondage to Freedom
From Darkness to Light
From Death to Deathlessness
From Ignorance to Innocence
From Misery to Enlightenment
From Personality to Individuality
From the False to the Truth
From Unconsciousness to Consciousness
The Goose Is Out
The Great Pilgrimage: From Here to Here
The Invitation
Light on the Path (Talks in the Himalayas)
My Way: The Way of the White Clouds
Nowhere to Go but In
The Osho Upanishad (Talks in Bombay)
The Path of the Mystic (Talks in Uruguay)
The Razor's Edge
Sermons in Stones (Talks in Bombay)
Socrates Poisoned Again After 25 Centuries (Talks in Greece)
The Sword and the Lotus (Talks in the Himalayas)
Transmission of the Lamp (Talks in Uruguay)
Walk without Feet, Fly without Wings and Think without Mind
The Wild Geese and the Water
Yaa-Hoo! The Mystic Rose
Zen: Zest, Zip, Zap and Zing

Personal Glimpses
Books I Have Loved
Glimpses of a Golden Childhood
Notes of a Madman

Osho's Vision for the World
The Golden Future

The Hidden Splendor
The New Dawn
The Rebel
The Rebellious Spirit

The Mantra Series
Hari Om Tat Sat
Om Mani Padme Hum
Om Shantih Shantih Shantih
Sat Chit Anand
Satyam Shivam Sundaram

Interviews with the World Press
The Man of Truth: A Majority of One

For any information about OSHO Books, please contact:

OSHO Media International
17 Koregaon Park, Pune – 411001, MS, India
Phone: +91-20-66019999 Fax: +91-20-66019990
E-mail: distribution@osho.net
Website: http://www.osho.com

For More Information

For a full selection of OSHO multilingual online destinations, see osho.com/allaboutosho

The official and comprehensive website of OSHO International is osho.com

For more OSHO unique content and formats see:

– OSHO Active Meditations: osho.com/meditate

– iOSHO, a bouquet of digital OSHO experiences featuring OSHO Zen Tarot, TV, Library, Horoscope, eGreetings and Radio. Please take a moment to do a one time registration which will allow you a universal login. Registration is free and open to anyone with a valid email address: osho.com/iosho

– The OSHO online shop: osho.com/shop

– Visit the OSHO International Meditation Resort: osho.com/visit

– Contribute in the OSHO Translation Project:oshotalks.com

– Read the OSHO Newsletters: osho.com/NewsLetters

– Watch OSHO on YouTube: youtube.com/user/OSHOInternational

– Follow OSHO on Facebook: facebook.com/osho.international.meditation.resort

– and Twitter: twitter.com/OSHO

Thank you for buying this OSHO book.